THE SHORT STORY AND THE
FIRST WORLD WAR

The poetry of the First World War has come to dominate our understanding of its literature, while genres such as the short story, which are just as vital to the literary heritage of the era, have largely been neglected. In this study, Ann-Marie Einhaus challenges deeply embedded cultural conceptions about the literature of the First World War using a corpus of several hundred short stories that, until now, have not undergone any systematic critical analysis. From early wartime stories to late-twentieth-century narratives – and spanning a wide spectrum of literary styles and movements – Einhaus's work reveals a range of responses to the war through fiction, from pacifism to militarism. Going beyond the household names of Owen, Sassoon, and Graves, Einhaus offers scholars and students unprecedented access to new frontiers in twentieth-century literary studies.

ANN-MARIE EINHAUS is Lecturer in Modern and Contemporary Literature in the Department of Humanities at Northumbria University. She is the co-editor of *The Penguin Book of First World War Stories* (2007) and has published articles on First World War writing, modernism, and canonization in journals such as *Literature & History*, *Modernist Cultures*, and *Zeitschrift für Anglistik und Amerikanistik*.

THE SHORT STORY AND
THE FIRST WORLD WAR

ANN-MARIE EINHAUS

Northumbria University

CAMBRIDGE
UNIVERSITY PRESS

CAMBRIDGE
UNIVERSITY PRESS

32 Avenue of the Americas, New York, NY 10013-2473, USA

Cambridge University Press is part of the University of Cambridge.

It furthers the University's mission by disseminating knowledge in the pursuit of
education, learning, and research at the highest international levels of excellence.

www.cambridge.org
Information on this title: www.cambridge.org/9781107038431

© Ann-Marie Einhaus 2013

First published 2013

Printed in the United States of America

A catalogue record for this publication is available from the British Library.

Library of Congress Cataloguing in Publication data
Einhaus, Ann-Marie.
The short story and the First World War / Ann-Marie Einhaus, Northumbria University.
pages cm
Includes bibliographical references and index.
ISBN 978-1-107-03843-1 (hardback : alk. paper)
1. World War, 1914–1918 – Great Britain – Literature and the war.   2. English fiction –
20th century – History and criticism.   3. Short stories, English – History and criticism.
4. War stories, English – History and criticism.   I. Title.
PR830.W65E38   2013
823'.91209358–dc23   2013000015

ISBN 978-1-107-03843-1 Hardback

Contents

Acknowledgements

I would like to express my heartfelt thanks to the many people and institutions who enabled me to complete this book and without whose help the process would have been so much more arduous and so much less enjoyable. First and foremost, I would like to thank Professor Timothy Clark and Dr Jason Harding at Durham University for all their help and advice, for their eagle-eyed attention to detail, and for never letting me get away with sweeping observations or unsubstantiated claims. I would like to thank Professor Barbara Korte at Freiburg for first introducing me to the short story of the First World War, for starting me off on my research, and for her generous and valuable advice along the way. I am indebted to the expert editorial guidance of Dr Ray Ryan and Louis Gulino at Cambridge University Press, and to the two anonymous readers for their helpful and constructive comments. I would like to thank Dr John Nash and Dr Victoria Stewart for their excellent and encouraging feedback on my doctoral thesis, out of which this book has developed. Needless to say, any shortcomings of the book are entirely my own. I am further deeply grateful to the Fritz Thyssen Foundation, the Arts and Humanities Research Council, and the Department of English Studies at Durham for funding different stages of the research for this book, and to Northumbria University for providing such a congenial environment to finish the manuscript. I would like to thank my colleagues in Freiburg, Durham, Newcastle, the International Society for First World War Studies, and the British Association for Modernist Studies for countless stimulating discussions and helpful feedback.

Needless to say, the process of researching and writing a book is never a purely academic one. Without ceaseless emotional and technical support from Ben Lowing, I might have foundered a long while ago. I couldn't possibly give the credit they deserve to all my friends in Freiburg and Durham who have put up with my moods and encouraged and diverted me whenever I needed it most, but my most particular thanks go to

Katharina Böhm, Peter Creasey, Thea Farkas-Baumann, Kathrin Göb, Katherine Heavey, Maebh Long, Jahnavi Misra, Emily Ridge, Dominic Wells, and Friederike Wursthorn. Last but certainly not least of all I would like to thank my parents, Margret and Wilhelm Einhaus, and my sister Elisabeth. I am very fortunate to have had such untiring and generous family support over the years, financial, practical, and emotional. This book is dedicated to them.

Introduction

The First World War has occupied a central place in British popular memory for almost a century. Hardly any other historical event has been referenced so frequently and remembered so consistently and single-mindedly. With a plethora of rituals and memorials in place, the First World War continues to be part of popular consciousness in Britain, and although many of these commemorative efforts have come to encompass other wars as well as World War I, such as the British Legion's annual Poppy Appeal, they remain intricately connected in the minds of most Britons with what is seen as the archetypal modern war. The 'Great War' that failed to end all war is still the first to be invoked in many pacifist protests. Yet contemporary remembrance of the First World War is affected by the same selective processes that characterise all historical events: a narrowing down of what actually happened, of a plethora of different experiences and stories of the war, to a powerful but reductive master narrative. This process has resulted in a myth of the war that condenses a complex four-year conflict fought on a variety of fronts by vast numbers of people from all over the world to a nutshell image that is easily summarised and remembered. Writing about the place of the First World War in British literature and culture at a period of a renewed interest in the war in the early 1990s, Samuel Hynes described the war's myth as a master narrative of 'a generation of innocent young men, their heads full of high abstractions like Honour, Glory, and England',[1] whose subsequent suffering and disillusionment served to establish an almost unbridgeable gap between pre-war Britain and the post-war world.

Taught in schools across Britain, used as the basis for innumerable films, documentaries, popular histories and television series, the myth of the war is intricately connected with the war's literature and centres on the Western Front trenches and the stricken soldiers and veterans described so powerfully in the war poetry of Wilfred Owen and Siegfried Sassoon. This Western Front narrative has demonstrated enormous staying power and is so deeply embedded in popular consciousness that it has so far resisted a variety of attempts by revisionist historians and critics to widen and nuance our view of the war. Dominic Hibberd, writing at the same time as Hynes, points towards this phenomenon when he states, 'There is no typical writer of the Great War; the literature which it produced was as vast and diverse as the colossal human effort which the war represented. Only a very little of that literature is still read today.'[2] For most Britons, their image of the First World War is informed largely by their familiarity with its poetry: Sassoon, Owen and Isaac Rosenberg, Edward Thomas and Rupert Brooke will be familiar to most readers who have been educated in British schools. For many, a selection of war novels and memoirs will also feature in their perception of the war, from Robert Graves's *Goodbye to All That* (1929) and Richard Aldington's *Death of a Hero* (1929) to Vera Brittain's *Testament of Youth* (1933) and Erich Maria Remarque's international bestseller *Im Westen Nichts Neues* [*All Quiet on the Western Front*] (1929). Film and television adaptations of these war classics have cemented both their appeal and imaginative hold over the war's popular memory in Britain. More recent literary treatment of the war reinforces these images, such as Sebastian Faulks's novel *Birdsong* (1993), adapted for the BBC and screened in January 2012.

Short fiction, on the other hand, rarely features in the war's literary memory, despite the fact that First World War short stories can be seen as 'particularly fruitful in terms of offering contexts through which readers can begin to complicate or question their responses to particular events and topics'.[3] While Rudyard Kipling and D.H. Lawrence might be tentatively named as writers who addressed the First World War in their short stories, few other names spring to mind. As this study shows, this is not due to ignorance or ill will, but results both from inevitable processes of selective reading and remembering, and from the particular circumstances affecting the production, distribution and consumption of the short story. Great War short stories encompass a wide variety of stylistic, artistic and ideological approaches. While this study looks at examples from the full range, in cultural terms it is the largely formulaic fiction published in magazines that is particularly interesting in its strategies of representing the war. Although later stories are a different matter, which will be treated separately in the final chapter of this book, First World War short stories in general (and magazine stories in particular) document a period in which a diversity of experiences and memories of the war were still existing side by side, with little precedence given to any one specific version. As Dan Todman points out, '[t]he inter-war years saw Britons wanting to remember very different versions of the war. Although none completely obscured the horror and the suffering inflicted by the war, the meanings derived from those experiences varied widely.'⁴

Although the war found expression in a number of literary genres, from histories to memoirs and novels, to the particularly abundant poetry of the war, none of these other genres fulfil quite the same snapshot function as the short story. Longer prose texts tended to be more panoramic and analytical in their treatment of the war, whereas poetry frequently sought to transcend the specific nature of one war and to appeal to universal human values and experiences – whether these are patriotism and sacrifice, or, in Wilfred Owen's famous words, 'the Pity of War'. Most war novels and memoirs of the inter-war period offer an in-depth view of the war's experience from the perspective of only one of its protagonists – often the archetypal junior officer (anti-)hero – and the canonised poetry of the war provides short commemorative texts useful for purposes of remembrance or anti-war protest. First World War short stories in all their diversity offer something else: a multi-perspectival view of the war which allows us to re-assess our current mythology of the war and to map a cultural history of the war's experience by scrutinising a genre located at the pulse and in the everyday sphere of its readers.

Due to their publication primarily in magazines, short stories were one of the most ephemeral genres in which the experience of the war was reflected. While they may not always be easily accessible to contemporary readers and researchers and sport gaps and oversights of their own, Great War short stories hidden in out-of-print story anthologies and back numbers of magazines can contribute significantly to completing our image of the First World War beyond the typical Western Front narrative. Short stories, particularly those published in popular magazines, were part of a narrative framework that offered readers a means of comparison for their own war experiences, a context within which they could locate themselves.⁵ These stories cannot be read out of the context of other war writing, but although they cannot be said to be a unified body of work, they fulfil distinct social functions jointly with but perhaps more effectively than longer narrative prose texts. Just like actual lives, war stories reflect the multi-layered nature of war experience and both challenge and confirm the war's mythology. Their contribution during and immediately after the war was to help readers shape their own narrative identities as survivors and witnesses of war by placing them in a context of readily available fictional war narratives. Their very diversity allowed even those whose experiences have since come to be marginalised or forgotten to discover themselves in what they read, to compare their experiences to fictional models, or to model their own behaviour on that of fictional characters.

Why is it, then, that First World War short stories have been largely disregarded for so long? This question takes us into the heart of research on the war's mythology, bound up as it is with what one might call the literary memory of the war. The war texts that have come to form such a potent part of the Western Front myth of World War I – the wartime trench poetry and disillusioned novels and memoirs of the late 1920s – are literary testimonies of immense power, in an ideological and often also an artistic sense. Because most of us have been reared on these writings in our perception of the war, it is hard to look beyond them and beyond the mythology of the war of which they form such an integral part. Difficulty also results from the fact that these texts are by no means giving us a *false* image of the war. Just as the myth of the First World War is reductive rather than factually incorrect, these canonical war texts are simply limited in the view on the war that they offer readers, restricted as they are to a predominantly male military or military-related experience of the conflict. The challenge lies in complementing them to gain a better view of the whole picture, rather than discarding these canonical war writings altogether in favour of a wholly new perception of the war. Short stories, as Andrew Maunder has argued, can 'offer a fuller picture of the war; snapshots that give us access to a different world view'.[6] They can shock and disturb as much as the most graphic war memoir, such as the privately published 'The German Prisoner' (1935) by James Hanley, in which two British soldiers torture and kill a youthful German soldier, or I.A.R. Wylie's 'All Dressed Up' (1930), which shows the devastating consequences of trying to turn reluctant civilians into soldiers. They can also throw new light on writers we thought we knew, such as Jessie Pope, better known as the much-reviled covert addressee of Owen's 'Dulce Et Decorum Est', whose short stories betray a much more nuanced and sensitive side of this writer of racy recruitment poems.[7]

Over the past decade, the First World War short story has slowly gained in critical acknowledgement, primarily but not exclusively through the publication of specialised anthologies, such as Trudi Tate's *Women, Men and the Great War* (1995) and the *Penguin Book of First World War Stories* (2007, eds. Barbara Korte and Ann-Marie Einhaus). The most recent and most groundbreaking anthology in this line is Andrew Maunder's *British Literature of World War I: The Short Story and the Novella* (2011), which forms part of a series of editions of little-known war texts and focuses on forgotten short stories mostly by popular writers. The anthology market and its impact on the reception of First World War short stories will be discussed in depth in Chapter 3. Naturally, these new publications on the short fiction of World War I must be seen before the backdrop of a wealth of critical material on the First World War and its cultural and literary history, as well as criticism on the short story as a genre. This study owes a great debt to a range of seminal studies of the past three decades, such as Samuel Hynes's *A War Imagined* (1990), Claire Tylee's *The Great War and Women's Consciousness* (1990), Rosa Maria Bracco's *Merchants of Hope: British Middlebrow Writers and the First World War, 1919–1939* (1993), and Vincent Sherry's *The Great War and the Language of Modernism* (2003) to name but a few, as well as to some groundbreaking studies in the war's cultural history, including Janet S.K. Watson's *Fighting Different Wars: Experience, Memory, and the First World War in Britain* (2004), Dan Todman's *The Great War: Myth and Memory* (2005) and Adrian Gregory's *The Last Great War: British Society and the First World War* (2008), which in turn lean on earlier work such as Bernard Bergonzi's *Heroes' Twilight* (1965) and Paul Fussell's *The Great War and Modern Memory* (1975). Although I may in places disagree with their conclusions, my own perspective on First World War writing has evolved from three decades of revisionist research in the war's literary and cultural history, and any disagreements primarily result from my looking at a different genre and new source material than these previous studies. While my work on the short story of the First World War builds on these earlier studies, it also endeavours to negotiate between acknowledging existing research and avoiding to simply repeat lines of argument that are already well-established. There may be the occasional moment of disappointment on finding that a particularly evocative story has not been included in the present study, or that its analysis and previous critical treatment have received less attention than they seem to merit. The purpose of my study is explicitly to move away from texts that are already well-explored towards texts and aspects of the war that have so far received little or no critical attention. References to existing critical material are consequently often kept down to a minimum to afford more room for the treatment of hitherto unexplored material.

The overall aim of this book is two-fold. One of its purposes is to engage with the existing mythology of the war by opening up a wealth of fictional writing about the war that is also a source of alternative cultural history. It also endeavours, however, to answer a number of more specific questions. The key concern of this study is why a genre as productive and popular during the First World War as the short story did not become part of the war's literary memory, unlike, for instance, the similarly prolific poetry. Following from this central question, a secondary concern addressed is how far the specific genre characteristics of the short story on the one hand, and the stories' treatment of the subject of war on the other, are at the root of their non-canonicity. Last but not least, this book strives to determine how these matters change over time, bearing in mind that short stories about the war are still being published. Its main proposition is to view short stories about the First World War as crucial contributors to two important social functions: on the one hand, they helped contemporary readers reflect on, evaluate and come to terms with their own experience of the war by offering a wide range of different fictional interpretations to choose from, and on the other, they constitute for modern readers a cultural archive of the war that can challenge and add depth to the myth of the war and its literary canon.

Although Andrew Maunder has recently opened up the field of First World War short fiction both through his anthology and a chapter on war stories in *The British Short Story* (Liggins, Maunder and Robbins, 2010), there exist at present no book-length critical studies of World War I short fiction. The few monographs or articles on the wider subject of First World War literature that discuss some of the war's short stories do so briefly, in an incidental manner, and only as a supplement to discussions of longer prose texts or poetry. Recently, excellent work has been done on magazine short stories in particular, mostly with a specialised research interest in mind: Carol Acton has contributed a fascinating essay on the treatment of the First World War in popular magazines for young working-class women,[8] and Michael Paris's work explores the juvenile literature of the Great War, its origins and continuities.[9] None of this recent work, however, has set out to take a systematic look at the short story of the war in particular. It is in this sense that this book makes its contribution to existing research, in opening up a vista on short stories of the war as a whole, with regard to a wide variety of forms and subject matter, as well as their peculiarities of publication and reception.

In book-length studies of the war's literature, short fiction does not usually feature or receives only passing attention, mainly in connection with modernist writers such as D.H. Lawrence, Virginia Woolf or Katherine Mansfield. Early influential studies such as Bernard Bergonzi's *Heroes' Twilight* (1965), Paul Fussell's *The Great War and Modern Memory* (1975), as well as Samuel Hynes's *A War Imagined* (1990), and indeed more recent works such as Sarah Cole's *Modernism, Male Friendship, and the First World War* (2003) and Santanu Das's *Touch and Intimacy in First World War Literature* (2005), largely favour other genres over short fiction, particularly the prose memoir, the autobiographical novel and the poetry of the war. Historical studies, on the other hand, tend to either draw on oral history interviews and contemporary news reports, or work with literary texts that already form part of the established canon. The resulting selective approach, which often takes recourse to the same limited range of literary testimonials, has the potential to unwittingly skew our critical engagement with the war. Exploring the short-story genre as a new field of writing about the war contributes to opening up new avenues for critical inquiry.

While this book is by no means the first to critically engage with the mythology of the First World War, it draws on a wide range of new primary material and adopts a wider temporal scope, leading it up to the end of the twentieth century. Most existing studies focus on already canonised war fiction, or adopt a very specific angle on the war's literary heritage, such as gender roles, class, memory, or propaganda. A comparable approach to the one of this book is taken in Janet Watson's *Fighting Different Wars* (2004), but Watson's aim is primarily to revisit 'classic' war texts rather than to work with new literary material, and her analysis is informed by a particular interest in class distinctions with regard to the war's experience. Brian Bond, in *The Unquiet Western Front: Britain's Role in Literature and History* (2002), similarly limits himself to reinvestigating canonical war texts from an historical angle. Adrian Gregory in his more recent *The Last Great War: British Society and the First World War* (2008) explores new material alongside classic war texts, but as an historian uses exclusively non-fictional sources from newspapers and oral history transcripts. Jane Potter's *Boys in Khaki, Girls in Print: Women's Literary Responses to the Great War 1914–1918* (2005) is one of the few literary studies to also examine popular narratives of the war, but Potter's study has a specific interest in publishing history and primarily focuses on gender issues in soldiers' and nurses' memoirs, whereas my own approach is deliberately broader.

Accounts of the history and theory of the short-story genre mostly fail to address First World War-related short fiction beyond some modernist work. Adrian Hunter's *Cambridge Introduction to the Short Story in English* (2007), necessarily reductive, restricts its exploration of early twentieth-century short fiction to modernist, experimental fiction. Paul March-Russell in *The Short Story: An Introduction* (2009) acknowledges the critical bias amongst academics in favour of the modernist, 'plotless' short story, but nevertheless devotes his chapter on early twentieth-century short fiction to modernist narratives, helping to perpetuate the idea that the First World War invariably triggered stylistic innovation when he says 'One of the many casualties of war [...] is the linear narrative: the ability to tell a story straight is irredeemably affected by the stop-start procedure of trench warfare, in which intense bursts of violence are contrasted with long periods of boredom'.[10] The sole exception to this rule is the aforementioned *The British Short Story* (2010) by Emma Liggins, Andrew Maunder and Ruth Robbins, which devotes a section to First World War stories in the realist style. Their selection, however, is necessarily confined by the bounds of a book chapter and consequently focuses on only a few well-researched representatives of familiar literary positions: 'soldier-writer' 'Sapper' H.C. McNeile, 'war-lover' Rudyard Kipling and 'outsider' Radclyffe Hall. While the authors challenge the idea that war writing was necessarily modernist, the aim and scope of their book does not allow for in-depth critical engagement with the war's mythology or the potential of First World War short fiction to challenge and complement existing cultural assumptions about the war.

This study adopts a largely thematic approach to the subject of First World War short stories, covering a range of topics that seem of particular pertinence. The stories treated in this book account for a wide variety of writers from within British society: men and women, combatants and non-combatants, young and old, commercial and coterie, comic and serious, mainstream and avant-garde; a diversity that hopefully reflects much of the actual, heterogeneous experience of the war in Britain. The noticeable bias of this study is in favour of the home front and the popular magazine market, the most productive arena for short story writers addressing the war. The majority of stories about the war were written for a wide audience and published in popular media; coterie stories also addressed the First World War, but did so with a different ideological and aesthetic agenda. As a result, modernist short fiction about the war is treated mainly as a foil for the larger number of 'popular' narratives.

Although the number of Great War stories published after 1945 fell sharply compared to the prolific output of the decades between 1914 and the Second World War, a steady drizzle of stories still appeared, in particular around the ninetieth anniversary of the First World War. In analysing such a wide range of stories, one has to draw clear distinctions between the different periods of writing. Whether or not short-story writers had personal memories of the war, second-hand or only third-hand reminiscences; what political or ideological agenda informed their writing; what media they published in and which audiences they targeted; all these factors change radically over time and affect the texts and their possible readings. I have consequently tried to differentiate between those stories published during and in the wake of the First World War, those published in the aftermath of the Second World War, and those that appeared comparatively recently, in the last two decades of the twentieth century and at the beginning of the new millennium.

At the outset of this volume, it also seems appropriate to explain the use of the term 'British' as used in this study. By 'British' I refer to writers who were either citizens of, or spent the greatest part of their adult lives in England, Scotland or Wales. On occasion, this includes writers such as New Zealander Katherine Mansfield or Mary Borden, an American by birth. The restriction to British writers was on one level a necessity to limit the number of stories to be addressed, but it also reflects a particular interest in a specifically British cultural experience of the First World War. Just as the conflict was experienced in different ways by individual participants or witnesses, what one might call national experiences and remembrance of the Great War differ considerably. The 'memory culture' of other English-language countries that participated in the war frequently focuses on different aspects of its experience: in Ireland, the war is overshadowed by the violent struggle for independence; in the United States, as well as in many European countries, the Second World War has largely eclipsed the first; in the former dominions Canada, Australia and New Zealand, the memory of the war quickly became inextricably bound up with a nascent sense of national identity and the birth of a new, independent nation. Similarly, countries such as Jamaica and India – whose substantial participation in the First World War has only recently become the focus of historiographical attention – experienced the war in relation to a growing sense of nationalism and movement towards political independence.[11] To attempt to combine all these divergent experiences and memories in a single study is nigh on impossible, as these differences inevitably inform the literature written about the war in any of the participant countries. With regard to colonial testimonials, particularly from countries in which English was not the first language and where the majority of the population was non-literate, it is moreover hard to come by contemporary accounts of the war other than letters and the occasional memoir, as fictional narratives addressing the First World War by colonial participants from Africa, Asia and the West Indies are rare. Santanu Das points to this problem when he comments on Gail Braybon's verdict that 'more words have been written about the British war poets than about all the non-white troops put together' by observing that 'the fact remains that the war poets have written more words about the conflict than all the non-white troops put together'.[12] Consequently, this book limits itself to the British experience and memory of the war as evidenced in its short fiction, with all the regrettable bias in terms of subject matter and approach this entails: beyond a few casual (and casually racist) asides, non-white colonial troops are virtually invisible in British First World War short fiction.[13] However, while non-white colonial troops and workers involved in the war received only marginal treatment in British magazines and story anthologies, at least British war stories do offer us views of white British participants in and theatres of the war beyond the Western Front.

Last but not least, I should add that defining the short story is a difficult and contentious issue, and it serves no practical purpose to become embroiled in lengthy debates over the nature and aims of the genre. Consulting any one of the more recent works on the short story, one will inevitably come across the realisation that the short story, more than perhaps any other literary genre, is extremely hard to define, and that its definition has changed so often over time that it is virtually impossible to agree on any other common denominators than that a short story ought to be a piece of prose fiction, and that it ought to be relatively short. Even its shortness, however, can vary between a few hundred and several thousand words. It is partly this difficulty of definition that troubles all histories and critical studies of the short story because it is hard to decide which stories to include and exclude, how to compare them and most of all, how to discern what Dominic Head calls a 'developing aesthetic'[14] of the short story. For the purpose of this study I will regard as a short story any self-contained, short, fictional narrative published in a periodical, anthology or collection, regardless of internal features such as style and structure.[15]

In terms of organisation, the first chapter of this book introduces the theoretical framework on which the study is based. This framework combines aspects of short-story genre theory (particularly issues pertaining to form and publication of short fiction), memory studies (and the evolution of a mythologised remembrance of World War I in particular), research on modernism (as a critical starting point for analysing First World War fiction), and canonisation (in relation to genre attributes on the one hand and the social functions of literature on the other). A cornerstone of the first chapter is the mapping of a new kind of reader-response theory based on Paul Ricoeur's concept of the social function of narratives as fictional 'laboratories' for rehearsing experiences and decisions. The idea of narrative fiction as a testing ground for reality offers an ideal tool for interrogating the social and formal dimensions of First World War fiction. By focusing on their implied reader, the subsequent analysis of short stories from the research corpus can identify expectations regarding the experience of war created by short fiction. Because short stories were published in a plethora of magazines and newspapers and because they were consequently one of the most readily available genres at the time, the expectations they raised had the potential to shape readers' experience and memory of the war.

Chapter 1 also outlines the historical context of the study and provides an overview of First World War writing across different genres and of writing about war and invasion prior to the outbreak of the war. It further gives an account of the development of the war's memory and how this relates to the formation of a literary canon of First World War writing. In terms of canonicity, Great War stories are located in a 'cultural reservoir' of war writing rather than in the canon of First World War writing as it is currently taught in schools and universities. The chapter offers reasons for this existence of World War I short fiction next to rather than in the canon and discusses the purpose and desirability of trying to include them in the canon proper. The work of German cultural historian and literary critic Aleida Assmann is used to establish a new take on canonicity, particularly her distinction between a passive 'reference memory' (i.e. available but unread sources) and an active 'working memory' (i.e. canonical and frequently re-visited sources) within the larger framework of a society's overall cultural memory. The chapter closes with an investigation of assumptions about the relationship between modernism and First World War writing and suggests a reconsideration of these issues.

Chapters 2 and 3 move from a theoretical to a practical grounding of the study and introduce the publishing context of World War I stories from 1914 to the present day. As short stories are limited to magazines and anthologies in terms of their potential publishing outlets, their means of publication and their position inside or outside the canon are closely related. To do justice to this close relationship, these chapters discuss the interrelation between publishing environments in different media and the formal and ideological features of war writing, focusing in particular on differences between popular media and avant-garde publications. In historical terms, they trace changes in the publishing environment for short stories from the early twentieth century to the early twenty-first century and relate these to the changing nature and impact of short stories addressing the First World War. The two chapters also investigate readerships and ideologies behind these publications, with particular focus on a range of short-story anthologies (general, academic and specialised in war fiction) and two sample magazine publications, the *Strand Magazine* and the *English Review*. Following up concerns raised in Chapter 1, Ricoeur's ideas on the narrative configuration of reality and an investigation of implied readerships are applied to the magazine and anthology market, mapping changing target audiences and audience concerns. The critical scrutiny of anthologies, including academic publications, will serve specifically to show how these perpetuate a restrictive view of World War I literature as limited to a modernist-experimental versus realist-pacifist binary, which is only gradually relaxing. The final section of Chapter 3 in particular scrutinises the relationship between formal modes of telling stories about war and their reception and social functions. It establishes connections between subject matter, style and genre. The main argument here is that central concerns of wartime and inter-war Britain were negotiated in a variety of ways through its short fiction so as to offer readers a multitude of possible foils and interpretations for their own experience or memory of the war. Themes include loss and mourning, remembrance, love and personal relationships, physical and psychological damage, ethical dilemmas, fears of espionage and racial degeneration, and the depiction and implications of violence. This section also investigates different subgenres of the short story and how these are used in different ways to negotiate these concerns: romance, spy thriller, melodrama and adventure story, as well as the modernist psychological sketch.

The core chapters of the book are Chapters 4 and 5, which use the theoretical and contextual premises established in the first three chapters for wide-ranging readings and analyses of war stories written and published between 1914 and 1956. These readings illustrate in greater depth previously made points about stylistic and ideological diversity, readerships, social functions of war fiction, canonisation and the relationship between war writing and modernism. The notion of the implied reader and the use of narrative fiction as a means of (re-)configuring readers' and writers' own experiences inform these readings, all of which investigate different narrative strategies of addressing their implied readers' concerns, particularly the use of familiar genre patterns. Chapter 4 continues to illustrate the intimate relationship between formal presentation and the functionality of a text introduced in Chapter 3. Focussing on stylistic matters on the one hand and the issue of the implied reader on the other, this chapter provides close readings of a range of short stories from several popular subgenres to show how these popular forms are used to negotiate central concerns of their implied audiences, both during and after the war. The chapter falls into three subsections addressing a variety of issues. The first section looks at short stories dealing with subjects of loss, grief and mourning as a pertinent problem in wartime and post-war society. Stories discussed in this section range from immediate wartime responses to some later stories tracing continued grief and its gradual transformation into the inter-war and post-war period. The second and third sections concentrate on physical and psychological damage sustained in the war and demonstrate how the romance genre in particular was used to negotiate injury and disability by placing these in the context of safe, reassuring formulae.

The fifth chapter complements Chapter 4 by offering further close readings of individual short stories, in this case focusing on the negotiation of moral and ideological dilemmas through the medium of short fiction. Chapter 5 is divided into three subsections dealing with the conflict between personal and military obligations, espionage fears and the treatment of 'enemy aliens' in Britain and representations of violence and the figure of the soldier. Through its wide-ranging selection of primary material, Chapter 5 in particular illustrates how short fiction offered readers a range of alternative interpretations of the war and thus a variety of foils for their own experiences of the conflict. This chapter also illustrates the stylistic and formal variety of short fiction available.

The final chapter of the book extends the analysis of the preceding chapters to a selection of inter-war and post-war stories, written and published from the late 1930s to the present. Following a similar structure as the preceding chapters, readings investigate changes in outlook, interest and topics of post-war short fiction, as opposed to the bulk of earlier stories. Topics covered include continued mourning, remembrance and memory building, and the use of the war as a de-personalised historical marker. The chapter also addresses the increasing difficulty to clearly identify subgenres of the short story in contemporary short fiction addressing the war, with the crime story as the notable exception. Chapter 6 particularly distinguishes later stories about World War I from short fiction written in closer temporal proximity to the conflict in terms of their social and aesthetic agenda. A selection of close readings illustrates the move from short stories responding to immediate interests of an intended readership embroiled in war to a more reflective interest in the commemoration and memory of the war. In relation to these new interests the chapter addresses the continued development of the war's mythology in contemporary literature, with a particular focus on the second 'war books boom' of the 1980s and 1990s, during which novelists such as Pat Barker, Sebastian Faulks, and Children's Laureate Michael Morpurgo addressed the war in their fiction, and which also sparked a number of short stories on the subject of the Great War. Reading this book, many more possible themes and topics will spring to mind, but I hope it offers a representative selection of what has preoccupied readers and writers in Britain dealing with the First World War from 1914 to the present day.

CHAPTER I

Canon, Genre, Experience, and the Implied Reader

GREAT WAR SHORT STORIES AND THEIR LITERARY CONTEXT

Just as Great War writing in general cannot be regarded as if it existed in a literary and historical vacuum, short stories of and about the war cannot be analysed separately from writing about the war in other genres. Next to the war memoirs of the 1920s, poetry has been one of the most important literary genres to play a part in the popularisation of the war and in the shaping of its cultural memory in Britain. Accordingly, a closer look at the poetry and prose that found its way into the canon of Great War literature after 1914 may reveal the qualities of Great War writing that were most remembered once the conflict was over. Why did the war's poetry, and to a lesser extent its novels and memoirs, have such an impact on the way we remember the conflict when its short fiction is all but forgotten? And how did this 'literary' remembrance of the First World War come about?

While Britons during the inter-war years held a variety of beliefs about what the war had been like and what it had achieved, the 1920s and 1930s experienced a public remembrance culture that regarded the war as a tragedy in terms of loss of life, but, as Dan Todman suggests, could not yet bring itself to declare the war to be wholly futile due to the perceived need of bereaved relatives to believe that their sons, brothers and husbands had died in a worthy cause.[1] Todman argues that while the 1960s are generally seen as the period in which the myth of the war first came into being, it is more accurate to say that this was the point in time where renewed interest and a resulting surge of new publications, film and television programmes, the anti-Vietnam War movement, the gradual demise of bereaved relatives and increased veteran activity combined to cement a version of the war that had existed since at least the 1920s.[2] The decades from about 1960 onwards witnessed the gradual formation of the memory of the war as the senseless slaughter in the Western Front trenches that has evolved into such a powerful mythology.[3]

The canonised, disillusioned war poets have been part and parcel of the war's myth since at least the 1960s: they are the so-called trench poets whose poetry has come to be regarded as the authoritative voice of truth about the First World War, despite the fact that they constitute a minority among those who wrote and published poetry during the war.[4] Hibberd and Onions link the canonisation of the trench poets as the war poets per se to their perceived ability to bear first-hand witness to the war.[5] Regardless of the extent to which war poetry has helped to form British cultural memory of the war, it is certainly true that the British focus on the trenches in public perceptions of the First World War is reflected in the war's literary canon. While the Western Front constitutes the largest part of British remembrance culture, the home front – and with it all non-combatant experience of the war – remains in a marginalised position and has mainly been popularised as a negative contrast to the 'real' war at the front.[6]

Apart from its strong mutual relationship with the memory and remembrance of the war, the most prominent quality of First World War poetry is its prolific nature. War poems far outnumber texts from all other genres, including the short story: Catherine Reilly's groundbreaking bibliography *English Poetry of the First World War* (1978) lists more than 3,000 individual war poems by more than 2,000 poets. Edna Longley describes poetry as the unprecedented 'mass medium' of the First World War in Britain which, despite the fact that most of the war poems composed during the war have since been 'remaindered by history', offers scope to be 'read, imitated, and quoted in shifting contexts'.[7] Her observation aptly captures the phenomenon of Great War poetry in Britain, which stimulated satire even during the war itself, and continues to thrive in Britain up to the present day. Longley also stresses the strong anti-war element connected with Great War poetry today, quoting as an example the anthology *101 Poems Against War* (2003), published just before the Iraq war, which prominently features Wilfred Owen's poetry.[8] Longley suggests various reasons poetry became the most important genre of the war – primarily its faculty for 'improvisation' and 'rapid response' – contrasting it with prose in a wartime context by arguing that 'as it proved from Brooke to Owen, poetry's symbolic and mnemonic force reaches where prose cannot touch'.[9] Short stories are also quickly written and can respond to war experiences with great immediacy, yet their impact on the memory of the war, especially when compared to the trench poetry, is negligible. Besides their relative brevity and the possibility to respond quickly, those war poems perpetuated by inclusion in authoritative anthologies and school syllabi must have had a further quality that ensured their lasting precedence over short fiction. A potential characteristic that makes poetry more suitable than short prose may be its tendency to be more easily adaptable, more universal in its rhetoric and outlook; qualities that are exemplified in Wilfred Owen's poetry:

[For] all that Owen's poems make reference to poison gas, dugouts and artillery bombardment, they are much less specifically rooted in a description of trench warfare than, for example, Sassoon's. Owen's effort to transcend the context of the trenches in poems such as 'Anthem for Doomed Youth' and 'Strange Meeting' made his work more easily applicable to subsequent conflicts, or to war in general. The reader does not require specific knowledge of the First World War to draw out a layer of meaning based on Owen's horror at the mutilation and death of young men.[10]

Even those war poems that attempt to portray warfare realistically are still bound by certain poetic conventions; they still make extensive use of symbolic imagery and metaphor, rhetorical devices that help to see what is referred to in the poem in a more abstract manner. It is not surprising, as Todman also observes, that the composer Benjamin Britten chose a selection of poems by Wilfred Owen for his composition *War Requiem* (1962), designed as a musical memorial for the dead of both world wars and as a statement against war in general. Indeed, Great War poetry by poets such as Owen, Sassoon, Isaac Rosenberg, Robert Graves and Ivor Gurney came to be seen increasingly as anti-war in general, not anti-First World War in particular: it has long since turned into a pacifist message that could be applied to the Vietnam (or, as we have seen above, the Iraq) war just as well as to the war that formed its actual historical context. Esther MacCallum-Stewart notes this phenomenon in her work on contemporary children's literature dealing with the First World War, and observes that in the wake of the anti-war movement of the 1960s,

[t]he writing of the First World War writers and poets was [...] adopted as synonymous with the notions of futility and the pity of conflict. Direct links were made between the war poets such as Siegfried Sassoon, Robert Graves, and Wilfred Owen and the ongoing conflict in Vietnam. This led to the adoption of the First World War as a metonym for *all* wars.[11]

Although Owen and his fellow soldier poets often referred very specifically to the unique conditions of trench warfare – the poison gas attacks and helpless immobility – that were not to be repeated in the same form, their descriptions were sufficiently non-specific to encompass all modern warfare. By contrast, the short stories of the Great War tend to be much more specifically rooted in the social and political climate of that particular war, but even more importantly, their language and subject matter are recognisably those of their time of writing. Since most short stories were published shortly after being written, writers of short fiction could rely on their audience's familiarity with current events, resulting in frequent allusions and a lack of explanation of the bigger picture of the war. These qualities date the stories and discourage readers who do not share the knowledge taken for granted by the writers. The topics addressed by these short stories are also frequently too mundane, too trivial to be read in the same universal manner transcending specific historical conditions that one can apply to a poetry of death and sacrifice. Many stories deal with formulaic notions of romance and adventure, or with small, everyday matters such as food rationing and separation. Significantly, those short stories written during the war that survived in the literary canon, such as Katherine Mansfield's 'The Fly' (1922) or D.H. Lawrence's 'Tickets, Please' (1919), foreground not the specific conditions of the war, but more universal issues of human psychology and human interaction.

Short stories and poems alike depended on the periodical press and on anthologies for publication. Hynes lists *The Times*, the *Morning Post*, the *Daily Chronicle* and the *Westminster Gazette* as publications 'where war poems appeared as regularly as first leaders', and observes of wartime anthologies of poetry that they 'appeared with astonishing rapidity – three in September 1914, another in November, twelve in 1915, six more in 1916'.[12] This trend continued throughout and after the war, and it is in these anthologies that we can see most clearly how the formation of a canon of First World War literature and the shaping of a popular remembrance culture of the war go hand in hand – always bearing in mind that all war poetry was not equally well received and that only a fraction of it became part of the war's literary memory.[13] Compared to poetry anthologies, story anthologies were much rarer, and most short stories of the war did not possess the same pacifist, ideological potential as those poems of the war that were repeatedly anthologised. Consequently, although both war poems and war stories appeared in the same media during and after the war, war poetry (albeit a highly selective part thereof) fared better at establishing itself as part of the war's myth in the long term, both as a result of the more profitable nature of poetry over prose anthologies, and because of its more universal outlook.

Longer prose texts addressing the war are as selectively read as Great War poetry, and only a small number of texts are taught in schools and universities, mainly novels and memoirs of the late 1920s. Works such as Siegfried Sassoon's semi-autobiographical Sherston novels (published between 1928 and 1936), Graves's *Goodbye to All That* (1929), Richard Aldington's *Death of a Hero* (1929), or Blunden's *Undertones of War* (1928) were war books perpetuated by republication, critical attention and their close connection with the emerging myth of the war. Naturally, however, prose fiction about the First World War was not limited to this comparatively small number of disillusioned texts published ten years after the end of the conflict. Despite claims that the war could not have been addressed before the late 1920s because the traumatic experiences it had occasioned for writers and readers alike had first to be overcome, people did read about the war even in the early 1920s, in short stories as well as novels. These stories and novels do not try to hide or ameliorate tragic or unpleasant aspects of the war, but nevertheless strive to present them in the light of meaningful sacrifice – a stance infinitely more valuable to a large readership that had to come to terms with the loss of friends and relatives than the bitter, ironic outlook of the fiction of disillusionment published during the 'war books boom' of the late 1920s.[14] Early examples are John Hay Beith's novel *The First Hundred Thousand* (1916; initially published as a serial in *Blackwood's Magazine* under Beith's pen-name Ian Hay) and its two sequels published in 1917, all of which present the war from a soldier's perspective, but in a cheerful, down-to-earth vein, even after fictional protagonists and real-life author alike had been transferred to the front. From the beginning of the war, novels and short stories were written and published that endorsed the war in the same manner earlier fiction had supported the colonial wars of the nineteenth century and stood in the same tradition of heroic and patriotically inspiring war writing.

A particularly good example of this is Ernest Raymond's inter-war novel *Tell England* (1922), which Cadogan and Craig have described as 'probably the most representative novel [of the war] in terms of public-school honour and classic chauvinism'.[15] In *Tell England*, Raymond relates in positive, affirmative tones the sacrifice of two English public-school boys who volunteer for service and meet their death in action in the Dardanelles campaign. Their death is presented not as the futile waste that became the general interpretation from the late 1920s onwards, but as a meaningful offering in accordance with notions of honour, patriotism and spiritual integrity. Rosa Maria Bracco notes that other novels, expressly written for a middle-class adult audience, interpreted the war in a similarly affirmative light, particularly after its end, although George Simmers has since shown that all 'middlebrow' writing about the war was not necessarily untroubled by concerns about the war's effect.[16] In his studies on juvenile adventure fiction and what he calls the 'pleasure culture of war',[17] Michael Paris establishes that war continued to be considered an exciting and worthwhile pursuit for boys and girls alike after 1918, despite the fact that the realities of modern warfare were frequently outlined in graphic detail.[18] Such narratives of the war were published well into the Second World War and even after its end, encompassing both new editions of older texts and post-war stories by younger writers, often veterans of the Great War.[19]

Paralleling the poetry of the Great War, only a small fraction of the war's prose has been canonised, namely those works that support the myth of the war as a tragically futile endeavour, or that showed a certain degree of formal innovation. Prose fiction and particularly short stories following 'traditional' patterns and referring back to pre-war modes of endowing the conflict with meaning tend to have been marginalised and have not found their way into the canon of Great War literature. Most short stories addressing the war fall into the realm of popular fiction, and that, alongside their more transient form of publication, their lack of formal innovation and a refusal to treat the war as entirely futile, may be responsible for their quick descent into obscurity.

CULTURAL ARCHIVE, NARRATIVE CONFIGURATION, AND THE IMPLIED READER

Given how much the First World War has come to be associated with its literature, and how far the poetry of the war in particular has shaped popular memory of the conflict, canonicity is an issue of central concern to the study of First World War writing. The idea of a literary canon has undergone much scrutiny over the past decades, without resulting in a universally acknowledged consensus. Given the complexity of factors contributing to processes of canonisation, it is helpful to assume that there is no such thing as a universal literary canon. The everyday practicalities informing canon formation are not the least reason to be doubtful of the concept of a literary canon. A literary text may be of supreme aesthetic value, but as long as it fails to be printed and made accessible to the right kind of audience, it has no hope of entering any canon at all. Publishing and marketing concerns, outlets of publication, the question of who reads a text and for what reason; all of these factors have a significant impact on canonisation. Not the least of these are accessibility and longevity. Publication and availability are a problematic issue attached to the short story that distinguishes it clearly and radically from the novel. A novel will usually be published (sometimes following previous serialisation) in one autonomous piece, and republished as long as it sells. A short story, on the other hand, is usually first published in a newspaper or magazine, and for its republication depends entirely on the choices made by anthology editors. The exception are short stories by particularly successful authors (who are mostly also successful novelists), which may be reprinted in a collection of short stories by that author, but will usually lag far behind that author's novels in sales. The self-contained publication of a short story, while possible, usually only happens at the costly initiative of the author.[20] This makes short stories a particularly transient genre, and many of them are absent from critical studies simply because they disappeared from view almost as soon as they were published. In most cases, scholars and critics devote their attention to stories written by well-known authors, seen as supplementing their longer prose, or stories that serve to exemplify particular literary trends. Availability through republication in turn also tends to have an impact on the curriculum, since only widely available texts are likely to be taught in schools. As John Rodden points out, 'a well-edited collected volume can facilitate the institutionalizing of new works and the growth of a reputation'.[21] Publication and anthologisation consequently have to be regarded as important factors in canonising a text, which will be examined at greater length in Chapters 2 and 3.

Despite all these caveats, it is hard to deny that processes of canonisation are constantly at work, shaping what is read and discussed in schools and universities, among lay readers and critics. This is as evident in the field of First World War writing as in any other area of literature. How, then, can we approach the fact that selective processes are clearly taking place, without applying restrictive conceptions of canonicity? One possible solution is to regard canonicity as a concept closely related to the process of cultural memory formation, which also facilitates a reading of First World War texts in relation to the war's evolving mythology. Such a take on canonisation allows for a range of factors, not least the accessibility of a text, and can be achieved by adapting Aleida Assmann's theory of cultural memory.[22] Assmann outlines two types of memory: the so-called working memory ('Funktionsgedächtnis'), and its complement, the 'reference memory' or 'cultural reservoir' ('Speichergedächtnis'). These two types of memory are seen as constituting the two layers of the cultural memory of a group or society.[23] Distinguishing between them allows for a distinction between the large body of items – texts, images, events, memories or similar – that is theoretically accessible to a given group and those items that are an actual part of its active consciousness.

The cultural reservoir is likened by Assmann to an attic in which cultural artefacts are stored but not normally accessed.[24] In real-world terms, one would have to think of all those texts as part of the cultural reservoir that are available in libraries, archives and private collections, but remain on the shelves and in the store-rooms without being read regularly by a significant number of people. Short stories of the First World War, potentially accessible in newspaper archives and old collections, are a good illustration of the cultural reservoir. As we will see, particularly short stories written by and for personal witnesses of the war conform exactly to Assmann's definition of cultural artefacts, in that they have 'lost their immediate addressees; they are de-contextualized and disconnected from their former frames which had authorized them or determined their meaning'.[25] The working memory, on the other hand, comprises those texts which are continually revisited and read by members of a given group or society – such as the war poetry of Wilfred Owen. Their constant revisiting amounts to a selective social process of canonisation,[26] meaning that these texts remain in the working memory only as long as they coincide with social interests and values.[27] Canonisation in this sense takes on a distinctly communal character: the canonised texts are included in a canon because they are relevant to the society of which that canon forms a part, while those texts remaining in the cultural reservoir have no such current relevance. At the same time, all texts in the cultural reservoir may be transferred into the working memory as soon as they can serve a social purpose. Assmann stresses that working memory and cultural reservoir cannot exist one without the other. While the working memory is backed up and at times 'corrected' by the information stored in the reservoir, the reservoir itself would be meaningless without the possibility that its contents might become part of the working memory at some point in the future.[28] As Assmann observes, the cultural reservoir provides a rich background for the working memory or canon that ensures its lasting significance.[29] Ongoing feminist revision projects dating back to the 1970s and 1980s, exemplified by the establishment of Virago Press and the systematic republication of texts by neglected female writers, are an example of a deliberate bid to shift material from the cultural archive to the working memory. In its own way, this study constitutes another such revision project with regard to popular short fiction addressing the First World War.

Broadly speaking, the working memory of the war offers an overarching narrative of the war; a generalised tale that has come to reflect and shape public consciousness of the Great War and channels individual memories into a unified story. Such a myth of the First World War is not simply a fiction or fabrication, but rather a 'simplified narrative that evolves from a war, through which it is given meaning', a 'socially necessary' tale that chooses of all divergent narratives and experiences of the war the one best suited to the society that re-tells and perpetuates it.[30] The cultural reservoir, on the other hand, to which First World War short stories largely belong, complements that dominant narrative of the war with its plethora of divergent narratives which challenge, confirm or run parallel to the war's working memory, but form no active part of it unless they are for some reason extracted and introduced to a wider audience.

One reason to transfer a text from the cultural archive to the working memory is the wish to make sense of an experience, like the need of those who had lived through the war to assign meaning to their experiences, or the attempts of later generations to throw light on their grandparents' and great-grandparents' war. In *Oneself as Another* (1990), Paul Ricoeur scrutinises the functions and benefits of narrative for reflections on identity and character, and ultimately its bearings on human actions and ethical choices.[31] He argues that human beings interpret their lives by means of plot patterns borrowed from fictional or historiographical narratives. According to Ricoeur, 'self-understanding is an interpretation; interpretation of the self, in turn, finds in the narrative, among other signs and symbols, a privileged form of mediation'.[32] Interpreting life as a text, as a narrative that is being written as we live it, helps the self establish its identity across the span of an entire life.[33] By providing a framework for establishing and confirming identity, narrativity helps us solve one of the main problems Ricoeur posits in his analysis of selfhood and sameness, that of a need to establish continuity of character and thus identity over time.[34] Ricoeur introduces the idea of narrative as a 'laboratory of moral judgment' in which we can test our judgements and desires against their potential consequences.[35] The process of narrative configuration, of configuring events and occurrences through narration, is a sense-making process, a way of attributing meaning, for those who either narrate or read/follow the narrative. The totality of one's life may be threatened by adverse and unforeseeable events, such as an accident, but through narrative configuration, even adversities can be incorporated into a life's history as a meaningful occurrence that has some connection with its before and after: an adverse event 'only becomes an integral part of the story when understood after the fact, once it is transfigured by the so-to-speak retrograde necessity which proceeds from the temporal totality carried to its term'.[36]

Given that the war was widely perceived as a rupture, even a 'gap in history',[37] Ricoeur's concept is excellently suited to a reading of First World War fiction as an instrument of creating meaning through narrativity. Coincidence, according to Ricoeur, is turned into fate through narrativity.[38] Ricoeur adopts Alasdair MacIntyre's idea of the 'narrative unity of a life', which is, as he says, 'governed [...] by a life project, however uncertain and mobile it may be, and by fragmentary practices, which have their own unity, life plans constituting the intermediary zone of exchange between the undetermined character of guiding ideals and the determinate nature of practices'.[39] Ricoeur suggests that because of the instability and elusiveness of 'real' life we need narrative as a means of rewriting our lives into more stable, uniform patterns. Even unsettling narratives challenging widely held beliefs can fulfil this function for the individual reader by confirming personal experiences that run counter to communal opinion, and by thus offering alternative means of interpretation. Such a rewriting happens retrospectively, is always open to revision and offers the means of dividing life into 'chapters' that can be closed off and left behind as provisional endings before the grand ending, death.[40]

Great War short stories are narratives that were widely accessible and sufficiently varied to provide interpretative patterns to which their readers could compare their own experiences and on which they could mould their own impressions and memories. This also has a dimension of putting isolated personal experiences into a larger perspective, and of giving meaning to the personal by relating it to the general. In the broadest sense, it is in this light that I am looking at the stories included in this study: as a means of interpreting the war, of coping with its manifold aspects and consequences, and of striving to express and experiment with insights and experiences unique to the war. That these stories have come to be part of the cultural archive of the war rather than its working memory does not reflect their value as narrative models to wartime readers, or the interest they hold for interpreting the experience of World War I from the perspective of the early twenty-first century.

In Ricoeur's theory of narrative configuration, the readership rather than the writer of a text is given prominence, linking the theory to the field of reader-response theory and particularly the work of German literary scholar Hans Robert Jauss. Jauss's reader-centred approach to texts, formulated among others in a collection of his early essays, *Toward an Aesthetic of Reception* (1982), centres largely on the idea of readerly expectations. Jauss has argued that what a reader takes away from a text is strongly influenced by what he brings to it in the first place, an approach also taken by Ricoeur:

Ricoeur's principal interest was what the reader takes away from the narrative work, an effect that Hans Robert Jauss called an *aesthetics of reception*. Understanding of the narrative work and self-understanding overlap; to receive and understand the work is also to receive an understanding of self and the complexity of temporal existence. The relationship between narrative and the understanding of temporal existence is characterized by the intersection between the world of the narrative composition and the understanding that the reader brings to the engagement with the text.[41]

According to Jauss, every text is read against what he calls a 'horizon of expectations' surrounding any given work at the time of its first publication, which is made up of existing literary and cultural standards. Combining Jauss's work on reception and reader-response theory with Ricoeur's conception of narrative texts as a means of configuring reality highlights the importance of what readers brought to short stories about the war at their time of first publication. It also helps us appreciate that contemporary readers' responses and expectations differed vastly from what we bring to these stories today. To readers with their own first-hand experience of the war, whether at the home front or as combatants, any fictional account of the war needed to somehow relate to their own memories, knowledge and experiences. I am arguing here that writers, particularly writers of magazine fiction who were conscious of their potential readers' expectations for commercial reasons, were fully aware of this and modelled their writing on an implied audience with such a shared, communal knowledge of the war. The wartime and inter-war short stories discussed below were capable of being means of narrative configuration of their readers' reality exactly because they assumed such knowledge and took into account the great variety of experiences the war engendered. Later stories addressing the war, on the other hand, work with different assumptions and reflect the gradual change in perception of World War I within British society as time passed. By this I do not mean to suggest that these stories are mere reflections of changing trends; rather, they themselves assist in the process of change. The formation of a literary canon of First World War literature and of the war's mythology were mutually influential. My basic assumption, based on what Jauss terms a 'horizon of expectations', is that writers are consciously or unconsciously working to such expectations, which inevitably change over time and are thus beyond their continued control. This assumption underpins the analysis of First World War short

fiction in the following chapters. While it is impossible to quantify readers' actual responses beyond the very general notion that what was frequently published must have sold well and would have been read by large
audiences, it is possible to infer a horizon of expectations from the texts
and their contexts. By making frequent references to newspaper articles,
historical source material and writing about the war in other genres, I
am looking at the different kinds of questions that contemporary and
subsequent generations of readers may have put to these short stories and
continue to put to them, in the light of the answers the stories can and
do provide.

One of the reasons this book focuses primarily on what can be called
popular or even formula literature – magazine short stories written for
those in search of light entertainment – is that such stories were particularly widely available. Moreover, as Jauss points out, it is rarely the
avant-garde literary masterpiece that best expresses contemporary moods
and sentiments. On the contrary,

> an important work, one that indicates a new direction in the literary process,
> is surrounded by an unsurveyable production of works that correspond to the
> traditional expectations or images concerning reality, and that thus in their social
> index are to be no less valued than the solitary novelty of the great work that is
> often comprehended only later.[42]

My argument for studying magazine fiction and modernist writing side
by side, and my main reason for retrieving popular narratives from old
anthologies and magazine back numbers, is that both conservative and
innovative literary texts are needed to appreciate the diversity of discourses
that informed the war's experience. Popular literature was crucial in creating the horizon of expectations against which modernist war stories were
pitched and which modernist and disillusioned war writing went on to
gradually alter and adapt. Formula literature in general and magazine stories in particular often constitute excellent examples of Ricoeur's notion of
narrative configuration in action. Popular First World War stories offered
idealised representations of both home front and frontline(s) that reassured and comforted those faced with hardship or doubt; romance stories addressed anxieties about loosening morals and romantic attraction
by channelling war-related sexual tensions into the socially acceptable
domain of courtship and marriage; frontline stories attempted to depict
the experience of combat for civilian readers and rehearsed difficult moral
decisions. By addressing all aspects of war and depicting new developments such as widespread war work amongst women, popular war stories

did their bit to reconcile readers to the profoundly disturbing experience of the (arguably) first total war.

Modernist and avant-garde stories similarly engaged with the war and its impact, but by different means; either striving to find new ways of representing the challenging new experience of modern warfare, or exploring underlying motives, psychological reactions and emotional responses to a conflict of unprecedented scale. Their audience, however, was much smaller than that of popular magazine fiction, and their strategies of representation not necessarily easily accessible or comforting to those reading primarily for pleasure, distraction or reassurance. In the preface to her collection *The Demon Lover and Other Stories* (1945), Bowen points out that '[p]eople whose homes had been blown up went to infinite lengths to assemble bits of themselves – broken ornaments, odd shoes, torn scraps of the curtains that had hung in a room – from the wreckage. In the same way, they assembled and checked themselves from stories and poems, from their memories, from one another's talk.'[43] Although she is speaking from a post-war perspective, Bowen's perceptive observation of wartime society illustrates beautifully the idea of narrative (re-)configuration. Short stories thus take their place next to oral communication, poetry and material evidence in validating and interpreting memories, and completing again what has been ruptured. In a certain sense, what Bowen describes is a miniature version of Assmann's cultural reservoir; a personal archive to be referred to as and when needed to invest personal experiences with meaning. In this light, even what might be deemed trivial reading not only served as 'the perfect vehicles for sustaining the hearts and minds of the population'[44] during the Great War, but allowed for the continual reassessment and validation of readers' own experiences and memories. As Michael Roper has put it, 'one possible motivation for story-telling [was] as a means of actively managing painful experiences from the past'.[45]

If one applies Assmann's concept to First World War literature specifically, the British canon of Great War writing emerges as roughly equivalent to a working memory of the war, while all those texts – like most short stories of the war – which do not form part of that canon constitute the war's cultural archive. These are a body of texts and sources about the experience of the war, and about the cultural or literary treatment of this experience, that can be drawn on to amend, substitute or complement the working memory of the war. Given that, as we move further and further away from the war as a lived experience, World War I is increasingly consigned to cultural rather than personal memory, it seems desirable to encourage any initiative in teaching and scholarship that might lead to the inclusion of new texts. First World War short stories in particular can help us reclaim many of the different facets of the British experience of the war that would otherwise remain buried, both literally with the war's eye witnesses and their direct descendants, and metaphorically in archives and library store rooms.

WHICH CANON? SHORT FICTION AND FIRST WORLD WAR LITERATURE

With respect to First World War writing, canonicity cannot be restricted to a purely academic understanding. Widespread attention and reception, not necessarily restricted to an academic environment, are to be seen as major indicators of the canonicity of a text. Both the academy and the intended reader have to be acknowledged as important influences in the canonisation of a text, and in the case of First World War short fiction they contribute to the development of two largely separate canons: a 'literary' canon of largely experimental war writing (a scholar's canon), and a socio-cultural canon of texts concerned with an 'authentic' retelling of the war's experience (a reader's canon). While factors such as literary quality do play an important role in the canonisation of a text, even a text of superior literary quality needs to be either widely received over a longer period of time (which is usually the case when it can recognisably serve relevant cultural and/or social functions), or it needs at the very least to be read and received by the right kind of audience, i.e. an audience that has the resources to ensure the text in question remains in print, and is introduced into educational syllabi.

The scholar's and the reader's canon of First World War writing deserve some further scrutiny before we move on to taking a closer look at different kinds of short stories. Where a scholarly canon has a pronounced interest in stylistic and structural properties of texts, the reader's canon of First World War writing is primarily a socio-cultural canon where content is a more important criterion than form, and aesthetic considerations are secondary to the 'truthfulness' or authenticity of a text. There is generally a certain tension present between plot, style and subject matter in First World War writing: short stories often use the war as a plot intensifier and have a greater interest in formal characteristics, whereas other, especially non-fictional war texts have little interest in form beyond its relationship to the perceived authenticity of a text. War as a topic appears to demand realism, genre demands artistry.[46]

While contemporary critics also expected war memoirs to be well written, their main concern was the veracity of the author's account of his war experiences, or, with fictional prose, the authenticity of what was depicted in comparison to life at the front. Readers and critics alike expected their war books to show them war as it really was, or rather, as they expected it to be, a desire and a disparity, as Kate McLoughlin has shown, shared by many authors of war books throughout history.[47] Although he declares that his particular praise is reserved for narratives he considers 'particularly well written',[48] Cyril Falls in *War Books* (1930) more often than not censures a novel whose author, he feels, 'appears to know singularly little of certain of the details which he describes'.[49] Robert Graves found himself criticised for the factual inaccuracy of his war memoir *Goodbye to All That* (1929), a hastily dictated volume composed in the midst of his separation from his first wife and under severe financial strain. In response to this criticism, Graves stressed the practical difficulties faced by memoirists of the war given the lack of reliable sources. It had been his inaccuracies about battles and frontline topography that had most irked some reviewers and critics, and Graves pointed out subsequently the impossibility of keeping a diary in the trenches. He also noted the undesirability of relating only pure fact: 'I would even paradoxically say that the memoirs of a man who went through some of the worst experiences of trench warfare are not truthful if they do not contain a high proportion of falsities.'[50] Siegfried Sassoon deliberately recorded his war experience in the form of a series of autobiographical novels, which yet claimed to be fictional memoirs (and were thus imbued with a sense of factuality while being fictional). An example from a frontline other than the Western Front are the experiences of T.E. Lawrence as recorded in *Seven Pillars of Wisdom: A Triumph* (1926), whose veracity was first questioned by Richard Aldington in the disparaging *Lawrence of Arabia: A Biographical Inquiry* (1955). Although most of his allegations of falsehood or embellishment were later disproved by either witnesses or official documents, Aldington's book hit hardest where a war book was most vulnerable, in that it questioned the truthfulness of Lawrence's account, combined with claims that Lawrence was homosexual. Lawrence's exploits were nevertheless immensely popular particularly with a juvenile audience, perhaps – as Dorothea Flothow suggests – because they took readers away from the dreary modernity of the trenches to the exoticism of desert warfare, and to individual heroics rather than mass drudgery.[51]

Fictional accounts of the war, whether in the form of a novel or a short story, always competed with texts claiming to be non-fiction and based entirely on autobiographical experience. Since non-fictional texts claim for themselves a depiction of reality that may by necessity be narrated but is by definition factual, war memoirs and autobiographies potentially promised an account of the war that was considered more 'truthful' than that provided by fictional texts. Evelyn Cobley notes that those writing about their own experiences of the frontline in the First World War wrote 'to provide an alternative history which was scrupulously accurate in its depiction of everyday events',[52] frequently driven by feelings of survivor's guilt or the need to retrospectively embed what had happened into safe narrative frameworks. In these attempts, the vast majority of writers chose a documentary mode, whether in the form of explicitly non-fictional memoir or fictional autobiographical novel.[53] In entering the British canon of First World War literature, short stories addressing the war were thus in competition (aesthetically, ideologically and commercially) with a plethora of other texts with higher claims to truthfulness and authenticity: while short stories are, firstly, fictional texts, and were secondly in most cases written by civilian writers, other texts – such as war poetry written by poets with frontline experience, or memoirs and autobiographical fiction written by war veterans – are seen to convey a more authentic account of the war.[54] Andrew Maunder also observes how, particularly during the early stages of the war, '[f]actual books seemed preferable to fictional ones because their readers could at least claim to be taking the conflict seriously rather than trying to escape it'.[55] The development and change of the Great War canon in British culture can and must be seen as intricately connected with changing public perceptions and commemoration of the First World War, and in particular its evolving mythology.[56]

First World War literature, and poetry of the war in particular, has become an important part of English literary studies and has been a staple element of modern British school curricula since the 1960s.[57] Although the range of exam boards and set texts in Britain result in difficulty in terms of gathering empirical evidence, British popular memory of the war appears to be strongly shaped by the teaching of the war's 'trench poetry' and a select number of other texts in secondary schools across the country.[58] In *The Pity of War* (1998), the historian Niall Ferguson relates how his early exposure to the poetry of Wilfred Owen in school, aged fourteen, cemented his interest in the First World War.[59] However, war writing taught in schools does not necessarily reflect the actual experience of the Great War or its literary output.[60] The poems of Rupert Brooke, for instance, who later on came to be regarded as merely the naive victim of patriotic enthusiasm, can be seen as far more typical of World War

I writing than the now vastly more popular Wilfred Owen.[61] Historian
Brian Bond agrees with Rosa Maria Bracco that literary critics and scholars, namely those who are in a position to influence the formation of a
literary canon, 'have too often focused on enduring literary merit to the
neglect of the more ephemeral popularity of competent middlebrow writers'.[62] This neglect results largely from the conflicting interests of literary
criticism and social historiography: where Bond, Bracco and others see
a plethora of texts yielding rich insights into popular attitudes and concerns regarding the First World War, literary scholars often see works of
popular fiction repeating predictable patterns and catering to mass tastes
rather than developing complex new aesthetics. Theories of cultural and
literary production introduced and refined by Bourdieu and Ken Gelder
place emphasis on target audiences; and different First World War texts
do indeed hold different merit depending on the audience they originally
targeted and the readings applied to them today.[63]

By the 1980s, Great War writing had become almost synonymous with
pacifist, anti-war writing, and evoked clear images of the horrors of modern warfare. The eminence of the First World War as a literary topic is
due primarily to the war's importance for British cultural memory: the
conflict is widely remembered as the ultimate catastrophe of the twentieth
century that marked the loss of innocence and entrance into the age of
mechanised 'total' warfare. Corresponding to this perception of the First
World War as a locus of fundamental change for modern society, its literature is frequently perceived as exemplifying the turn from traditional,
realist Victorian and Edwardian writing to more experimental, modernist
writing, despite the fact that most narratives and poetry about the war
adhered to traditional patterns even after 1918. The formation of a canon
of First World War literature began during the inter-war years, particularly
the late 1920s and early 1930s, when most of the now canonical 'classic'
war novels and memoirs appeared after a period of relative silence on the
war. These texts of the so-called war books boom reiterated the stance on
the war that had previously been adopted by the more war-critical among
the trench poets, and condemned the war as a futile endeavour and senseless mass-slaughter of young, promising men. Janet Watson argues that
this evaluation of the war was by no means exclusively a result of the war
years themselves, but mainly resulted from the socio-economic difficulties of the inter-war years which helped to create the illusion of pre-war
Britain as a better world terminated by the conflict.[64] She claims that the
now canonical memoirs and autobiographical novels by Blunden, Graves,
Sassoon and Remarque were invariably 'much more about life after the

war than about the war itself',[65] and demonstrates this by contrasting diary entries and retrospectively reworked versions of the same incidents in the writings of Sassoon, Graves and Vera Brittain.[66] Literary war texts that came to be included in the canon, whether poetry, novels or memoirs, were characterised by a uniform condemnation of the war, and by certain stylistic traits that recur throughout canonised Great War writing regardless of its degree of experimentation: gritty realism, the frequent abandoning of narrative sense, an ironic narrative voice, descriptions founded on personal experience of the war (frequently referred to as a factor of 'truth', or veracity of narration), and a certain universality in their (pacifist) representation of war.[67] Watson stresses that the greatest interest critics have in Great War texts is orientated towards the future, to how war books can help prevent further war and/or help to come to terms with the past conflict to be able to leave it behind.[68] She thus directs our attention to the fact that all popular readings of Great War literature remain closely connected to the idea of a moral message, an obligation on the part of the authors to subscribe to a pacifist ideology. This attitude is also visible in the work of scholars such as George Parfitt, who repeatedly condemned war novels on the grounds that their authors had 'failed to learn' their (pacifist) lesson from the war, that they glorify it when they should be condemning it.[69] The book's explicitly moral stance is perhaps also visible in its dedication to Parfitt's uncles who fought in the war, a recurring feature of critical studies, including Fussell's dedication of *The Great War and Modern Memory* to a friend killed in action in 1945.

GREAT WAR SHORT STORIES: BETWEEN COTERIE AND MASS MARKET

The Great War as the ur-catastrophe of modernity is commonly seen to have necessitated a literature capable of representing modern reality and consciousness in new and different ways, and there appears to be widespread agreement among literary critics that modernism offered the best means for this undertaking. Modernism and the First World War are frequently considered hand in hand. Not only did literary modernism coincide with the war and the inter-war period, it also reacted to the war in texts such as T.S. Eliot's *The Waste Land* (1922), Virginia Woolf's *Jacob's Room* (1922), or David Jones's *In Parenthesis* (1937). Jones's poem is a particularly interesting case as it combines traditional reference frameworks with modernist structure and style. On the continent, the Dada movement attempted in far more radical ways to find a new language for the experience of modernity and to openly oppose the war by its own nihilistic 'war games of the mind',[70] but it did not find a following in Britain, where modernism prevailed as the main current of alternative artistic expression. Characteristics associated with the literature of high modernism, such as fragmentation of narrative structure, an interest in psychology and the dynamics of human interaction and the mind, undoubtedly all lend themselves to the purpose of representing modern experience. Hynes goes as far as saying that the First World War and its sense of radical discontinuity 'entered post-war consciousness as a truth about the modern world',[71] including post-war literature, and links the myth-making war books of the late 1920s directly to literary modernism in that they 'share a sense of history'.[72]

A broad range of authors wrote about their war experiences using narrative or poetic techniques associated with modernism, often in the short form,[73] and their writing is felt to express most poignantly the experience of modern warfare. It is often conveniently forgotten, however, that modernist experimental writing about the war crucially depended on a departure from existing models of expression. A vast array of non-modernist war fiction published during and after the war created the literary context – the 'horizon of expectations' – that helped contemporary and modern readers situate modernist responses to the conflict as a commentary on or counterpoint to these established models. Without the continued existence of alternative models of expression against which to offset innovative approaches to rendering the experience of war, modernist war writing would lose much of its edge. At the same time, there is much overlap and not always a clear dividing line between the different 'schools' or trends in war writing. In fact, as we will see below, modernist, realist and popular writers frequently addressed very similar topics, and writers commonly regarded as modernists do not necessarily always provide the most radical literary rendering of cultural concerns.

While some writers relied on modernist techniques, the majority of short story writers during and after the war continued to engage in conventional, plot-based story telling. Jay Winter criticises an understanding of the cultural history of the war as purely modernist on the grounds that even radically modernist writers of the period did not break entirely with the more traditional values and styles by which they were surrounded, but rather interacted with and transformed them, resulting in not so much a cultural and artistic rupture as a gradual development. Especially with respect to mourning and commemoration, traditional modes of expression prevailed over modernist forms in the inter-war years.[74] First World

War short stories support Winter's claims. They do not form part of the British working memory of the war partly because they largely address issues such as loss and fear by employing established, comforting patterns and formulae rather than techniques of fragmentation and alienation. However, it would be misleading to contest their value as literary documents of the war's experience on these grounds. Speaking in terms of Jauss's concept of a literary and contextual 'horizon of expectations', these conventional, mundane texts about the war may not be 'works that correspond to modern taste',[75] in particular modernist critical values. However, while they do not speak to contemporary critics and readers in the same way a modernist approach has come to do, they did speak to readers at the time through their use of familiar contexts and references. The modernist-experimental narratives privileged today, by contrast, are avant-garde in the most literal sense, in that they offer interpretations of wartime reality that only became relevant to readers as perceptions of World War I gradually changed, resulting in an adjustment of readers' and critics' expectations. The canonicity of modernist literary writing about the First World War, then, reflects subsequent developments in literary taste much more than contemporary preferences of those who had experienced the war for themselves.

The first half of the twentieth century was a heyday of short story writing and publication, owing much to the popularity of fiction magazines and periodicals, which lasted in Britain until roughly the late 1940s. Short-story writer Stacy Aumonier ventured as far as saying that 'the art of writing short stories is probably the only art in which the demand is far greater than the supply'.[76] In a writing manual, publisher and author Michael Joseph describes the circumstances as extremely favourable to the aspiring short story writer in 1923, stating that '[a] wide and increasing market awaits the writer's work. The already large number of fiction magazines is being added to practically every month, thus testifying to the public demand for fiction of this type'.[77] The early twentieth century saw the emergence and continued popularity of a great variety of short story subgenres, read by large and varied audiences. Readerships ranging from upper- to working-class, from avant-garde to popular, each with its own publication outlets, offered a fruitful market for short fiction. Publishers, with a view on profit as well as literary profile, were unwittingly contributing to the marginalisation of the popular short story by emphasising its market value over its artistic merits.

Of all early-twentieth-century story types the modernist short story has received the most critical attention. Claire Hanson, echoing Joyce, identifies as the central feature of modernist short fiction 'a single moment of intense or significant experience'.[78] Hanson stresses the impact of modernism on the social standing of the short story in general, arguing that '[i]n the modernist period the short form came to have, for the first time in its history, a status almost equivalent to that of the novel'.[79] Although modernist short stories constitute only a small portion of the stories written in the first half of the twentieth century, they are now the most canonised. Despite the fact that contemporary readers often found fault with modernist fiction 'on the ground that it has no plot and contains no action',[80] influential critics seized upon the new ideas and formal experimentation of the modernists and, like A.C. Ward, decided that it was the 'sluggish perception' of the readers that was to blame for their unfavourable reception among popular audiences.[81] Michael Joseph reacts to this contemporary difficulty of understanding modernist stories when he regrets, in the introduction to his writing manual, that he has had to 'omit reference to writers of the calibre of Tchehov [sic], Henry James, Katherine Mansfield, Rebecca West, Walter de la Mare, Aldous Huxley, G. B. Stern, May Sinclair, Maurice Baring, and Elizabeth Bibesco'.[82] He explains that, while these authors 'are playing an important part in the development of the modern short story', their avant-garde conception of short story writing would 'not help the would-be contributor to the magazines'.[83] Joseph explicitly posits modernist stories against the 'magazine short story'; against a kind of good, readable prose for a public interested in quality entertainment but without particular literary ambitions.

This notion of the short story as an essentially modernist form, conceived perhaps in the wake of New Criticism's regard for modernist fiction and perpetuated in a range of more recent critical studies, has contributed significantly to the marginalisation of much that British short fiction has to offer. Rita Felski notes that modernist affiliations were increasingly seen as visible signs of a 'repudiation of the past and a commitment to change and the values of the future',[84] whereas traditional narratives were perceived as anti-modern and thus of less value. Essentially, Felski argues that modernist texts came to be privileged in the canon because of their status, audience and affiliations, pointing to 'the formalist and antireferential emphasis of New Criticism as an institutional practice and technology of reading'.[85] New Critical ideas about what a short story ought to be came to dominate the emerging canon of short fiction and led to a bias in favour of stories that fulfilled expectations of innovation in terms of style, structure or subject matter, to the detriment of conventional tales regardless of their narrative quality. As Paul March-Russell observes, this trend continues into late twentieth-century criticism of the short story, visible in a tendency on the part of academics 'to favour what Eileen Baldeshwiler has termed the "lyrical" story over the "epical"',[86] that is, the smaller number of character-based, psychologically oriented stories over the great number of plot-based short narratives. Just as the canon of First World War literature came to be selected according to the principle of alleged truthfulness or authenticity, the short story canon became dominated by the criterion of innovation.[87]

Assuming that a privileging of modernist texts has taken place certainly helps to make sense of the process of canonisation (or lack thereof) of twentieth-century short fiction. Dominic Head has argued in favour of seeing the short story as the quintessential modernist form.[88] Head identifies fragmentation and a preoccupation with an episodic rendering of events, as well as 'a stress on literary artifice in the short story which intensifies the modernist preoccupation with formal innovation',[89] as major features of early twentieth-century short fiction. In effect, Head claims that although the short story evolved over time like other genres and changed accordingly, it reached its climax in literary modernism, which it epitomises in both its formal properties and outlook. There is much to be said for Head's argument, in that the short form was certainly extremely congenial to the aims and approaches of high modernism, and it is conspicuous that those short stories of the First World War which have found their way into the canon, into critical studies and literary histories in however marginal a position are almost invariably stories connected with modernism. I would argue, however, that this is mostly the result of our tendency to forget that the short story was equally well suited to the needs and skills of those who wrote popular, plot-centred magazine fiction, who similarly found its brevity to be conducive to their purposes. The perceived modernist monopoly on the short form is essentially a matter of literary status, in that we remember canonised modernist short fiction but forget its prolific contemporary, the magazine story.

Only a minority of writers responded to the war in an innovative way that could potentially be termed modernist. Although the Great War 'is invoked as a factor in some of the most radical departures of modernism' that are included in the canon of texts taught at universities, 'the texts dealing directly with that war remain marginal'.[90] I would claim that this is primarily because those texts that deal with the war in the most direct manner are also those that depict it in the least experimental, most traditional ways. Most texts, and most short stories in particular, follow traditional patterns that adhere to straightforward plots, closed endings, and conventional techniques of characterisation and description, but processes of canonisation and the selectivity of scholarly critical interest have led to a selection for curricula and literary histories of those texts that do address the war on modernist terms, thus giving the misleading impression that the war invariably provoked formal innovation. The majority of war writing, and certainly the majority of short stories, are no more 'modernist' in their stance on the war and its effects than they are in terms of formal properties. They are, simply and perhaps disappointingly to modern readers, works of popular fiction written for purposes of entertainment and reconciliation, propaganda and moral edification, but not with any express aim to reflect the experience of modern warfare and its effects in artistic terms. Rather than the defining literary movement of the period, as modernism has come to be viewed in retrospect, we ought to consider it as but one aspect of an 'increasingly diverse literary market'[91] at the time. Modernist short stories and their accompanying sense of disillusionment about the war are in a minority compared to the great number of stories interpreting and rendering the war in different, more conventional ways, not only during but also after the conflict. It is essential not to slip into a simplified, dual understanding of the cultural history of the war as 'modern' vs. 'traditional', an understanding that is not supported by the evidence of short stories addressing the First World War, as these stories cover a wide range of stylistic and ideological positions not only located firmly within either the modernist or the popular, traditional camp, but also in a variety of in-between stages.

Magazine stories were supposed to entertain and to sell well, and consequently valued a thrilling plot and engaging action over the psychological acuity called for by New Critical standards. As we will see below with regard to First World War short stories, short fiction published in popular weeklies or monthlies, such as the *Strand Magazine*, often differs from more artistically minded stories published in journals with a smaller circulation, such as the *English Review*. Two writers as different in their artistic ethos as D.H. Lawrence and 'Sapper' H.C. McNeile may both be writing about war injuries, but their approach to the subject, their depiction of it and reasons for choosing to write about veterans' disabilities vary considerably. Far from being problematic, this divergence between stories written of and about the First World War, and their great variety of subjects, outlook, style and agenda are their greatest benefit to the cultural and literary historian. In Chapter 2, we will be looking at two very different stories addressing the same topic of mourning, Katherine Mansfield's 'The Fly' (1922) and Ben Ray Redman's 'The Enduring Image' (1930). Contrasting

Mansfield's modernist masterpiece with a popular magazine story like Redman's gives us an idea of the varied and differentiated nature of First World War stories. The fact that most of these found themselves excluded from the war's working memory is mainly due to issues of alleged authenticity and representation. That they did not enter the canon of short fiction either is a result of the non-conformity of the vast majority of these stories to what a 'good', modern(ist), short story ought to be. The following chapters will provide an overview of the publishing context of First World War short fiction to establish some understanding of the environment in which First World War short stories were (and are) published. Such a contextualisation not only helps shed light on the different kinds of stories this study is concerned with, but adds a more practical grounding to my discussion of coterie and canon compared to the popular and the cultural archive, given that the impact of the continued publication and availability of some literary texts rather than others on our perception of the war can hardly be overestimated. As Andrew Maunder has noted, 'the fact that the influential post-war novels and autobiographies by Aldington, Sassoon and others have tended to remain in print since first appearing has had several effects. It has added to their power, but equally has prevented significant literary impressions of the war from capturing the public imagination.'[92] We can hardly underestimate the impact of what is published, and how, on the way in which we remember the First World War.

CHAPTER 2

The War in the Magazines

THE PUBLISHING CONTEXT OF BRITISH GREAT WAR SHORT STORIES

In the prefatory note to his collection *Far-Away Stories* (1916), William J. Locke stated as his reason for republishing some of his short stories that he did not want them 'to remain buried for ever in the museum files of dead magazine-numbers – an author's not unpardonable vanity'.[1] The writer's remark, casual as it may seem, exemplifies a core problem of the genre: by definition, a short story is a story that will not be published on its own for a variety of reasons, commercial and otherwise, and consequently depends on magazines and collections. Magazines and newspapers are the most ephemeral media in which war stories were published.[2] The majority of periodicals are read and then discarded, meaning that unless a magazine story is republished in another, more lasting medium, it will disappear into a few libraries and archives, most likely never to be read again. Anthologies and collections of stories by individual authors tend to have a longer shelf life, but appeal to a more restricted audience.[3] Story anthologies often target either a specialist audience of critics[4] or a student audience in an educational context. Authors' collections are most likely to appeal to readers familiar with the respective writer's other work.[5] All of these, however, are restricted audiences, and as with periodicals and anthologies the impact of the individual short story is dampened by its position amidst other texts.[6]

A brief thought experiment can illustrate the influence of its publication environment on the reading of a short story. Joseph Conrad's war story 'The Tale' lends itself to such an experiment because of its republication in a number of anthologies and collections. Conrad's story is a tale within a tale: a navy officer on leave meets his lover, and to end an emotionally draining conversation, the woman demands a story to make her forget the grim realities surrounding the lovers. The officer's tale, however, inevitably returns to the war. In the early days of the war, a naval officer (a thinly veiled 'fictional' version of the embedded narrator himself) commands a ship hunting for German spies, submarines and illegal supply ships. He comes across a neutral Scandinavian ship in dense fog, whose captain he strongly suspects of smuggling supplies for German submarines. Talking to the captain of the ship, the officer's suspicions are strengthened into certainty, but he cannot find sufficient material evidence. The captain of the neutral ship claims to be lost, stranded in the fog dangerously near the English coast. Acting solely on his intuition, the naval officer provides the captain false coordinates and orders the suspicious ship to set out again immediately, against the Northman's wishes. The ship duly hits a ledge of rock and sinks. The naval officer finishes his tale by expressing anxiety about the justness of his decision. Because he can never have absolute certainty as to whether or not the crew of the neutral ship was guilty of collaboration, he will have to live with the responsibility of his decision for the rest of his life.

'The Tale' conveys an idealised conception of war and warfare, both indirectly through the naval officer's disgust at sabotage (he is described as being 'in revolt against the murderous stealth of methods and the atrocious callousness of complicities that seemed to taint the very source of men's deep emotions and noblest activities'),[7] and directly through the officer's statements on war, which he compares to love: 'Everything should be open in love and war. Open as the day, since both are the call of an ideal which is so easy, so terribly easy, to degrade in the name of Victory'.[8] Conrad here presents us with an idealised vision of how war should be waged, only to show that in war even a man with the best intentions may find himself in a situation where his ideals become questionable and he is exposed to the risk of erring fatally. The intuition that prompts the naval officer to send the suspicious ship to its doom is imbued with a strong sense of righteousness: 'At that moment he had the certitude. The air of the chart-room was thick with guilt and falsehood braving the discovery, defying simple right, common decency, all humanity of feeling, every scruple of conduct.'[9] According to his instincts, the naval officer is right to act as he does, following as he is his own humanity of spirit – and yet he finds himself tormented by doubt:

I believe – no, I don't believe. I don't know. At the time I was certain. They all went down; and I don't know whether I have done stern retribution – or murder; whether I have added to the corpses that litter the bed of the unreadable sea, the bodies of men completely innocent or basely guilty. I don't know. I shall never know.[10]

In a tone that frequently borders on the elegiac, Conrad combines appeal-ing magazine fare – the mystery of a nebulous love affair and thrill of a crime story – with the discussion of serious moral anxiety.

'The Tale' was first published in the *Strand Magazine* in October 1917. In this issue, Conrad's story appeared next to various fiction and non-fiction contributions, including two more war stories and a short one-act play. The two other war stories were both contributed by well-known authors of the time: Frederick Britten Austin's story 'They Come Back' envisions the end of the war and subsequent fraternisation of social classes in Britain, resulting in a utopian version of British society in which each man receives his dues according to his merits. May Edginton's 'War Workers', on the other hand, is a comic story about two prim elderly spinsters who secretly covet a parcel of expensive lingerie donated to their welfare committee by a famous actress. The short play finally is a polemic propaganda effort set in Germany and illustrative of German 'frightfulness', in which a scientist presents to the Kaiser a resurrected German soldier whose body has been patched up and who, now a soulless fighting machine, ends up throttling the emperor himself to death. Read in the company of these texts, and considering that the story itself is accompanied by the same kind of melo-dramatic illustrations as the other contributions, 'The Tale' reads like a standard magazine thriller. It has a love interest in the frame narrative, a strong touch of melodrama, the trappings of detective fiction, and the suspense of a mystery story. Its finer points, on the other hand – such as the apt description of a taunting moral dilemma – pale in comparison with the dramatic nature of its plot. Conrad, who had to support a family, would certainly not have refused to write a story appropriate for publica-tion in as lucrative and well-paying a magazine as the *Strand Magazine*.[11]

When we consider it in a different context, however, our reading of 'The Tale' changes significantly. Subsequent to its magazine publication, the story appeared in Conrad's posthumous collection *Tales of Hearsay* (1925). The collection consists of four stories, written between 1884 and 1917, of which 'The Tale' is the only story addressing the First World War. The other stories are set in Russia after the Napoleonic Wars ('The Warrior's Soul', written in 1917), in Poland struggling against Russian autocracy ('Prince Roman', 1911), and on a ship bound for Calcutta ('The Black Mate', 1884). All of these stories, regardless of their setting and plot, are essentially character studies, exploring in their turn the nature of mercy and compassion, courage and human folly. Placed alongside three other stories by Conrad, it is exactly this quality of 'The Tale' as a psychological investigation of ethical behaviour which comes to the fore, while its more sensational elements become merely instrumental to the portrayal of the narrator's dilemma.

A third context again subtly alters our possible perception of 'The Tale'. After its appearance in *Tales of Hearsay*, the story was included in the anthology *Great Short Stories of the War* (1930), edited by H.C. Minchin with a foreword by Edmund Blunden and comprising war stories by authors of mixed nationality, including German.[12] Collected among sixty-five other stories, all chosen carefully for their critical outlook on the war, emphasis on its futility and the importance of humanity and compassion in the midst of the horror of war, 'The Tale' again changes its focus and becomes an anti-war story. The tormenting doubts of its main protagonist take on a new meaning beyond personal trauma; transformed into a political statement, they reveal the destructive effects of war both in terms of the loss of lives and the emotional scarring of the survivors.

The different publication outlets for short stories affect not only the way a story is read initially, but also the longevity of its reception. From at least the 1880s onwards, magazines promoted the publication of short stories next to serialised novels, and the more periodicals catered for specific audiences, the more varied a selection of stories was published.[13] In the early twentieth century and particularly in the inter-war period, a plethora of British magazines was published weekly, monthly or quarterly, and their flourishing coincided with a period of immense commercial success for the short story. The magazine market dwindled and never recovered, however, during and after the Second World War.[14] Although their publication in magazine format made short stories accessible to a wider readership, the format was also detrimental to the short story's prestige as a genre. Literary critics in particular regarded magazine publication as a doubtful means of achieving large audiences, a context of purely commercial entertainment 'planned for obsolescence' that aimed to provide 'distracted reception in brief moments between other activities'.[15] The more artistic magazines, such as the *English Review* or the *Criterion*, were certainly too expensive to be discarded immediately and were frequently collected in bound volume format, somewhat limiting the validity of these observations. However, the short story's standing will be lowered rather than improved as long as readers and critics believe in the inferiority of magazine publication. Bourdieu also points to the damaging effect of saleability on a text's prestige. He observes that the economic principle in the field of literary production is reversed: his field of literary production constitutes an environment 'where the only audience aimed at is other producers', in which 'the economy of practices is based, as in a generalized game of "loser wins", on a systematic inversion of the fundamental principles of all ordinary economies', [16] and where the only 'literary' capital that is worthwhile to critics is of a symbolic rather than monetary nature. Rather aptly, the dwindling of the magazine market paradoxically decreased the short story's audience but increased its literary prestige – not least of all because it is now seen as primarily an experimental literary form. Given that the durability and influence a text enjoys depends not only on how many people read it, but also on who these readers are, a short story published in a popular magazine may be commercially successful and read by a wide audience, but unless it is republished elsewhere, it will quickly sink into oblivion. The publication of a short story in an anthology, on the other hand, potentially secures for this story a more lasting reception. In short story anthologies and collections, short stories receive specialised attention, but at the same time they still compete with a greater number of very diverse texts. Although some of the now canonical modernist short fiction stood a better chance of republication by virtue of its authors' personal connections with literary editors and patrons, and the arguably greater desire on the part of modernist writers to perpetuate their work in a collected (and collectible) volume, most commercial magazine stories at best found their way into a single annual selection of the periodical they first appeared in. Since the Second World War, from the 1960s onwards in particular, story anthologies have frequently targeted an educational audience. In contrast to anthologies of poetry or general literary anthologies like the Norton series, however, there is no such thing as a single authoritative short story anthology widely read and discussed in schools or universities.

Collections of short stories by single authors differ from multiple-author anthologies in that their unifying factor is the writer, not necessarily an underlying theme or subgenre – although many writers, especially in the first half of the twentieth century, wrote short story cycles or sequences with a specific theme and/or recurring characters. In authors' collections, short stories that have already appeared in a magazine may be supplemented by previously unpublished stories, thus widening the range of texts available. At the same time, the audience of such collections is as limited as that of most anthologies: the more popular the writer, the larger its audience; the more obscure, the smaller the readership. Story collections are moreover harder to publish than novels, because where novels have 'a good chance to reach and surpass the break-even point for publishers', short story collections rarely do. [17] Valerie Shaw provides some examples of successful short-story writers, such as Katherine Anne Porter and A.E. Coppard, who felt they had to 'resist' publishers' wishes for a novel.[18] Most recently, Paul March-Russell summarised a survey carried out by the British Council in 2003, which confirmed publishers' wariness of publishing short-story collections by first-time authors. By contrast, the 1920s and 1930s were a period when 'publishers [were] beginning to look with a more favourable eye on short stories'.[19] Nevertheless, this was seen as an agreeable change in attitude rather than a general trend for the first half of the twentieth century, as early-twentieth-century publishers had previously 'fought very shy of the volume of collected short stories'.[20]

WARTIME AND INTER-WAR PUBLICATION: THE *STRAND MAGAZINE* AND THE *ENGLISH REVIEW*

During the 1910s and 1920s, the *Strand Magazine* was one of the most popular magazines in Britain to publish short stories. The *Strand Magazine* was largely apolitical with a focus on entertainment and self-improvement, but during the war years it displayed the staunchly patriotic attitude adopted by the British press generally. Each monthly issue contained between five and ten stories by British and international authors, often in serial or semi-serial form. Its proprietor, George Newnes, was the son of a minister and worked as a haberdasher before making his fortune with his first publication venture, *Tit-Bits*, in 1881. His endeavour 'to give wholesome and harmless entertainment to hard-working people craving a little fun and amusement' stemmed from a first-hand knowledge of the reading tastes of the working population.[21] As a rule, most of these stories either describe feats of physical daring, miraculous escapes, exotic adventures or romance overcoming varying obstacles. Although the *Strand Magazine* had started off as a periodical primarily of interest to male readers, most issues by 1914 also contained one story expressly aimed at children, and a range of romance stories designed to appeal to female readers, making the *Strand Magazine* a family magazine with content suitable for all ages and interests. This desire to offer stories for a range of tastes continued during the war, when most stories followed the same basic patterns and simply adopted a wartime setting for standard romance, adventure or detective plots. Short fiction in popular magazines such as the *Strand Magazine* was almost invariably formula literature, following specific generic conventions. As Jane Potter observes for popular romance, such pre-war formulae were 'easily transformed for use in wartime' by the writer of magazine fiction.[22] Modelled on American fiction magazines such as the *Saturday Evening Post*, the *Strand Magazine* quickly became 'a perennial best-seller', and arguably 'exercised an important and beneficial influence upon English short-story writing'[23] by offering lavish remuneration to those writers whose stories met its editorial requirements.[24]

Besides short stories, the *Strand Magazine* published reportage and celebrity commentaries on current affairs, as well as interviews, informative and lifestyle articles. In his introduction to a 1992 collection of short stories first published in the *Strand*, Frank Delaney outlines the magazine's editorial policies:

Readability was all. Newnes's success lay in taking care that each reader should emerge from the pages having shared easily in public entertainment, while privately – though not furtively – having acquired socially useful knowledge.[25]

Delaney estimates the number of readers who perused the magazine every month at two million in the immediate pre-war period, multiplying sales figures by the number of readers assumed to have shared each copy sold.[26] On the basis of these figures, Delaney claims that '[h]ardly an adult of measurable literacy could have been unalert to the magazine's existence'.[27] Although the editorial choices of the *Strand Magazine* certainly reflect the opinions and political outlook of its proprietor and editorial staff more than the public consciousness of Britain in the abstract, the selections in the *Strand Magazine* nevertheless may be seen to have shaped and reflected public opinion of its middle-class readers to some extent. These middle-class readers included those who had volunteered and were on active service in the army: like many periodicals, the *Strand Magazine* encouraged its readers to sponsor gift subscriptions for soldiers at the front or donate their own copies after reading, and in March 1917 published a special 'Humour Number' for soldiers at the front.

The *English Review* had a much smaller circulation than the *Strand Magazine*, but it was one of the commercially more successful and longer-lived literary magazines in Britain. Whereas many artistic magazines were of short duration – the best-known example is the much more radical *Blast*, of which only two issues were published – the *Review* survived for twenty-nine years, founded in 1908 by Ford Madox Ford (then Hueffer) and discontinued only when it merged with *The National Review* in 1937. The *English Review* published a wide range of avant-garde authors from Britain and overseas.[28] Before the outbreak of the First World War, in the early 1910s, it had a peak circulation of 15,000 to 18,000 copies.[29] During the war years, the *English Review* was edited (and from September 1915 onwards partly owned) by Austin Harrison. Harrison had studied languages in France and Germany and had previously worked as editor and journalist for *The Times*, the *Manchester Guardian* and Reuters news agency. In these jobs, he spent several years in Germany and some time in Russia. Before being invited to edit the *English Review*, Harrison edited and wrote for Lord Northcliffe's *Observer* and *Daily Mail*, first as political editor, later as drama critic. In his editorial choices, he was not only a convinced internationalist and champion of authors censored at the time for their sexual explicitness – his unofficial title for the magazine was 'The Great Adult Review' – but also a keen political observer who used his position as editor to comment at length on the war and the state of the British nation. On the basis of his first-hand knowledge of pre-war Germany and particularly German press censorship, Harrison was a harsh critic of the country. He had published a critical book on the German political agenda, *The Pan-Germanic Doctrine*, as early as 1904, and after the outbreak of the war published a second volume of political commentaries and articles, most of which had first appeared in the *English Review*, under the title *The Kaiser's War* (1914). Unlike the *Strand Magazine*, the *English Review* did not primarily publish short fiction. Out of an average number of twelve to sixteen items, only two or three would generally be short stories (although this is admittedly still a comparatively large percentage compared to the editorial policy of other magazines) and three to four poems, which were consequently outnumbered by non-fiction contributions. This reverses the policy of the *Strand Magazine*, where the straightforward entertainment provided by short fiction was interspersed with non-fiction articles. The *English Review*, by contrast, placed a stronger emphasis on (as its name suggests) reviewing and political commentary.

Although the *Strand Magazine* and *English Review* are different types of magazine, there are similarities which make both publications particularly suitable as examples of the publishing context of Great War stories. Given their respective target audiences, both magazines were perused by a large readership. Likewise, both magazines reflect the patriotic, anti-German stance that dominated British public opinion into the 1920s, despite the fact that the *English Review* combined its professed abhorrence for German militarism with ample criticism of the British government. At the same time, the different editorial programmes of the two magazines – light entertainment on the part of the *Strand*, serious reading and criticism in the *English Review* – allow an insight into two divergent target groups of readers. Although it might be argued that a focus on these two magazines excludes the working-class experience of the war, this is only partly true. The 'middle-class' readership of the *Strand Magazine* encompassed a much wider section of early twentieth-century society than the term suggests, from 'the most humble shopgirl to newspaper proprietors'.[30] Moreover, as Carol Acton and Michael Paris have shown for working boys' and girls' magazine fiction, working-class war fiction differed from its middle-class counterparts in degree rather than kind.[31] Whereas the *Strand Magazine* was light reading for a wide variety of readers from the lower-middle to (potentially) upper classes, the *English Review* was pitched at an intellectual audience with an interest in international politics and art. Harrison's envisaged audience comprised 'a wide range of readers, from graduates of the Board schools created about the time of his birth to university and professional men and women',[32] in London and beyond. Although advertisements and the subject of many articles betray a bias towards the upper middle class to whom Harrison himself belonged, he explicitly desired as readers those 'who have made Dent's Everyman series a success'.[33]

The Strand Magazine

The *Strand Magazine* did not immediately react to the war with the same fervour as *Punch* or *John Bull*, although it had published Arthur Conan Doyle's sensationalist invasion tale 'Danger!' as recently as July 1914. The October number of 1914 featured a reportage on an American girl's zeppelin flight over Germany with no reference to the war whatsoever – a rather remarkable fact considering that fictional responses to the war such as Arthur Machen's 'The Bowmen' appeared as early as September 1914 in the pages of the *Evening News*. The first war story to appear in the *Strand Magazine* was Frederick Britten Austin's adventure story 'The Air-Scout' in the November issue. Even this story does not specifically relate to the ongoing conflict; the two opposing nations remain unnamed and any relation to the war that had begun only three months previously is implied rather than explicit. The most likely reason for the *Strand Magazine's* delayed reaction to the war is that it had to plan ahead to ensure lasting good quality in its contributions: the *Strand Magazine* at that point went to press five weeks ahead of publication.[34] Consequently, stories and articles were bought in advance, and were not always up to date. In addition, authors as well as editors had first to react to the war, and stories addressing the conflict needed to be written and submitted before they could be published. During the last months of 1914 and the whole of 1915, the war is reflected in the *Strand Magazine* for the most part in articles and commentaries on topics as varied as German cultural achievements, English war heroes, military decorations and similar issues, such as a short series introducing the British Empire's Indian allies and their determination to aid the British war effort.

In terms of fiction, the war found its way into the December 1914 issue in the shape of only one war story, Edgar Wallace's 'The Despatch-Rider', in which an emancipated and headstrong English 'flapper' is caught up in the war during a motoring tour of France, and is reunited with her estranged fiancé when she carries dispatches for the army in an unofficial capacity during the first turbulent weeks of the war. 'The Despatch-Rider' is a typical example of an adventure story with added love interest in the usual style of the *Strand Magazine*, and employs the war setting as a means of heightening suspense before the lovers are reunited.

Throughout the year 1915, the war is represented on the fictional side almost solely by a series of stories by popular writer Richard March, whose pre-war (anti-)hero, humble office-worker Sam Briggs, enlists in the army and is dispatched to France after a series of humorous and edifying exploits in training camp.[35] Only five out of the twelve 1915 issues include other war-related stories, most of which use the war as a mere backdrop for romance or humour and are set on the home front. From January 1916 onwards, however, March's Sam Briggs serial is replaced by one to three (rarely more) independent short stories per issue addressing the war in various ways. There is a clear tendency for these stories to fall into established categories: comic stories or romance using the war as a backdrop, science-fiction stories involving new war technology, 'heroic' stories contrasting Allied courage and chivalry with German atrocities, and perhaps the most popular category, spy stories about German agents in Britain. Some stories, most notably a number of shorter tales by professional soldier-writer 'Sapper', are also set at the front, but although they do not attempt to hide the unpleasant aspects of warfare, they stress its comical or bizarre aspects rather than its horrors. Authors also began to prematurely envision the end of the war: Britten Austin's stories 'They Come Back' (October 1917) and 'Peace' (September 1918) describe the end of the war from a British and a German point of view respectively.

Following the Armistice, there is a sudden increase in stories dealing with alleged German atrocities in Belgium and Northern France, such as E. Temple Thurston's 'The Nature of the Beast' (December 1918), Lewis da Costa Ricci's 'The English Way' (January 1919) or Britten Austin's 'A Problem in Reprisals' (March 1919), all of which direct readers' attention back to perceived crimes of the former enemy and speak out against forgetting these past proofs of German 'frightfulness'.[36] A wish to influence public opinion with regard to the impending peace treaty may have prompted the publication of such stories at this point in time. It is moreover interesting to note that stories set partly or entirely during the war continued to appear in the *Strand Magazine* until well into 1919, particularly romance stories. Again, a possible explanation is that editorial choices were made in advance, and that material which had been bought or commissioned before the war ended had yet to be published. The publication lag of war fiction in the *Strand Magazine* reflects the situation of a society that had grown accustomed to war only to find itself suddenly and disconcertingly confronted with the task of returning to peacetime conditions. Of the large body of stories published between August 1914 and December 1920 that do not address the war in any way, many are set either in the United States (frequently written by American authors) or in other neutral countries. Alternatively, their action unfolds in a preserved pre-war Edwardian Britain, most notably in the frequent contributions by P.G. Wodehouse, whose only *Strand Magazine* short story with a (civilian) wartime setting was 'A Prisoner of War' (1915). It is particularly striking that the special 'Humour Number' of the *Strand Magazine*, published in March 1917 and expressly recommended as ideal reading material to be posted to the trenches, includes no war story whatsoever – despite the fact that an ample supply of humorous war stories were written and published both before and after this issue. The most likely explanation is that the editors felt soldiers on active service would rather be distracted from the war than reminded of it.

Their publication even in as widely circulated a periodical as the *Strand Magazine* did not ensure lasting fame for these war stories. To secure long-term reception, they depended on republication in collections and anthologies, but only two out of the approximately 140 war-related stories that appeared in the *Strand Magazine* between August 1914 and December 1920 were chosen for Geraldine Beare's anthology *Short Stories from the 'Strand'* (1992): Conrad's 'The Tale', and D.H. Lawrence's 'Tickets, Please'.[37] In his introduction to the volume, Frank Delaney reveals that they were not chosen for their connection with the war (which, especially as far as 'Tickets, Please' is concerned, is tenuous in any case), but because of their literary quality and capability to reveal insights into the respective writer's literary development as well as their authors' status.[38] Three other, more specialised anthologies of stories published in the *Strand Magazine*, Geraldine Beare's *Crime Stories From the 'Strand'* (1991) and *Adventure Stories From the 'Strand'* (1995), and Jack Adrian's *Detective Stories from The Strand* (1992), display similar editorial choices, in that most popular authors of the time are also noticeably excluded.

The vast majority of stories included in the *Strand Magazine* take the war as a backdrop rather than a central subject, and are essentially formula literature following Ken Gelder's definition of popular fiction: they are clearly aimed at a mass audience, and written for commercial purposes.[39] *Strand Magazine* short stories are for the most part entertaining tales that employ the war as a setting for standard plots and often formulaic conflicts and resolutions; they cater for home-front needs, provide a welcome distraction, reinforce a sense of the justness of the British cause and address the realities of war in a manner designed to reassure readers. These stories rarely delve into the realm of psychological or political observation beyond a general approval of Britain's war aims and policies, and the value of soldierly sacrifice. Even Lawrence's 'Tickets, Please' did not startle its magazine readers with undue formal innovation; although the subject matter of vengeful women ticket collectors may have been disquieting, the story's narrative structure is straightforward and relies on a traditional third-person narrator.

The English Review

Considering Austin Harrison's background in journalism, it is not surprising that the *English Review* addressed the war mostly through the non-fictional genres of reportage and commentary. As early as September 1914, the *Review* introduced a new section headline separating general contributions from explicitly war-related pieces. Initially, this rubric was titled 'The Kaiser's War' (September 1914), rapidly changed to 'The Kaiser's World War' (October 1914) and finally to 'The War of Liberation' (November 1914) – an ambiguous headline that might refer both to occupied Belgium and France, and to notions of liberating civilisation from the threat of German militarism. This latter heading remained in use until 1917, when it was changed first to 'Imperial Reconstruction' (April 1917) and then to 'War and Reconstruction' (June 1917 to July 1918) before the concept of a special war rubric was abandoned in mid-1918.[40] This section contained almost entirely non-fictional contributions, including, in September 1914, two scathing editorial commentaries by Harrison denouncing the cultural politics of the German emperor and setting out the tasks of the Allies as liberating Belgium and stamping out German militarism.[41] Nevertheless, later articles and commentaries prove that the magazine was by no means uncritical of how the war was conducted on the part of Great Britain. In a series of articles published in the summer of 1915, Harrison agitated for the introduction of conscription, and claimed in all his war-related articles that recruitment on a voluntary basis would be no use against the highly organised German war machine. In his column on financial issues, regular contributor Raymond Radclyffe rarely failed to criticise the handling of war expenses by the government, both before and after Lloyd George took over as prime minister from Asquith in December 1916. Regular reports from the war zone by correspondents such as H.M. Tomlinson, and by active service personnel writing under a pseudonym (as those on active service were prohibited from publishing) supplemented these political commentaries from the home front and provided first-hand insights into life at the front.

The dominance of non-fictional contributions is not to imply that no war-related literary contributions found their way into the *English Review*. Indeed, the magazine's poetry section was the first to respond to the outbreak of war: in the August number for 1914, Aleister Crowley contributed a sequence of humorous poems parodying the style of various English poets from Chaucer to the early twentieth century, rewriting the chorus of the popular nineteenth-century music-hall 'Jingo War Song' by G.W. Hunt. The September issue opened with John Masefield's poem 'August, 1914', now famous for its wistful celebration of a pre-war idyll. Poetry by active service personnel was published continuously throughout the war, although it did not always have the war as its subject. In January, March and September 1918, and once more in February 1919, the poetry section of the *English Review* was given over entirely to 'Soldiers' Poetry', featuring exclusively poetry by active soldiers and officers, with Siegfried Sassoon as the best-known but by no means the most prolific contributor.

Although most short stories in the *Review* did not touch upon the war, some war-related stories were published at intervals, such as a sketch by R.B. Cunninghame Graham entitled 'In a Backwater' (October 1914). This piece is more or less indistinguishable from reportage and centres on the reception of the war news in a rural community. A farmer in the Home Counties, preoccupied with his wheat harvest and the recent death of his wife, is further troubled by the war news he gleans from his *Daily Mail*. He is particularly horrified at reports of hundreds of dead soldiers and horses lying in Belgian cornfields, and his somewhat slow and rambling conversation with the story's unnamed narrator returns to this image time and again. Another story by Cunninghame Graham, 'Brought Forward', appeared as the second war-related story in the February number of 1915 and describes how the death of his close friend and colleague in action prompts a Scottish worker to enlist, seeking to avenge his friend. The story can be read as recruitment propaganda complicated by Graham's socialist background, visible in its appeal for a working-class solidarity that was more commonly evoked as part of an internationalist, pacifist Labour rhetoric. D.H. Lawrence's well-known story 'England, My England' (October 1915) also appeared in the *Review*.

Further war stories published were Stacy Aumonier's 'The Grayles' (March 1916), a bittersweet tragicomedy about a pacifist family whose only son enlists out of a mistaken belief that his father and sister want him to fight, and returns disabled; Gilbert Frankau's 'A Rag-Time Hero' (January 1917), a scathing satire on cowardice and patriotic hypocrisy; and 'Casualty' by Arthur Eckersley (April 1917), dealing with the anguish of a young recruit who is disabled in an accident just before his dispatch to the front and suffers in the knowledge that he cannot uphold the long military tradition of his family. Two short stories by Hugh Pollard, 'Morphine' (February 1918) and 'Hazard' (May 1918), address the small yet painful tragedies and moral dilemmas of war, dealing with a doctor whose attempt to cure one man from a drug habit leads to horrific suffering for a dying soldier, and a desperate game of cards which determines who is to command a suicidal attack. Alec Waugh's 'An Autumn Gathering' (May 1918) already adopts a sympathetic attitude towards Germany, as it relates the story of two young German lovers parted by the war. D.H. Catterick's 'Reginald' (October 1918) depicts the esteem felt by a group of British marksmen for a particularly devious German sniper, and their regret at having to kill him. Other, later stories scrutinise the effect of war on human behaviour and character, such as Blamire Young's 'Clarence' (December 1918), in which a boisterous officer is put to shame by the far more real, if less glamorous, achievements of a lowly NCO. Arthur Mill's 'Wreckage of War' (March 1919) is a short, disillusioned sketch of a soldier returning from war service in the Near East to find England a sad and desperate place and his friends and acquaintances all altered for the worse. '"For it"', by A.E. Mander (October 1919), which follows a young lieutenant from training camp to the front and his eventual death, begins with the explicit warning 'When we are drifting into the next war – *let us think of the last*'. A more psychological interest in coming to terms with loss, injury and circumstances altered by the war is visible in three further stories: Baroness von Hutten's 'Mothers' (January 1920) compares different ways of coping with the loss of an only son, ranging from suicidal despair to grim determination; 'The Old Dovecote' by David Garnett (February 1920) shows how even those who returned from the war to a loving home sound and whole may yet feel that the home to which they were looking forward to returning has changed beyond recognition, and D.H. Lawrence's 'The Blind Man' (July 1920) is a study of how war-related blindness has subtly changed the relationship and power balance between a husband and wife and the wife's best friend.

The long intervals at which these stories were published during and especially after the war show that Harrison continued his pre-war policy of promoting diversity and artistic quality, as does the fact that the many stories published without any reference to the war include works in translation by internationally renowned authors such as Anton Chekhov and Yone Noguchi, whose story 'The Skin Painter' appeared in the December issue of 1917. The war was dealt with in articles and commentaries on current affairs, but largely kept out of editorial selections of literary contributions. On the whole, war-related stories were even scarcer in the *English Review* beyond December 1918 than during the war, as the war and its after-effects, particularly the peace conference and Treaty of Versailles, continued to be addressed in articles and commentaries rather than short fiction. Those war stories that were included for the most part differ strikingly from those published in the *Strand Magazine*, in that they do not simply adopt a wartime setting for a pre-conceived adventure or romance plot. Instead, these stories concentrate on a psychological analysis of motives and reactions, attempting to shed light on issues such as the decision to enlist, on war-related fears and the sense of social obligation the war inspired in many.

Lawrence's 'England, My England' is a representative example of an *English Review* war story. Its basic plot is easily summarised: a young married couple, who have been slowly growing apart as the result of fundamental differences in character, are irrevocably estranged when the eldest of their three young daughters is crippled in an accident. When the war breaks out the husband enlists with his wife's approval. Mentally more than physically unsuited to be a soldier, he suffers from the crudities of military life and his wife's readiness to feel dutiful towards him as a soldier but not as a man, and he is killed soon after being sent to Flanders. This story exists in two versions, an early version published in the *English Review* and an extensively revised one published after the war in *England, My England, and Other Stories* (1922).

In the early magazine version, whose mere 5,900 words make it less than half as long as the collected version of almost 13,000 words, the focus on the war is conspicuously stronger.[42] This earlier version is divided into two parts. The first and shorter part is set in England and describes the process of marital estrangement, whereas the second and considerably longer section of the story is set in training camp and at the front. In the *Review*, the closing paragraphs of the story describe not only the husband's death in great detail, but also his killing of three German soldiers with his service revolver before he himself is stabbed to death and viciously mutilated. In the revised version, more than three quarters of the story are devoted to describing the early relationship, marriage and gradual estrangement of the couple, while only a short section at the end of the story describes the husband's enlistment, training and death at the front, where he is killed by a shell and found already dead by passing German soldiers. The focus of both versions of 'England, My England' is on the emotions and psychological motivations of the protagonists' actions, but whereas the early version published in the *Review* shows a greater interest in the main protagonist's reaction to the war, the later version places greater emphasis on the disintegration of his marriage and the intricacies of the estrangement between two lovers.

'England, My England' in its earlier version reflects the overall nature of war stories in the *English Review*. Like Lawrence's story, most stories in the *Review* dealing with the war address it as the source of interpersonal or psychological problems rather than using it as a backdrop for romance or adventure plots, and strive to convey 'the horror of what one becomes through participating' in war rather than the horrors of war itself.[43] Although they are otherwise as diverse in their choice of subject matter and setting as the stories published in the *Strand Magazine*, their focus on the effects of the war in a psychological sense sets them apart from the typical *Strand Magazine* tale. Whereas *Strand Magazine* stories are largely specimens of formula fiction, stories in the *English Review* are more likely to deviate from a plot-based, generic structure. Some of these stories for instance adopted a sketch-like structure and resemble reportage in their focus on observation rather than action. Even plot-based stories do not fit comfortably into the moulds of formulaic subgenres. Despite its subject matter, Lawrence's 'England, My England' certainly cannot be read as an adventure or romance story. Of the much smaller number of stories published in the *English Review*, a larger percentage still ring familiar with a modern audience. This is mainly because the *Review* published a number of authors who have come to be associated with the modernist movement whose stories were subsequently reprinted in topical collections.

WAR STORIES IN BRITISH WARTIME AND INTER-WAR ANTHOLOGIES

Whereas the selection criteria of fiction magazines tend to depend on fairly loosely defined editorial policies, story anthologies assemble short fiction under often arbitrary common denominators such as their writers' nationality or gender; topic or genre; ideological outlook or time of writing.[44] Both, however, must be seen as primarily commercially motivated. When many established periodicals, including the *Strand*, ceased publication, editors and publishers tried to establish new outlets for short fiction. As a consequence, inter- and post-war Britain witnessed the publication of a range of anthology series such as John Lehmann's *New Writing* series (1936–1943), or the English Association's *English Short Stories of To-Day*,[45] but between 1918 and 1945, only very few stories addressing war were included in these new story anthologies. In three 1920s anthologies,[46] no stories are included that address the First World War in any way despite the continued publication of war stories in magazines. Published at the end of the decade, Edward J. O'Brien's *Modern English Short Stories* (1930) does include a small number of tenuously war-related stories amongst its twenty-eight contributions, but these stories, such as 'Mr Franklyn's Adventure' by J.M. Allison, as a general rule merely allude to the war. Only Katherine Mansfield's 'The Fly' and 'The Lock' by Edward Sackville West scrutinise the after-effects of the war on the human psyche. The only other story dealing straightforwardly with the Great War appeared in the first anthology of the *English Short Stories of To-Day* series: 'Defeat' (1939) by Geoffrey Moss deals with the friendship between the English narrator and a German officer, interrupted by the war for more than ten years and revived in French-occupied Rhineland. The story appeared at a politically sensitive time after the remilitarisation of the Rhineland, as it describes in sympathetic detail some of the complications of occupation and popular sentiment in defeated Germany, particularly among returned army officers who face the complete breakdown of their careers. General anthologies and annual collections of short fiction were clearly not a fruitful outlet for war stories, as they quickly oriented themselves to either established classics of the genre, or new fiction that no longer cared to address the war.

However, as general anthologies abandoned the theme of war, dedicated collections of war fiction continued to publish short stories addressing the First World War. The anthologies considered in this chapter were published between 1915 and 1936, and specialise either in First World War writing or in texts about war generally. Many anthologies of war writing are mixed collections not of short fiction, but primarily excerpts from longer works such as novels or histories, often mixed with war poetry. This preference for excerpts from longer prose works over genuine short fiction is, as we will see, a recurring theme, which illustrates both the marginalised position of short fiction and the dominance of a pacifist-realist bias with regard to the canon of First World War literature. A large number of the anthologies examined here are directed explicitly at children and young adults, just as a high proportion of war literature generally is aimed at young readers. Because of the marked tendency of war writing towards the historiographical or autobiographical, most war anthologies include a significant number of excerpts from longer works of non-fiction or auto-biographical fiction.

Considering the political outlook of stories published in wartime periodicals, it is not surprising that those anthologies of war stories published during the war itself also took a positive, patriotic stance towards the war and focussed on tales of heroic conduct, courage and endurance. Jane Potter has argued that although commercial viability was an obvious necessity, most of the London publishing houses during the war felt obligated both by a general sense of social responsibility and by personal stakes in the war – such as the war service of close friends, family or employees – to consider patriotic issues. Even those publishers who opposed the conflict understood the need to support soldiers and civilians under the burden of war.[47] The fact that preference was given to texts that took a positive slant on the war and stressed the value of patriotic sacrifice has been noted repeatedly for anthologies of war poetry and holds equally true for story anthologies.[48] Indeed, the most important aim of these anthologies seems to be to stress the valour and daring of the British troops, a goal eloquently put in their titles, ranging from *Thrilling Deeds of Valour: Stories of Heroism in the Great War* (1916), *The Post of Honour: Stories of Daring Deeds Done by Men of the British Empire in the Great War* (1917), to *Wonderful Stories: Winning the V.C. in the Great War* (1917). Emphasis is also put on the veracity of the accounts given in the short stories, corresponding to post-war concerns about the authenticity of war writing. Implicit in most titles, and explicit in a number of prefatory notes and introductions, is the claim that these stories can be taken as eyewitness accounts of what has really happened. Walter Wood, editor of the collection *Soldiers' Stories of the War* (1915), claims in his introduction:

All of the stories in this volume are told by men who were there personally, and who, with one or two exceptions – cases of soldiers who had returned to the front – read the typescripts of their narratives, so that accuracy should be secured. The narrators spoke while the impressions of fighting and hardships and things seen were still strong and clear; in several cases full notes had been made or diaries kept, and reference to these records was of great value in preparing the stories. When seeing an informant I specially asked that a true tale should be told, and I believe that no unreliable details were knowingly given.[49]

The fact that Wood was able to publish a second volume as a sequel to his collection only a year later – *In the Line of Battle: Soldiers' Stories of the War* (1916) – seems to prove that his concept was successful. Arthur St John Adcock's collection *In the Firing Line: Stories of the War by Land and Sea* (1914) represents its stories as quasi-journalistic accounts of the war in its earliest stages. Supplementing his own writing with ostensibly real letters and diary entries by British soldiers, Adcock paints a gruesome picture of German atrocities in Belgium. His anthology was part of the *Daily Telegraph* War Books Series, begun prior to the outbreak of the First World War and consisting to that date of fifteen volumes, mostly dealing with the British colonial wars. The Great War was thus placed securely in the context of previous conflicts.

A further striking feature is the wide geographical range of the short stories included in wartime anthologies. Modern popular memory of the war centres almost entirely on the Western Front, and it is the poetry and prose of soldiers who served in France and Belgium that is remembered as canonical war writing today. The texts collected in wartime anthologies stand in stark contrast to this selectivity in that they cover the war in all its theatres, from Flanders to Mesopotamia, and a wide variety of branches of the British military. The anthology *Thrilling Deeds of Valour* (1916) alone, a richly illustrated, patriotic collection aimed at children, includes stories set amongst the Royal Engineers, among British midshipmen in the Dardanelles, Australian soldiers on the Gallipoli Peninsula, on a war cruiser in the Atlantic, and among Russian troops capturing a German general. It also comprises an account of the exploits of the flying corps, of British army nurses and doctors in the Balkans and of British troops in Mesopotamia, and even includes a home front story set on the Shetland Islands. Similarly, *Wonderful Stories: Winning the V.C. in the Great War*, which had gone into a second edition by 1917, contains stories from all fronts, including the Balkans, Mesopotamia and service branches such as the navy and the submarine corps. Through their wide range of settings, these stories offer a means of imaginary participation for all readers. Regardless of where friends and relatives were deployed, readers were certain to find a corresponding tale. In wartime anthologies of Great War short stories, there is no sign of editors' and writers' choices being narrowed down to the Western Front, although there is a visible emphasis on the combatant experience of the war. However, all aspects of the war, including home front and nursing, find consideration and are included in collections in what may be an attempt to portray the war with all its facets, particularly for young readers. The way in which the war is represented is part of a continuing tradition of heroic war writing and the comparatively new field of war reportage that developed during the colonial wars of the mid to late nineteenth century.[50]

The end of the war did not bring about a sudden, radical change in short story anthologies and their editorial choices. Collections such as Sir James Edward Parrott's *The Path of Glory: Heroic Stories of the Great War* (1921) retain the wartime focus on heroism and British moral and physical superiority. This particular anthology comprises nineteen stories and sketches, all written by Parrott and selected from his *Children's Story of the War* (1915–19) in ten volumes. A foreword by the author dedicates the book to 'The Unrecorded Brave of the Great War' and describes in great detail how Britain, believed by the Germans and its own citizens to have lost its strength and patriotic valour, rose to the challenge of the war, made the most gallant sacrifices and emerged from the war victoriously.[51] The stories are all purportedly true accounts of actual events during the war and supply names and dates for a greater appearance of authenticity. They are obviously written for children and strive with great pathos to provide positive role models. As was the case with most wartime anthologies, this collection includes stories on a wide range of services and theatres of war: from Allied women and children assisting British soldiers, over flying corps, navy and British submarine crews (dramatically dubbed 'Heroic Toilers of the Deep'), to medical officers, nurses and colonial troops from India. Even after the end of the war, and in the midst of public debate over issues of public commemoration and private grief, a positive evaluation of the recent conflict seems to have been possible, especially in the light of having to make sense of loss and change.[52]

A number of anthologies of war stories published in the early 1930s continue this trend of positive evaluation. These form a striking contrast to the harsher, disillusioned interpretation of the late 1920s war memoirs and several collections of stories published around the same time by the same authors who had reworked their war experiences into novels and autobiographies. Whereas Richard Aldington's collection *Roads to Glory* (1930) paints an unremittingly dark picture of the war, Junior Allan's anthology *Humorous Scottish War Stories: Selected from the 'Daily Mail'*, published in the same year, takes pains to illustrate the humour and wit with which Scottish soldiers supposedly encountered the hardships of the Great War. Although the 'bitter experiences of that eventful time'[53] are acknowledged in the editor's foreword, his selection of stories does not present the war in the light of utter futility that informs Aldington's prose. In a similar vein, Wingrove Willson's anthology of sea stories, *Naval Stories of the Great War*

(1931), expressly does not seek 'to glorify warfare', but to provide its audience of young readers 'with some idea of the perils and privations faced by the sturdy men who kept the seas for Britain in the dark days of 1914–18' and to inspire in them 'a kindly thought for the heroes who sacrificed so much and fought so bravely 'neath our glorious flag'.[54] Here, too, war is not presented as a matter to be trifled with and its costs are acknowledged, but the moral necessity of British involvement in the war is not questioned. The collection once again stresses heroism and comprises stories by various authors, dealing with feats of (in this case naval) daring such as the blocking of Zeebrugge harbour in April 1918.

Not all inter-war anthologies, however, continue this positive evaluation of the war. The year 1930 also saw the publication of H.C. Minchin's aforementioned hardback anthology *Great Short Stories of the War* (1930). This substantial volume, introduced by Edmund Blunden, collected a wide selection of Great War short stories (and some excerpts from novels) by authors of different nationalities, including German and Austrian. Although it also includes a small number of stories in a traditional heroic mode, such as Bartimeus's 'The Port Lookout', it is dominated by stories of the 'school of disillusionment'[55]: Richard Aldington and Liam O'Flaherty are represented by particularly disturbing depictions of the frontline, as are their French and German counterparts Henri Barbusse and Erich Maria Remarque. Even those stories included that were contributed by usually more light-hearted authors such as Stacy Aumonier ring a tragic note: Aumonier's 'Them Others' stresses the tragedy of personal loss and the universality of grief and anxiety across national boundaries. In his prefatory note, Minchin claimed that *Great Short Stories of the War* was 'the first substantial collection of short stories of the Great War to be published', hoping that it would have a lasting value and influence while admitting to the fact that '[m]uch that has been written recently about the war is for the hour only and will cease to be'.[56]

CHAPTER 3

Post-War Publication and Anthologisation

ANTHOLOGIES AND MAGAZINES AFTER 1945

Given that war stories offered fictional accounts from almost any theatre of war and a range of different perspectives, they were likely to provide a means of narrative configuration in Ricoeur's sense for most of their contemporary readers regardless of the setting or nature of their own war experience. Popular stories in particular, like those published in the *Strand Magazine* or *Blackwood's Magazine*, moreover continued to follow established narrative patterns, thus guaranteeing an additional element of reassurance for war-fraught nerves. This function gradually became redundant after the end of the war. While inter-war anthologies of war stories do not entirely run counter to the emergent mythologisation of the war and related processes of canonisation, these publications still offer a more varied outlook on the war, and are more in keeping with war-time attitudes than one would assume. Unlike short stories published by the comparatively small number of critical, disillusioned war memoirists, these anthologies mostly uphold the war as a hard but essentially necessary (and potentially even beneficial) experience. After 1945, the publication of Great War stories was affected by the altered publishing scene, new tastes and topics. Whereas the majority of wartime and inter-war short stories appeared in magazines and periodicals, after 1945 short stories more often than not appeared only in anthologies or collections.

The Second World War had a significant effect on the reception and (re)publication of First World War writing, in that writers of the later war frequently referred to the earlier conflict and saw themselves in comparison and contrast to earlier writers, particularly the trench poets.[1] Poetry, novels and memoirs of the First World War were read with renewed interest during and after the Second World War, and poems such as Vernon Scannell's 'The Great War',[2] written after the end of World War II, stress the dominance of the memory of World War I in the popular imagination and point to the fact that the later conflict by no means eclipsed the ear-lier one, neither in public memory nor in literature. However, while First World War poetry remained a strong literary reference point to poets and novelists, general short-story anthologies that did not explicitly adopt war as their theme rarely ever included First World War-related stories after 1945. Looking at specialised anthologies of war fiction, on the other hand, one cannot fail to notice the influence of the Second World War and the myth of the Great War that gained strength and authority from the 1960s onwards, under the influence of the anti-war movement that was trig-gered by Vietnam. Anthologies of the 1990s and early twenty-first century in particular adopt an internationalist stance and are rarely restricted to just English or British authors. They further tend to include post-World War II writing on the First World War in a bid to pay tribute to recent literary trends and make the collection in question more marketable to a contemporary audience by including well-known authors' recent work. This editorial policy is in keeping with critical trends that regard mod-ern literature on the subject of the First World War, such as Pat Barker's *Regeneration* trilogy (1991–5), as an extension of the canon of Great War literature. Todman describes these books, which take great pains to supply distinct and 'realistic' descriptions of the Western Front, as almost equiva-lent to 'a second "war books boom"'.[3] Their treatment as war books may initially seem strange, but many of these late-twentieth-century works either consciously engage with or unconsciously document the way in which we remember the war. As the selection of short stories discussed in the final chapter shows, they either challenge or reinforce existing myths, justifying their critical treatment alongside 'genuine' (i.e. contemporane-ous) First World War fiction.

One of the most successful post-war anthologies of war writing judg-ing by sales and re-publication is Ernest Hemingway's *Men at War: The Best War Stories of All Time* (1942), which was first published during the Second World War but was reprinted and republished in new editions no fewer than seven times between 1952 and 1979. Hemingway's introduc-tion to the volume has a strong political agenda and reflects his determi-nation to see German militarism stamped out in his lifetime, but at the same time takes war as an essential, if deplorable, part of the experience of being human, drawing on Hemingway's own war experience:

The editor of this anthology, who took part and was wounded in the last war to end war, hates war and hates all the politicians whose mismanagement, gullibility, cupidity, selfishness and ambition brought on this present war and made it inevi-table. But once we have a war there is only one thing to do. It must be won.[4]

The pieces included range widely from fictional accounts of prehistoric battles to contemporary conflicts, and although the selection varies with every new edition and older pieces are partly replaced by more recent accounts, a small number of First World War pieces are consistently included in all versions. Most accounts are excerpts from novels or memoirs, however, such as T.E. Lawrence's *Seven Pillars of Wisdom* (1922) or Frederic Manning's *Her Privates We* (1930), and the only British Great War short story that is consistently included is Aldington's 'At All Costs' (1930). The texts included are also all combatant accounts of the war, and largely take a disillusioned stance that confirms canonical notions of World War I as a futile endeavour and large-scale mismanagement. The practice of substituting excerpts from longer prose texts for actual short stories, so noticeable in inter-war anthologies, continues in the post-war era. The main reason excerpts are privileged over genuine short fiction appears to be the factor of recognition and re-affirmation, leading to the perpetuation of the war's myth on the one hand and of its canon on the other. By constantly drawing on the same literary sources – amongst which novels and memoirs are much more prominent than short stories – these anthologies strengthen existing preconceptions about the war, and thus cater to the desires of a reading public brought up to a certain perception of the First World War that they wish to have confirmed, not challenged.

Further examples of this practice are not hard to come by. Jon E. Lewis's paperback *Mammoth Book of Modern War Stories* (London: Robinson, 1993) contains fifty-six stories by international authors, covering wars from the American Civil War onwards in roughly chronological order. Many of the 'stories' are, again, not short stories but excerpts from 'disillusioned' novels and memoirs. In the foreword to the volume, *Daily Telegraph* war correspondent Robert Fox states that 'the best writing about action is from those who have been through the turmoil of combat themselves.'[5] Fox here reiterates the notion that war writing is always first and foremost writing about combat. By implication, we find once more the idea that it is authenticity and veracity one should be looking for in a war story. The editor of the volume, Jon Lewis, recognises a distinct tone in fictions of particular wars, and shows that he has internalised the idea of Great War writing as essentially disillusioned and anti-war in adding that 'World War I stories – like World War I poems – are a distinct body of literature, imbued with a sense of disillusion, and contempt for the slaughter through which the troops were put',[6] in stark contrast to what he sees as the more affirmative stance on war as necessary and just in Second World War stories. For the selection of Great War writing in his own anthology, this is certainly true, as Lewis has chosen almost exclusively pieces by (soldier-) writers of the late 1920s 'disillusioned school' and avoided any such stories or excerpts that might challenge established negative perceptions of the war: carefully selected excerpts from Sassoon's *Memoirs of an Infantry Officer* and Manning's *Her Privates We*, from Remarque's *All Quiet on the Western Front* and Henri Barbusse's *Under Fire*; Aldington's cynical short story 'At All Costs' and Liam O'Flaherty's violent front-line tale 'The Alien Skull'. Those stories or excerpts included in the anthology by writers who usually wrote on the war with an affirmative stance, such as Bartimeus, H.T. Dorling or W.E. Johns, are uncharacteristically value-neutral and concentrate on rendering the particular war experiences they relate in a vivid, realistic manner.

A more recent example of a bias in favour of longer, disillusioned war fiction in keeping with existing tropes is the *Vintage Book of War Stories* (1999), edited by Jörg Hensgen and introduced by Sebastian Faulks, widely known in particular for his First World War novel *Birdsong* (1993). The volume collects almost exclusively excerpts from novels, and the selection of material for the anthology is justified in an historically precarious manner by Faulks, who echoes the myth of the war as futile slaughter 'of ten million men for no apparent reason'[7] and, like Fox, stresses the close connection of what he regards as 'good' war writing with journalism and by implication a 'true' account of war:

Many English novelists of the Great War were acting as auxiliary reporters: 'Look,' they were saying, 'no one really told you before what it was like' – and their ambitions were essentially journalistic. Those who went artistically further found what they could do constrained by the static nature of trench warfare. It is not surprising that, not only surveying an unprecedented human holocaust but watching it from the hole in the ground for months on end, these men produced such introspective books.[8]

Faulks's preface unwittingly highlights a commercial interest on the part of publishers to tap into the existing mythology of the war. It also demonstrates that veracity and authenticity (embodied, as Faulks suggests, in war reporting) continue to be considered important characteristics of 'good' war fiction, even if, in Faulks's opinion, it is not necessarily able to go 'artistically further'. Next to classic war texts such as Sassoon's *Memoirs of an Infantry Officer*, contemporary fiction on the First World War is represented by an excerpt from Pat Barker's novel *Regeneration* (1991), but not a single genuine short story of or about the First World War has been included in the anthology. The term 'story' in the title is clearly not regarded as referring to short stories, demonstrating once more a general marginalisation of short fiction, along with the marginalisation of writing that is non-modernist, non-disillusioned, or both.

Contemporary war-story anthologies aimed expressly at young readers add a distinctly moralistic stance on war to the usual selectivity. This stance is not entirely new: it is telling that Owen's draft preface for his collection of war poetry initially explicitly named children as a target audience, stating 'All a poet can do today is [to] warn [children] That is why the true [War] poets must be truthful'.[9] Contemporary editorial choices reflect the twofold desire of entertaining and educating young readers while ensuring commercial viability. At the same time, these anthologies break with the trend of substituting excerpts from novels for genuine short stories, most likely because the majority of children's anthologies comprise purposely written stories. A clear moral message is visible in the selection of stories and in prefaces and introductions alike, and the First World War is often presented alongside a wide range of other conflicts, as in Tony Bradman's paperback anthology *Gripping War Stories* (1999). Bradman's collection incorporates stories about war from Native American warfare to the war in the Balkans and strives to emphasise that the destructive nature of war is universal. In her essay on recent children's literature addressing the First World War, Esther MacCallum-Stewart points out the close connection between established perceptions of the First World War in particular (and war in general) as destructive and futile, the moral premises of education and commercial exploitation of popular subjects. MacCallum-Stewart notes that as a consequence of British educational policies regarding the war and its intensification through the existing pacifist mythology of the First World War, children's literature addressing the conflict 'suffers from a desire to say the right thing',[10] a desire certainly well-meant on the part of children's writers and editors, but nevertheless resulting in a somewhat narrow perception of the war. As she points out, a positive representation of the war is deemed unthinkable, and previous positive interpretations are presented as morally reprehensible. Children's fiction addressing the First World War, such as Linda Newbery's 'The Christmas Tree' (1999) proves this point but also serves to add further nuances to MacCallum-Stewart's findings. Newbery's story repeats well-established tropes of leave-taking and generational conflict. The main protagonist, a young English girl, has to part from her brother, who has volunteered for active service against the express wish of their father. His joining up is presented in terms of the same heroic willingness for sacrifice that informed wartime fiction, and his individual courage is commended. The stress on personal loss and tragedy, however, is marked and seems well suited to convey the cost of war to a young audience. Newbery's story is representative of much contemporary fiction about World War I in that it condemns war while honouring the memory of the war dead, in a manner comparable to our tendency to commend soldiers who fought in the First World War for their sacrifices and bravery while simultaneously regarding their efforts as futile.

A similar stance, and a similar format, are visible in Michael Morpurgo's *War: Stories about Conflict* (2005). This collection comprises fifteen stories about various wars by contemporary authors, written especially for children and young adults. Like Bradman's anthology, it has no introduction, only a short note by each author explaining how their interest in war was first aroused. Most give as their motivation childhood memories of the Second World War or its aftermath, and the First World War is duly eclipsed by the Second in this publication. The only story dealing with the Great War, Eleanor Updale's 'Not a Scratch', chooses a much more unusual subject in dealing with the fate of a First World War veteran who has contracted a permanent bowel disease from drinking polluted water at the front, and whose life – and the lives of his family – are permanently blighted by this embarrassing disability that does not fit in with the heroic idea of sacrificing life or limbs for one's country. This story engages with the working memory of the war in its own way by attempting to draw attention to a neglected aspect of the war experience that is not part of its cultural memory, namely the less glamorous yet deeply damaging sacrifices made by soldiers who survived the war but had to live with its uncomfortable legacy that could neither be alleviated nor publicly acknowledged:

After all, Sidney had been one of the lucky ones. It was a bit of an embarrassment, really. He hadn't had a story to tell. There was no family legend to pass down the generations. Lucky Sidney had come back from the Great War uninjured. Not a scratch.[11]

The overall moral stance of the story, however, nevertheless remains the same; the war and its effects on the lives of its survivors are condemned while their individual courage is commended.

Stories included in anthologies for young readers in the war and inter-war period actively encouraged admiration for soldiers and nurses and firmly embedded the Great War in the same context of British imperial history as previous and indeed later wars. Many children's magazines continued to publish First World War adventure stories right up to the Second World War, for instance the popular 'Captain Biggles' flying-ace stories.[12] Children's short stories and other writing for young readers about the Great War written since the 1960s turn these earlier tendencies upside down. Both *Twelve War Stories* (1980), edited by former secondary-school headmaster John Foster, and Jane Christopher's *War Stories: Major Writers of the 19th and 20th Centuries* (1999) collect short stories on war-related topics for use in schools. Foster's editor's note states that '[t]he object is to present the student reader with stories of quality, which give a realistic picture of what it feels like to be involved as a participant in an armed conflict, and thus to counterbalance the false pictures of warfare that are often presented on the screen and in war comics'.[13] 'Quality' literature is here employed to counteract images of war that the editor feels are false, and the texts chosen for this anthology are those that portray it as a thoroughly negative experience. In his wish to promote pacifist reactions to war in his student readers, and in a bid to ensure the realism of his collection – its veracity and authenticity – the editor relies on the didactic usefulness of soldiers' accounts in forming the young readers' attitude to war. He does not, however, consider the fact that the stories on World War I included in his anthology all stem from the particular group of junior officers, and as such cannot hope to be representative of more than that group's necessarily limited war experience: somewhat inevitably, Foster includes Aldington's disillusioned story 'At All Costs'; Robert Graves's story 'Christmas Truce', and Ian Hay's 'The Non-Combatant', an excerpt from his episodic novel *Carrying On – After the First Hundred Thousand* (1917) which was first published in serial form.

Christopher's anthology likewise comprises twelve stories covering a range of armed conflicts, with an introduction by the editor and a section with biographical information on the authors, recommended further reading, tasks and classroom activities at the end of the book. The First World War is represented by three stories: Liam O'Flaherty's 'The Alien Skull', Robert Westall's 'The Making of Me' and Katherine Mansfield's 'The Fly'. Christopher stresses that war is a topic with which every one of us is confronted almost daily in the news; that it is necessary to look beyond the factual information of the news reports to the human tragedies behind the images, and that short stories help us do this by providing new and different perspectives on a universal theme[14]:

The short stories contained in this anthology were written about different wars or destructive conflicts. The point here is that no matter the date, the country, or the number of people involved, all wars share main aspects in common: destruction, death, grief and hope.[15]

Finally, a different kind of commercial war anthology for juvenile and adult readers focuses entirely on the entertainment value of war fiction and forgoes any moral message or evaluation. The anthology *Heroic War Stories* (1988)[16] is a comparatively expensive hardback edition comprising twenty-three contributions – some short stories, but again mostly excerpts from war novels and autobiographies, triggering the desired recognition effect. Its title page shows a frontispiece with the inscription PRO PATRIA MORI superimposed over a crossed rifle and sword with barbed wire tangled around them, indicating a positive attitude to war that seems to clash with some of the editorial choices. The First World War is represented by excerpts from Remarque's *All Quiet on the Western Front*, Graves's *Goodbye To All That* and Frederic Manning's *Her Privates We*, all canonical Great War texts that are commonly seen to support a view of the First World War as tragic and senseless to equal degrees. These fictions of the Great War are placed alongside stories of the Napoleonic wars, American Civil War, Boer War, Second World War and other conflicts, and it is striking that, once again, sections from canonical war novels and memoirs were chosen over short stories to represent the First World War. Hayden McAllister's collection of thirty-six texts from various countries, *War Stories* (1997), repeats the pattern of this anthology and also includes next to no genuine short stories in its selection of fictional texts dealing with various armed conflicts throughout history. *The Best War Stories* (1985), on the other hand, an anthology of forty-nine pieces by authors from various countries, contains some short stories despite privileging excerpts from novels and autobiographies. This hardback collection addresses various conflicts from Roman conquests to modern African wars. The anthology includes two excerpts from longer texts dealing with the Great War, the seemingly inevitable excerpt from *All Quiet on the Western Front*, and H.T. Dorling's abridged novelette 'The Night Patrol' (1929). Genuine short stories chosen for the volume are Rudyard Kipling's 'Mary Postgate', 'A Friend of the Family' and 'The Gardener' – three stories ranging from overt hatred of the German enemy, to humorous treatment of the war, to coping with loss and grief; W.S. Maugham's espionage story 'The Traitor' (1928); three naval stories (including Conrad's 'The Tale'), and one 'disillusioned' short story, Aldington's 'At All Costs'. This selection of stories, particularly without the benefit of an introduction or foreword, is in its totality rather value-neutral and allows for both affirmative and critical evaluations of war in general and the First World War in particular, thus catering both towards modern mythology of the Great War as futile slaughter, and more affirmative voices in favour of war as adventure and a valid political instrument.

POST-WAR TEACHING AND SCHOLARSHIP

Academic collections of war writing also tend to substitute excerpts from longer prose texts and journalistic writing for genuine short fiction. Despite an often outspoken aim to widen the scope of inquiry to lesser known writers and texts, editors frequently opt for a large number of widely known fictional war accounts to supplement a small number of more obscure texts. While anthologies for young readers privilege the realist-disillusioned school of war writing, scholarly collections show a marked preference for modernist-experimental fiction. The result is a perpetuation of the existing binary to the exclusion of new material, particularly of popular fiction.

Academic anthologies, while they also need to sell, necessarily have other interests at heart than purely commercial anthologies, in that they usually foreground particular research interests. Accordingly, *The Penguin Book of First World War Prose* (1989), edited by Jon Glover and Jon Silkin, has the declared aim of making accessible a wide number of key texts that may not be readily available in other forms. This large-scale anthology of international war writing in prose includes texts as diverse as excerpts from novels, diaries, memoirs and autobiographies, journalism, letters, travel writing, critical essays and a small number of short stories, and represents most 'classic' First World War writers, including Robert Graves, Siegfried Sassoon, Frederic Manning, Vera Brittain, Edmund Blunden, Richard Aldington, Herbert Read, and Ivor Gurney, as well as the continental war writers Remarque and Barbusse. Out of ninety-nine texts included, only five are short stories, including Conrad's 'The Tale' and Aldington's 'Farewell to Memories'. Paradoxically, Silkin and Glover begin the introduction to their prose anthology with a reference to poetry, stressing its pacifist potential: 'In retrospect, the writing that has emerged from the war that was supposed to have ended all wars seems distinctive. No other poetry became, ultimately, as centred in its commitment to exposing the horror and absurdity of war; no other [...] so committed to infusing compassion with a determination to expunge war.'[17] In contrast to Great War poetry, Glover and Silkin claim, Great War prose 'is not [...] as unified in its attitudes, nor is the possession of excellence so clearly in the hands of those opposed to the war',[18] but they acknowledge that it does offer greater descriptive detail, an insight into the 'physical and moral education of individuals or groups' through shared war experiences, and a degree of contradiction less visible in the poetry.[19] Following a similar approach as Silkin and Glover's anthology, but with a pronounced emphasis on the short story genre, Trudi Tate's *Women, Men and the Great War: An Anthology of Stories* (1995) collects twenty-five English-language stories by a range of authors from a multitude of different backgrounds, including American writers such as William Faulkner, Ernest Hemingway and Edith Wharton. Many of the contributors are commonly regarded as modernist, such as H.D., Katherine Mansfield, D.H. Lawrence, Virginia Woolf, Wyndham Lewis and Mary Butts, but they are published along-side writers aiming at a wider readership, such as Rudyard Kipling and W.S. Maugham, and in this respect Tate strives to reflect the diversity of the war's short fiction.

Other anthologies of the 1990s follow a distinctly feminist or gender-centred approach and aim to make accessible women's writing on and of the First World War in particular as a statement against the predominantly male canon of Great War literature. Agnés Cardinal's *Women's Writing on the First World War* (1999) was the first such anthology and has an impressive scope: it comprises a selection of sixty-nine texts on the war and its effects by French, German, English and American women writers, including a number of short stories alongside letters, excerpts from novels and memoirs, short plays and essays. British short story writers are fairly well-represented in all sections of the volume: Part I, 'The War Begins', includes Radclyffe Hall's 'Fräulein Schwartz', chosen most likely for its sympathetic portrayal of a harmless German spinster trapped and persecuted in wartime England; another story by Hall, 'Miss Ogilvy Finds Herself', can be found in the final section of the collection, 'Retrospect', alongside Virginia Woolf's 'The Shooting Party'. A range of narrative styles are brought together in a section with the title 'Writing the War': Constance Holme's 'Speeding Up, 1917', Katherine Mansfield's 'An Indiscreet Journey' and Mary Butts's 'Speed the Plough' as formally innovative stories are balanced by three more plot-centred stories, A.E. Jameson's 'War Economy' and Blanche Wills Chandler's two short sat-ires 'A Pattern of Propriety' and 'A Little Nest Egg'. These latter stories are light-hearted, witty portrayals of wartime characters and the charming absurdities of wartime reality on the home front, and they are more repre-sentative of the bulk of fiction published in popular magazines during the war than any of the more experimental stories included.

Margaret R. Higonnet follows similar selective principles in the editing of her anthology *Lines of Fire: Women Writers of World War I* (1999). It is likewise an international selection, with many stories in translation from Russian, German, French and other languages of participant countries. The declared goal of Higonnet's anthology is to lead readers away from the prevalent focus on male combatant experience of the First World War. Angela K. Smith's *Women's Writing of the First World War: An Anthology* (2000) is similar to Higonnet's volume in aim, scope and selection but collects primarily English-language texts. Again, only a fraction of the texts included are short stories; the largest percentage of contributions are journalistic pieces, excerpts from longer works, or diary entries and letters, all organised topically rather than according to genre. Unlike Tate and – largely – Higonnet, Smith also includes previously unpublished writing by unknown writers. This new material, however, is still placed alongside a 'safe', well-known selection of established war writers. My personal experience as assistant editor of an anthology of Great War short stories (*The Penguin Book of First World War Stories*, 2007, with Barbara Korte) demonstrated that even publishers of a volume initially designed to 'rediscover' lost fictional accounts of the war will insist on a significant number of well-known names with the power to spark recognition in potential readers and prompt them to buy the book. Consequently, most of the authors included are familiar names, such as Kipling, D.H. Lawrence, Robert Graves, Arthur Conan Doyle, W.S. Maugham, Katherine Mansfield, Joseph Conrad and John Buchan, and only very few stories by lesser-known writers were added to widen the anthology's scope. As a result, even anthologies meant to broaden the field of inquiry into new areas of First World War writing often skew readers' impressions as they still largely consist of already established texts.

A recent exception is Andrew Maunder's aforementioned anthology of popular World War I short stories and novellas in the Pickering & Chatto series *British Literature of World War I* (2011). Maunder's anthology includes some material by familiar names such as John Galsworthy, Ford Madox Ford, Aldington and Herbert Read, but explicitly focuses on out-of-print material, particularly popular and magazine fiction by formerly best-selling writers who were well-known at the time but have since been largely forgotten. His aim is to make texts available that are no longer accessible except in copyright libraries and newspaper archives. Maunder's selection of stories includes gems such as Florence Barclay's novella 'My Heart's Right There' (1914), Richard Bird's public-school tale 'A Schoolboy Ranker' (1915), Jessie Pope's 'The Allotment Bride' (1917), and as a more 'literary' contribution, Ford Madox Ford's lesser-known story 'Fun! – It's Heaven', which appeared in the *Bystander* alongside Bruce Bairnsfather's war cartoons in 1915. The only disadvantage of Maunder's volume is the fact that it forms part of a costly five-volume series and cannot be purchased separately, resulting in a necessarily limited audience for this

specialised collection. Maunder's volume aside, however, the high percentage of stories included in scholarly anthologies that would generally be
described as modernist is a clear indicator of widespread interest in formally innovative fiction rather than the traditional modes of storytelling
that inform most stories about the war published from the 1910s to the
1950s. The tendency on the part of academic as well as commercial anthologies to include a larger number of already well-known texts is under-
standable in both practical and ideological terms: anthologies, notoriously
hard to sell, require a strong incentive for readers to purchase and/or read
them. Including a number of already widely known stories or excerpts
from critically acclaimed material promises a larger audience, which
potentially also benefits the lesser-known texts published alongside this
well-known war writing. At the same time, the constant republication of
canonised war texts results in a skewed impression of the war's literature.
The repeated appearances of these texts, which generally fall in either the
pacifist-realist or experimental-modernist camp propagate the impression
that literary responses to the war invariably took these forms. Anthologies
such as Smith's are a valuable starting point for a development away from
this narrow perception of war writing, but in order to challenge the existing binary and give the vast body of war fiction its due outside these two
fixed camps, scholarly anthologies and criticism need to move away from
their modernist bias more categorically than they have hitherto done. If
formal innovation continues to be championed over the complexity and
diversity of responses to the war, the rich social and ideological dimensions of war fiction addressed in the following chapters will remain largely
unappreciated. Maunder's anthology of exclusively popular war stories is a
timely reminder to editors seeking to widen the scope of their collections
that more material is available beyond the usual selection of texts.

MOOD, NARRATION AND TECHNIQUE

As Maunder's anthology shows, stories of the Great War adopt a variety of
approaches to the war beyond the modernist and disillusioned paradigms.
They differ in their formal properties, style, subject matter, and the generic
conventions they adopt. The concerns they address within the framework
of a range of genre conventions have naturally varied over time. Issues that
might have been at the forefront of readers' minds in the early months
of the war, such as the question of how to get involved in the war effort,
became less significant as the conflict progressed; after the end of the war,
reintegration, recuperation and the rebuilding of stable patterns began to

dominate over dealing with makeshift wartime arrangements and acute loss and grief.

Some of these stories belong more or less unambiguously to the realm of popular literature – such as most stories published in periodicals like the *Strand Magazine* – while others are more explicitly 'literary' fiction. This distinction follows a working definition of popular versus literary fiction provided by Ken Gelder, who builds on Bourdieu's theory of the divergent fields of restricted and large-scale cultural production.[20] Both Bourdieu and Gelder work on the premise that 'literary' texts are aimed at other artists in the first instance, and that other artists' praise is the highest measure of their success, whereas a 'popular' text is written to achieve commercial success. While it is perfectly possible to point out First World War stories which exemplify both ends of the spectrum, most stories will not fit comfortably into either category. The fact that a range of writers wrote for both artistic and popular magazines; the adaptability and complexity of a story such as Conrad's 'The Tale'; the necessity even on the part of many 'literary' writers to earn their keep by their pen, all disallow a narrow binary distinction between art and commodity. Bourdieu himself, whose work at any rate is very closely modelled on the particularities of the French culture industry, acknowledges that many factors determine the value of a work of art. While publishers, critics and influential fellow authors may be important to the making of a writer's reputation, the general public also play an important part in appreciating and evaluating art by purchasing or collecting it.[21] Gelder similarly draws attention to an important point when he notes that '[a]uthors of literary fiction can have bestsellers, too, and conversely, not every work of popular fiction sells successfully'.[22] Bearing in mind the permeable boundaries between magazine fiction and 'literary' short stories, there can be no absolutes when talking about First World War short stories, but a rough distinction between these two poles is still valuable to gauge the literary agenda and audience appeal of a short story. In the following, any references to the 'popular' or 'literary' nature of a story should be regarded as attempts to gauge their audiences, not as a value judgement. While it may be tempting to distinguish not only between 'popular' and 'literary' fiction but also between 'good' and 'bad' short stories, this kind of evaluation would be a gross misrepresentation of the material at hand. 'Popular' short stories, just as popular fiction in general, are not necessarily badly written or lacking in topical or contextual depth just because they were written for the appreciation of a broad audience. Many commercial short story writers were highly accomplished authors who produced intelligent, moving and complex stories about the war. Similarly, a story written with a small, select, 'literary' audience in mind is not necessarily a 'good' story purely by virtue of being experimental, unless one adopts innovation as the sole hallmark of value.

The comparison of stories published by the *Strand Magazine* and the *English Review* demonstrates that First World War stories were written for very different kinds of audiences, although it needs to be borne in mind that while *English Review* stories were more likely to be formally and stylistically demanding, few magazines could afford to publish the unreadable: like the *Strand Magazine*, the continued existence of the *English Review* depended on sales. Depending on the audience they were aimed at, First World War short stories follow varying approaches, resulting in some considerable differences in their narrating of the war. It would be wrong to suggest that all popular short stories of the Great War were unjustly forgotten merely for their topicality – aesthetic and stylistic considerations are also part of the process of canonisation, and many of these magazine stories were of indifferent literary quality. Different stories about the war, however, will tend to address the conflict in different ways, and with different goals in mind. The very diversity of First World War short stories bears witness to the complexity of experience informing them, and they offer an insight into numerous ways of narrating war experience at a time of profound crisis for British popular consciousness. On the popular end of the spectrum, we have stories using established patterns and formulae to provide reassurance and a safe context for embedding difficult and potentially traumatic subject matter, such as romance plots for the negotiation of war injuries. The *Strand Magazine* selection in particular exemplifies the popularity of traditional subgenres such as romance, adventure or detective fiction. John Cawelti notes for formula literature that it generally employs images, themes and symbols specific to its cultural and historical context, suggesting that 'popular' fiction not only tends to follow more rigid generic patterns, but is also closely bound up with the time of its writing.[23] It is partly on the grounds of this topicality, which results in a dating and subsequent forgetting of much magazine fiction, that literary critics tend to assume its inferior quality. Cawelti proposes, however, that the very qualities that tie popular fiction to the moment of its production may also be seen as its greatest assets.[24] At the literary end, we find stories that attempt to express a general sense of dislocation and insecurity, or specific experiences of the violence of war, through formal innovation and by employing modernist techniques. In between these two poles are a variety of stories that are hard to place in either camp, stories whose actual audiences (as opposed to their implied readers) are hard to determine in retrospect, and which at times combine stylistic innovation with traditional story patterns, or astute psychological observation with conventional narration. Modernist authors like D.H. Lawrence published stories in the *Strand Magazine* alongside commercial fiction, and they were not felt to be out of place.

A comparison of two stories is helpful to illustrate the range of narrative modes and approaches within First World War short fiction. Ben Ray Redman's 'The Enduring Image' and Katherine Mansfield's 'The Fly' both deal with the subject of grief and loss in the aftermath of violent death. Both stories depict ways in which a bereaved person copes with the loss of loved ones; both were written and published during the inter-war period. Redman's story was collected in his volume *Down in Flames* in 1930.[25] A young Scottish woman, Joan Gorden, is still mourning her fiancé Alan Leish three years after he has gone missing on a flying mission over Flanders. She spends hours on a cliff by the seaside that she associates with Alan and refuses in a friendly but determined manner the shy attentions of Alan's friend Kenneth, who has returned from the war with a crippled foot. With a pair of German binoculars Kenneth has given her, Joan habitually observes the sky from the cliff. The story takes a dramatic turn when one day Joan believes to be witnessing, through the binoculars, a ghostly vision of her fiancé's death, and in her painful excitement slips and falls to her death. Redman combines issues that were still at the forefront of his readers' minds – loss and continued grieving over the death of a loved one – with features typical of popular fiction: an element of idealistic romance in Joan's faithfulness to her dead fiancé that also echoes male anxieties over female faithfulness in the absence of the soldier; a supernatural element in the uncanny vision Joan has of her fiancé's supposed last flight through the German binoculars; and a sensational ending in which the story's heroine tragically falls to her death, the name of her dead lover the last word on her lips:

The glasses never left her eyes, and now she could see the pilot's helmeted head above the fuselage. His white face was straining downward. Trailing smoke and thin threads of flame, the plane plunged nearer; and that white face grew larger, more distinct. Then came for Joan an instant of racking unbelief, followed by a numbing surge of recognition. Staggering at the cliff's edge, she shrieked aloud a single name and tore the glasses from her eyes. [...] Gazing at nothing save an empty sky, Joan lurched forward. Loose earth and stones gave beneath her feet. With hands fluttering helplessly, she fell.[26]

The story is a conventional narrative told by an external narrator who offers intrusive interpretations of Joan's feelings and actions for the reader.

Beginning and ending on the cliff in Kintyre, the story has a simple circular structure and, with Joan's death, a closed ending in the most literal sense. Joan's death seems almost inevitable: her faithfulness to the dead lover forbids her to move on and live her life, because living would entail an eventual abandoning of her grief. The sensational ending of the story and its focus on plot and dramatic effect do not signify, however, that this is a badly written narrative. The character of Joan is drawn precisely and convincingly; the tentative advances of her fiancé's best friend and Joan's reaction to her loss are rendered aptly and sympathetically, with only occasional melodramatic flourishes.

Mansfield's 'The Fly', by contrast, was first published in the liberal American weekly *The Nation* on 18 March 1922, was subsequently collected in Mansfield's volume of stories *The Dove's Nest* (1923), and has been frequently anthologised since. In 'The Fly', a father and successful director of his own company – throughout referred to as 'the boss' – is suddenly reminded of his son, who was killed in the war, by a visitor's casual remark. While musing on his feelings of grief, he is distracted by a fly struggling to escape from his inkpot, which he eventually drowns in his ink. When he has disposed of the dead fly, the boss tries and fails to recapture his previous train of thought. Mansfield's story in general and the fly as metaphor in particular allow for numerous interpretations, and this openness and ambiguity of meaning is certainly a deliberate strategy, a refusal of strict patterns of interpretation. A reading of the story as a study of the nature of grief and mourning is particularly fruitful in the light of Mansfield's own experience of the First World War, in which her younger brother Leslie and numerous male friends were killed,[27] and it is from this comparatively narrow angle that I scrutinise 'The Fly'. The story can be seen as an illustration of how grief becomes less and less acute over time, how mourning may become a conscious effort as time takes the edge off the pain, using the fly and its gradual death as a symbol for a process of mourning that ideally ends in acceptance or forgetfulness. As a mourner desperately holds on to his grief as the last connection to the deceased, the fly desperately holds on to life, but with ever feebler efforts. Unlike Redman's story, 'The Fly' has no dramatic action, no sensational ending in which the story comes to a close. It ends on a note of puzzlement and bereftness, with the boss 'wondering what it was he had been thinking about before. What was it? It was ... He took out his handkerchief and passed it inside his collar. For the life of him he could not remember'.[28]

Mansfield's 'boss' increasingly finds mourning full of effort. Being startled into remembering his dead son by a visitor, he locks himself in his office afterwards, where he 'wanted, he intended, he had arranged to weep ...',[29] but finds himself unable to do so and is distracted by the fly instead. This effort is contrasted with earlier stages of his mourning process:

In the past, in the first months and even years after the boy's death, he had only to say those words ['My son!'] to be overcome by such grief that nothing short of a violent fit of weeping could relieve him. Time, he had declared then, he had told everybody, could make no difference. Other men perhaps might recover, might live their loss down, but not he. How was it possible? His boy was an only son.[30]

The subtlety of Mansfield's use of free indirect discourse and her general focus on the protagonist's own thoughts and feelings contrasts starkly with the more intrusive narrative voice of Redman's 'The Enduring Image'. Whereas we experience the boss's grief through his own thoughts and impressions, Joan's grief is mediated and interpreted for us by Redman's outside narrator:

It was three years since Alan had gone missing, and to her it might as well have been one day or twenty centuries. The sense of time had deserted her it seemed, leaving her poised in duration as some eternal gull might hold herself forever motionless against a ceaseless wind. But her suspension was effortless, unconscious. Events flowed past her, men and women came and went, her social self responded to them: she clasped hands, talked and walked, played bridge and golf, danced through long nights; and people would have said Joan Gorden still inhabited their world. But she had gone from them three years ago, as definitely and finally as Alan Leish had vanished in the Flanders sky. To her they were phantoms, and their world a dream. Reality for her lay in the past, and on this cliff where she and Alan had so often sat together; where they still sat, it sometimes seemed to her.[31]

Redman's interpretation of grief and mourning differs dramatically from Mansfield's. Joan's grief is eternal and unchanging, even in the face of continuing obligations and a new suitor for her affection – a tragic and yet comforting thought that presents love as an overwhelmingly strong force that can be relied on to keep the memory of the deceased alive. Mansfield's depiction is in many ways more realistic, as it shows the limitations of the human capacity to suffer, yet it is paradoxically less comforting than Redman's depiction of a grief so lasting it can only end in death. This may partly be explained by the fact that Mansfield shows the abatement of grief and lessening of its intensity not as a relief, but as a kind of loss in itself. Her multi-layered study of grief thus gains a complexity that is absent from Redman's more straightforward story, which, while also addressing the issue of grief, foregrounds a dramatic plot to capture the reader's interest.

In their different treatment of the same topic, 'The Fly' and 'The Enduring Image' illustrate some of the general differences between the many varieties of story adopting the war as subject: a tendency to integrate the war as part of daily life into stories otherwise following successful formulae or addressing issues of current interest to a wide readership in the predominantly popular selection of the *Strand Magazine*, as opposed to stories using the war to explore more fundamental psychological concerns, which constitute the predominant choice for the *English Review*. Naturally, these distinctions can never be absolutely authoritative. Jay Winter argues aptly that while modernist fiction, with its strong affinity to irony, paradox and dislocation, was well suited to express the experience of modern warfare during and in the aftermath of the First World War, it failed to offer consolation or healing of the trauma that war had inflicted on British society. On the contrary, traditional war writing such as elegiac poetry, 'while at times less challenging intellectually or philosophically, provided a way of remembering which enabled the bereaved to live with their losses'.[32]

The comparatively large number of humorous stories written about a conflict still largely interpreted as the ur-catastrophe of the twentieth century appears baffling, unless one realises the very urgent need, brought on by a continued crisis situation and in many cases self-conscious and not without precedent, to cater for positive thinking. This applies also to stories dealing with death and loss, which for the most part display the same 'aim of offering an explanation, or indeed a justification, for the deceased's involvement in a conflict that is still ongoing' noted by Victoria Stewart with respect to memorial volumes for dead soldiers.[33] In a short prefatory note to her Kiplingesque volume of social satires, comic author Blanche Wills Chandler expresses her aim to provide comic relief in the face of widespread despondency:

To have nothing better to offer as my share in the Great War than a collection of would-be funny stories, to cater for the merriment in these days of endless tragedy is a sorry part to play. But when an Editor recalls the expressions of approbation sent to him from the Front and when I remember kindly letters strangers have written to me, I take courage. If these sketches win a smile from one man in the trenches or lighten for one moment a heavy heart at home, I am not ashamed to have written them.[34]

Comic First World War stories were striving to assist their implied readers in coping with traumatic experiences, anxieties and emotional conflicts by placing them in a fictional context that allowed for an alternative, light-hearted interpretation of events. Stories like Chandler's, discussed in greater depth in Chapter 5, offered a temporary way out of everyday despondency. Even a 'disillusioned' writer like C.E. Montague, whose short story collection *Fiery Particles* (1923) appeared just one year after the publication of his programmatically named essay collection *Disenchantment* (1922), rendered the experience of the front line and trenches in a humorous manner.[35] His story 'The First Blood Sweep' is told by a shrewdly observant soldier-narrator. Protagonist Hanney, a young soldier fresh to the trenches, discovers that there is a raffle going on in which every man in the company draws the name of another, and wins ten pounds if that man is the next to die. Unfortunately, it is his platoon sergeant who has drawn his name, and Hanney fears Sergeant Gort may be tempted to deliberately send him on dangerous errands in order to win the ten pounds. To complicate the matter further, Hanney himself has drawn the sergeant's name. In the end, however, the sergeant dies first, sacrificing himself by taking over a dangerous sentry post in Hanney's stead. Although plot and subject matter of the story have tragic potential, its narrator unfailingly presents the comic side of things and adopts a tone oscillating between jocularity and sarcasm, as in his description of young Hanney's reaction to the disillusioning realisation that Gort, to whom he has taken an immediate liking, may well be anticipating his death with an eye on profit: '[T]he Kid's joy fell right in like a soufflé.'[36] David Cannadine has observed a similar tendency amongst British troops to joke in the face of danger and discomfort as a means of coping with the situation, often to the point of appearing callous or unfeeling in 'attempts to render horror and death bearable by making them funny'.[37]

Even more melancholy representations of the war, however, could be perceived as comforting and healing. To know that others shared the same experiences, that grief and loss were communal feelings embedded in a meaningful social context, could also fulfil a comforting function. As Kipling suggests in his poem 'London Stone', written for Armistice Day 1923, there is a sense of solace in the fact that others are visibly '[g]rieving as we're grieving'.[38] Martin Kearl in particular stresses the social dimension of grief and the importance of sharing loss and bereavement. He argues that society strives to put life-changing events (such as experiencing death) from purely personal, isolated experiences into shared experiences that are 'socially meaningful and personally less frightening' because they have a name and shared symptoms and are embedded in a safe, communal context.[39] His main argument is that grief is easier to bear for the individual if it is 'collectively shouldered', if only because sharing of grief offers a greater sense of continuity and security.[40] Short stories addressing the topical issue of death and bereavement, widely available in popular magazines, facilitated such a sense of sharing the burden of loss.

Short stories of and about the First World War differ not only in their way of treating specific subjects and their stylistic particulars. They also tend to adopt a variety of subgenres of the short story, or adapt generic conventions and formulae to suit their needs. Magazine short stories tend to be easier to assign to established subgenres such as the detective, ghost or supernatural story, romance, science fiction or spy story. Other stories are more elusive: while they deal with love, for instance, they do not necessarily follow typical romance patterns of love overcoming varying obstacles. Although many stories have elements of the supernatural, they are not necessarily ghost stories in the true sense of the word, in that they explore the nature of fear rather than employing fear as a narrative device. For this reason the 'modernist' story is usually regarded as more fluid in generic terms, as are the psychological story, the sketch and prose poem, character studies or reflections that are hard to place within any fixed subgenre. The difference between following and challenging genre expectations can be illustrated using two humorous front-line stories, Wyndham Lewis's 'The King of the Trenches' (written in the 1930s but first published in 1967 in an expanded edition of *Blasting and Bombardiering* by Calder and Boyars) and 'Sapper' McNeile's 'The Sixth Drunk' (1916).

Both stories are set at the Western Front and focus on the absurdity of modern trench warfare. In 'The King of the Trenches', Menzies, a young subaltern of half Peruvian and half Scottish origins, finds himself under the command of Captain 'Burney' Polderdick. Polderdick is a highly decorated professional soldier, amiable but to all intents and purposes stark mad, allegedly due to an old injury to the temple. Menzies watches with sympathy and detached amusement how Polderdick blunders and shirks, contrives to order trench mortar attacks at the worst moment, and escapes from every fight by feigning rheumatic attacks with a decided method to his madness. When things come to a head and Polderdick tries to defend a completely misplaced battery by insisting that he is the King of the Trenches, he is ordered back to England and Menzies experiences this as a personal loss. 'The Sixth Drunk' was first collected in Sapper's volume of short stories *Men, Women and Guns* (1916), but, like most of the author's stories, was most likely previously published in the *Daily Mail*. The story centres on Irish soldier Michael O'Flannigan, repeatedly penalised for being drunk and disorderly before his regiment is even posted to the trenches. Once he is at the front, O'Flannigan chiefly looks forward to his daily ration of rum. When a German infantry attack interrupts the issuing of the rum rations, the Irishman runs amok and single-handedly clears a whole trench of German attackers, inspiring his fellow soldiers to fight back and repel the attack. Mortally wounded, O'Flannigan dies a hero honoured by his regiment.

The differences between the two stories are located not only in their approach to the depiction of deviant behaviour in the trenches, but also in their modes of formal presentation. Lewis's narrator appears erratic, frequently repetitive, deliberately disjointed and at times contradictory. His introduction of the two main protagonists demonstrates these characteristics:

Why was the lieutenant pale? Why did he gaze so fixedly from beneath his new Gor'-Blimey? Because his mother came from Lima. That was also why his face was serious, and his nerves removed to a plane of reasonableness seldom reached by heat and shock. He had a certain gentle lisping breathlessness. Sandhurst had not curtailed his charm, which reached back to civilized Savannas.

He was astonished on the 4th May to see an unusual figure standing near him in the Trench. It was staring at his Flying Pig [a trench mortar battery], and twirling a stick. It twirled and twirled the stick and looked at the Flying Pig. Then it gave the fascinating siege ordnance before it a blow and exclaimed 'Ha! Ha!'[41]

Polderdick is perceived as a figure, an object rather than a person, and the narrator – focusing on Menzies's perceptions – deliberately uses the impersonal pronoun 'it' to refer to the major. Throughout the story, this detached stance is continued. Menzies observes Polderdick's exploits with anthropological interest, a sympathetic but impersonal curiosity. The peculiarity of the situation in which Lieutenant Menzies finds himself, the contradictions in his own character and particularly the madness of Captain Polderdick all transpire from this opening; the paradox of the 'civilized Savannas' contrasted with the British military establishment at Sandhurst in particular is a subtle yet unambiguous critique of the conditions Menzies encounters in the trenches. The story is told in scenes illustrative of Polderdick's peculiar behaviour rather than as a narrative built up towards a climax; it is a character study of Polderdick as seen through Menzies's eyes, and follows Menzies's speculations as mediated by the story's external narrator. 'The King of the Trenches' refuses to assign particular meaning to any event and instead stresses the bizarre elements of trench warfare. Front-line stories such as Sapper's 'The Sixth Drunk' follow a different narrative strategy: while they may also focus on the bizarre nature of modern war, they nevertheless adopt traditional narrative patterns, provide a specific event as the narrative focus of the story, and follow a coherent plot that imbues a seemingly senseless experience of war with meaning. In 'The Sixth Drunk', this event is O'Flannigan's unexpected moment of heroism, which creates a martyr despite the fact that it has been undertaken for the wrong reasons. O'Flannigan is also introduced to the reader in the beginning of the story, but in a far more explicit manner, in that we are given not only his name (we do not initially learn either Menzies's or Polderdick's name), but also a full report of his offences followed by a straightforward description of his physical appearance:

No. 10379 Private Michael O'Flannigan, you are charged, first, with being absent from roll-call on the 21st instant until 3.30 a.m. on the 22nd, a period of five hours and thirty minutes; second, being drunk; third, assaulting an N.C.O. in the execution of his duty.

The colonel leant back in his chair in the orderly-room and gazed through his eyeglass at the huge bullet-headed Irishman standing on the other side of the table.[42]

Unlike the narrative voice of Lewis's story, which centres on the perceptions of Lieutenant Menzies throughout, the external, third-person narrator of 'The Sixth Drunk' does not use O'Flannigan as the story's focaliser. Instead, the reader is guided through the story by ample comment and humorous interpretation of the protagonist's exploits and character. While Sapper's story with its heroic action, unambiguous narrator and clear plot fulfils expectations of a traditional soldier's tale and, as Jessica Meyer has argued, imbues the war with meaning in the sense that its hardships 'made men' out of civilians,[43] 'The King of the Trenches' appears to toy with genre conventions in its refusal to adhere to a coherent plotline, its meandering narrative style and focus on situation comedy rather than development of action. Both stories, however, facilitate narrative configuration of front-line reality by offering interpretive variety, precisely because of their different approaches to the subject of life at the front. In the following chapters, other short stories across a variety of subgenres are shown to perform similar acts of narrative configuration for the benefit of a wide and varied implied readership, ranging from the anxious to the bereaved.

CHAPTER 4

Negotiating Disaster in Popular Forms

GRIEF, MOURNING AND REMEMBRANCE

When it comes to the narrative configuration of reality, death is one of the most challenging experiences for literature to mediate. By constantly re-evaluating life in the light of its eventual end, and by creating narrative structures of meaning instead of a disconnected sequence of coincidences and events, its narrative rehearsal can help ease the acceptance of death, both our own and that of others.[1] Death and loss are the most obvious consequences of any armed conflict, and Great War short stories deal extensively with the experience of loss and bereavement, illustrating a variety of potential coping mechanisms. Their depiction of bereaved relatives both confirms and challenges Carol Acton's contention that '[p]rescribing and controlling grief through consolatory rhetoric that emphasises the meaning of death in the service of the state [...] becomes an essential element in the overall "manufacture of consent" through which the state persuades its citizens to participate in war'.[2]

The idea of keeping the dead alive through continuing remembrance in particular can be found in much wartime and post-war writing, most famously Laurence Binyon's 'For the Fallen', written as early as September 1914. The poem outlines a programme for continued remembrance in one of its best-known lines, 'At the going down of the sun and in the morning / We will remember them.'[3] The necessity to imbue the sacrifice of the dead with a purpose is visible in the rituals of Armistice Day.[4] In the field of the short story, one can even speak of an emergent (if short-lived) new subgenre of 'mourning stories'. Mourning stories, which may adopt characteristics of various other subgenres of the short story, have as their common denominator the treatment of loss and grief. In various different ways, they strive to depict the effects of death and loss, to offer either consolation or explanation, or at least a sense of commonly experienced bereavement. For the most part, they employ reassuringly familiar generic patterns and take recourse to traditional moral values. Their strategies of representation and consolation differ considerably, but the majority of stories reflect the attitude of respect and consideration for the feelings of bereaved relatives and in particular parents, many of whom seemed to 'derive comfort from the idea that their sons' deaths had been meaningful'.[5]

Perhaps the most straightforward approach to grief and mourning is the belief in spiritual solace. Adrian Gregory among others has shown that everyday religiosity was an integral part of British cultural life at the time, and that the high diction of sacrifice was 'deeply familiar to a Bible-reading and hymn-singing public', from the working to the upper classes.[6] Particularly but not exclusively stories written during the war adopt religion as an obvious means of consolation, as for example Annie Edith Jameson's 'The Parcel', first collected in her volume of stories *War-Time in Our Street* (1917). In this story, set in the small fictional Yorkshire village of Chigsby, two grandparents receive the news that their grandson Dick has died in action. The village community rallies round them, beginning with the postmaster's personal delivery of the telegram, to gifts of food and drink, and patient emotional support. The villagers admire Grandfather's fortitude and his pride in his dead grandson's sacrifice:

Grandfather and Grandmother breathed deep and hard, as those do who are suddenly winded. Then Grandfather rose, holding out his hand for the telegram.

'It was good on you to come yourself, sir,' he said. 'It's bad news ... bad news.'

There was a great dignity and fortitude about Grandfather as he stood there. The postmaster could not say anything, but his heart did dumb, unrecognised homage.[7]

Grandmother's reaction, on the other hand, is initially puzzling to those around her. Instead of accepting what has happened, she seems to cling to the mistaken hope that her grandson is 'alive somewhere',[8] based on a dream she has had of him the night before the fatal news. Initially, her friends and husband attempt to convince her to accept her loss, until they realise that she is referring not to Dick's continued existence on earth, but to his afterlife. Her belief in his further existence in heaven is the old woman's chief comfort, and her conviction eventually inspires her husband and friends with hope and endurance. The solace of life after death is stressed most overtly towards the end of the story, when the grandfather and a neighbour listen to the sound of the sea, which is being transcended by the spiritual 'noise' of the dead who have died in protection of England:

They listened to the booming of the sea, but their souls heard the deep and solemn chanting of our Choir Invisible. For it paces night and day round the shores of England now, so that we who hear that great hymn of hope and fortitude may remain undismayed.[9]

While this may seem a rather melodramatic presentation of spiritual comfort to the modern reader, the language of this story is the familiar language of hymns and church sermons, and the two main protagonists of the story offer two powerful models of potential solace. Grandfather exemplifies the virtues of patriotic fortitude and acceptance, which imply that the loss experienced is for a higher good, visible in his remark, after his grandson's death, that they 'wouldn't ha' kept him back'.[10] Grandmother supplements these 'male' virtues with her spirituality and firm belief in a life after death. Jameson's story is decidedly sentimental, yet it is also intensely humane and appeals through its deliberate simplicity. To an audience for the most part firmly rooted in a system of belief that allowed them to embrace the idea of an afterlife, it could certainly offer a sense of comfort.

Continued spiritual existence was also seen in terms of the dead living on in their loved ones' memories. The idea that those who died at least remained young and safe forever, and had merely exchanged a potentially painful and sordid earthly existence for a more rewarding spiritual one, is the driving force behind Anne Douglas Sedgwick's 'Hepaticas' (1918). Widowed Mrs Bradley, who is the focal point of this story, has a particularly close relationship to her only son, Jack. Mrs Bradley is devastated when Jack – who had enlisted at the outbreak of the war – returns home on his first leave and confesses to her that he has felt honour-bound to marry a chorus girl who is pregnant by him. She sees her son's happiness ruined by the insipidity of his wife, but for his sake takes in her new daughter-in-law, the aptly named Dollie. When Jack is killed in action just days after the birth of his son, his mother's grief is assuaged by the realisation that he will be spared a miserable future of bitter regret with a wife mentally inferior to him:

[W]hat was this strange up-welling of relief, deep, deep relief, for Jack; this gladness, poignant and celestial, like that of the hepaticas? He was dead and the dark earth covered him; yet he was here, with her, safe in his youth and strength and beauty forever. He had died the glorious death, and no future, tangled, perplexed, fretful with its foolish burden, lay before him. There was no loss for Jack – no fading, no waste. The burden was for her, and he was free.[11]

Not only is Jack safe from a life he would have had to share with a woman who could not have given him the companionship and support his mother feels he deserves, he also remains alive in and through her; she can see an active, constructive part for herself in mourning by keeping him alive, and taking over his burden in an act of maternal sacrifice. 'Hepaticas' has strong touches of magazine melodrama, particularly the trope of the fatal entanglement of a young man of good family with a chorus girl. These familiar features in the story's plot facilitate the intended readers' understanding of its message of hope, and their identification with the main protagonist. Jack's death does not come as a surprise, as it is foreshadowed by plot devices such as his father's early death and his mother's forebodings; conventions of family melodrama familiar to magazine readers. Other stories, too, stress that the dead may live on in the memory of those left behind. Redman's 'The Enduring Image', despite its tragic ending, is one such example.

Next to the solace of continued remembrance and keeping alive the dead through memory, patriotism offered potential comfort for loss and bereavement. Viewed in the light of patriotic sacrifice, a highly regarded public act, the death of a loved one may appear easier to bear for those affected, and indeed it was a sense of belonging to a national community of proud mourning that patriotic stories sought to disseminate. This idea is visible in a range of stories, such as John Hartman Morgan's 'The Lieutenant', collected in Morgan's programmatically named *Gentlemen at Arms* (1918), a consoling tale addressed specifically to readers of Morgan's own class and background that invokes the shared values of the upper and upper-middle classes. Patriotic sacrifice and valour are at the heart of this story, which follows its protagonist Anthony from his birth to his death at age twenty on the Western Front. With a family name that can be traced back to the Middle Ages, Anthony lives up to his heritage when, after his first year at university, the war breaks out and he enlists. A successful candidate in Officer Training, he is soon sent to the front and embarks on a model military career, which culminates in his earning the Military Cross after only a few months of active service. In a tragic turn, however, Anthony is killed after a short leave home, saving another man from certain death. The story focuses throughout on his courage and sense of justice, developed through his mother's instruction, and his equally keen sense of patriotic duty. Hartman Morgan was a Brigadier-General in the British Army, had been educated at Oxford and spent some considerable time in Germany as a student. His social and educational background is strikingly similar to that of his protagonist Anthony, and Morgan's ethos appears strongly based on a positive view of public-school education.[12] Young Anthony is firmly placed in the company of men who are cornerstones of the empire and keep alive the public-school spirit at home and abroad. It is in this spirit that Anthony volunteers for active service at the outbreak of the war, and his mother can bear the loss of her son because she understands and values his sense of patriotic duty. Anthony explains to her that he needs to join up because he cherishes the moral lessons she herself had taught him as a small boy, and 'from that moment she knew it was useless, nor did she try to dissuade him, for she would not have had it otherwise'.[13] Anthony's moral choices and his parents' acceptance of them are shown to be a matter of course; there is no room for doubt or alternative interpretations, as is visible in a description of how Anthony accepts his fate with an almost uncanny certainty:

One night he had to go out on patrol – a reconnoitring patrol, which is always a small affair and does not command the full complement of a fighting patrol. He sat in his dug-out writing a letter home on the flimsy of a 'messages and signals' form. The N.C.O. appeared at the dug-out and raised the screen of sacking. Tony folded up the letter, sealed it, addressed it, and marked the envelope, 'To be forwarded only in the event of my death.' Then he examined the chambers of his revolver and rose and went out into the night.[14]

'The Lieutenant' appears firmly embedded in a view of death on active service that developed during the latter decades of the nineteenth century and permeated British upper- and upper-middle-class culture. In Hartman Morgan's story we detect a sense that Anthony's death is preordained by his character and innate heroism. The same sense of predetermination can be observed in a range of war fiction, such as popular novelist Marie Connor Leighton's memoir of her son, Roland Leighton, *Boy of My Heart* (1916): patriotism and a belief in valour and duty may not make good the loss, but provide it with purpose and pride.[15]

In Stacy Aumonier's 'The Brothers', first collected in *Love-a-Duck, and Other Stories* (1921), it is not the heroic soldier at the front who dies for his country, but his invalid brother confined at home. When his older brother Giles joins the army and is sent to the Somme, the invalid Robin follows him in his mind's eye and begins to suffer the same injuries and symptoms as his brother, who is wounded at the front. While Giles recovers and eventually returns home unscathed, Robin dies as a result of his anxiety and the shared physical symptoms. A sympathetic friend who had witnessed Robin's mental and spiritual turmoil engraves on his headstone the words 'He died for England'.[16] The inscription initially puzzles Giles, but remembering with Milton that 'They also serve who only stand and wait', he comes to understand his brother's sacrifice and derives comfort from it. Robin himself had expressed his patriotic fervour to his friend, the sculptor Lawson, in unambiguous terms during an argument about the moral justification of the war, prior to an unsuccessful attempt to volunteer for active service himself:

Don't you think that we on this island have as great a right to fight for what we represent as any other nation? With all our faults and poses and hypocrisies, haven't we subscribed something to the commonweal of humanity? – something of honour, and justice, and equity? [...] As I walked up by the chalk-pit near Gueldstone Head, and saw the stone-grey cottages at Lulton nestling in the hollow of the downs, and smelt the dear salt dampness of it all, and felt the lovely tenderness of the evening light, I thought of Giles and what he represents, and of my mother, and what she represents, and of all the people I know and love with all their faults, and I made up my mind that I would fight for it in any case, in the same way I would fight for a woman I loved, even if I knew she were a harlot ...'[17]

The feelings expressed in 'The Brothers' are if anything more complex and moving than the sentiments voiced by Rupert Brooke in his sonnets of 1914, as Aumonier allows for doubt and ambiguities. His description of a young man falling victim to the war through indirect exposure to modern warfare is not as far-fetched an idea as it might seem. So-called 'civilian war neuroses' were not uncommon at the time, and they are described in a number of medical articles in *The Lancet* and fictional texts such as Rebecca West's *The Return of the Soldier* (1918) and Rose Macaulay's *Non-Combatants and Others* (1916).[18] The fact that 'The Brothers', like Sedgwick's 'Hepaticas', employs the language and sentiment of magazine melodrama facilitates its audience's understanding of the story.

A more aggressive way of dealing with loss is presented in Rudyard Kipling's 'Mary Postgate'. Written and first published in 1915 and subsequently collected in the author's volume *A Diversity of Creatures* (1917), 'Mary Postgate' remains a shocking tale to read and is one of the best-known First World War stories. In Kipling's tale, the eponymous Mary Postgate avenges the deaths of a young man she has reared like a son and a village girl killed by what she believes to have been a German bomb on a German airman she finds (or imagines to find) in her employer's garden amidst the debris of his crashed plane. Instead of helping him, Mary watches him die with a vindictive pleasure that closely resembles sadistic sexual arousal. In Tate's interpretation, 'Kipling's story brings the war into the centre of civilian lives, turning them into active participants'[19] – like Mrs Bradley in 'Hepaticas', Mary's grief over the loss of her beloved charge can take an active form, albeit in the destructive revenge she takes on an enemy whom she blames for Wynn's death. It is arguable whether reading 'Mary Postgate' would really have given comfort to anyone who had lost a loved one in the war, but the story certainly captures a sense of vengeful rage towards the perceived cause of that loss which would have been felt by many concerned.

Clearly, however, the hatred that offers at least temporary solace to Mary Postgate was not seen as an adequate long-term response to loss even by Kipling himself, whose own outlook changed after the war. Kipling's mellowed attitude is best visible in his 'The Gardener', first collected in *Debits and Credits* (1926). Kipling here portrays a woman whose illegitimate son Michael, brought up as her nephew, is killed in the war. The story follows her slow progress through the various stages of mourning, hampered by her deception, culminating in her visit to Michael's grave in Belgium. Even during her journey to the Belgian cemetery, Helen Turrell is unable to unburden herself of her secret. A fellow traveller confesses to her that the man whose grave she wants to see was her illicit lover, but although Helen can sympathise with the woman, she cannot bring herself to reciprocate the confidence and expose her own secret. It is only when a man she supposes to be a young gardener sees through her lifelong lie at the first sight of her that the reader is given the first explicit hint at the real relationship between Helen and Michael. There is a strong element of forgiveness and healing in the story, above and beyond the rather transparent analogy between the 'gardener' of the story and Jesus Christ as the ultimate comfort to the bereaved[20]:

He rose at her approach and without prelude or salutation asked: 'Who are you looking for?'

'Lieutenant Michael Turrell – my nephew,' said Helen slowly and word for word, as she had many thousand times in her life.

The man lifted his eyes and looked at her with infinite compassion before he turned from the fresh-sown grass toward the naked black crosses.

'Come with me,' he said, 'and I will show you where your son lies.'[21]

Helen, the bereaved mother, experiences her mourning process as to a great extent embedded in pre-existing structures of mourning and remembrance. She feels she is 'being manufactured into a bereaved next of kin',[22] and the news that there is a grave to be visited is perceived as but another step in this process[23]: 'So Helen found herself moved on to another process of the manufacture – to a world full of exultant or broken relatives, now strong in the certainty that there was an altar upon earth where they might lay their love'.[24] This step takes on an even greater significance in the light of Kipling's involvement with the War Graves Commission and his own experiences as a bereaved parent.[25] It certainly corresponded with agitated public debates on adequacies of remembrance, which are also touched upon in Mansfield's 'The Fly'.[26]

Helen's progress to the cemetery and through its maze, her confusion and denial when, even the day before visiting the cemetery, she fails to reveal her true identity as Michael's mother, symbolise her mourning process and its slow movement from denial to acceptance, culminating in the moment of (spiritual) recognition. This acceptance is not necessarily the end of Helen's grief, and we are not given any explicit reason to believe she leaves the cemetery comforted. Instead, the story ends on a supremely neutral note, with no hint as to Helen's feelings: 'When Helen left the Cemetery she turned for a last look. In the distance she saw the man bending over his young plants; and she went away, supposing him to be the gardener'.[27] It is the reader, not Helen, who is comforted by recognising in the gardener a symbol of Christ the Redeemer, inconspicuously present and compassionate towards those who grieve, whether or not they realise his presence. In this sense, the story also strongly builds on a pre-supposed spirituality of its readers as well as on a good knowledge of the New Testament, a knowledge that pervades much First World War writing across the full range of genres.[28] Recent studies such as Richard Schweitzer's *The Cross and the Trenches* (2003) and Michael Snape's *God and the British Soldier* (2005) conclude that although Britain was becoming increasingly secularised, religion was ubiquitous among First World War soldiers and civilians, with the presence of a New Testament in almost every soldier's pack, continued widespread Sunday School attendance, and a 'widely shared passion for hymnody' that guaranteed familiarity with religious topics and diction.[29] Such a shared basis of religious knowledge, if not necessarily actual religiosity, constitutes important literary and cultural tropes informing First World War writing that is often lost on modern readers.

Mourning stories such as these stand in contrast to some disillusioned renditions of the experience of loss, such as Richard Aldington's 'Of Unsound Mind'. The story was collected in Aldington's *Roads to Glory* (1930) and contributes considerably to the war-critical, disillusioned air of that volume. Evelyn, the main protagonist of this story, has left her tyrannical older husband for a young artist lover. The story relates her reasons for entering the unhappy and childless marriage, interspersed with bitingly satirical comments on rural high society. The lovers elope to London, and the outbreak of the war breaks up a complete idyll of idealistic and contented love:

Then came the deluge. It had seemed to them that they had foreseen everything, that no human power could destroy their happiness, since they were happy as long as they were together. They had forgotten the great collective hatreds of and stupidities and crimes of the world. [...] Evelyn and Ronald were among the many who paid the debt for which they were not responsible; for such is the justice of gods and men.[30]

The young couple are presented as innocent victims of a greater evil that is visited upon them, helpless in the face of adverse circumstances. Ronald reluctantly joins the army when social pressure becomes unbearable and the lovers part miserably. Amply foreshadowed by the tone of the story, Ronald is killed in the Battle of the Somme, and the devastated Evelyn drowns herself in the Thames. The coroner's verdict, '"Suicide"', with the humane rider, "while of unsound mind"'[31] echoes the verdict of her husband's friends after her flight. Aldington's story presents the loss of a loved one in the war as an insurmountable obstacle, a calamity not to be overcome. There is no comfort in this ending, and none seems to be intended. While other writers offer models for dealing with loss and grief and strive to provide comfort for their readers, Aldington's aim is to 'write off' in story form his own bitterness and trauma, not to help others come to terms with the consequences of the conflict.

A more unexpected kind of grief is that for a dead enemy. Mourning for a dead comrade is a common trope of inter-war literature, and as we will see below, many war stories also dealt with a sense of trauma mixed with guilt in veterans who felt haunted by enemy soldiers they had killed. A.W. Wells's story '"Chanson Triste"' (1924), however, varies this motif by relating the story of an unlikely friendship between a British and a Bulgarian soldier, cut short when the British narrator unwittingly betrays the Bulgarian's place of retreat. Prompted by a concert performance of Tchaikovsky's 'Chanson Triste', the narrator remembers his secret wartime friendship with Bulgarian soldier Dimitri across enemy lines in Greece. Having stumbled across a secluded hut used by Dimitri to read and write away from his regiment, the two men had exchanged books and letters using a secret hiding place, but their friendship ended tragically with Dimitri's death at the hands of the narrator's own company on the night they had agreed to finally meet up in person. As he has not been able to share his loss with anyone, the narrator feels unable to let go of his grief, which is inevitably mingled with guilt and self-reproach:

Certainly nothing has given me relief up to now. One, two, three, seven years ago it must be since it happened, and at a spot four or five thousand miles away, to which I am never likely to return; and yet there still come days, nights, sometimes even weeks, when the whole thing will break out in my brain again as though everything took place only yesterday.[32]

The narrator touches upon two crucial points with respect to the relationship between mourning and writing about war: first, the potentially therapeutic effect of writing about one's own war experiences ('I have sometimes thought that if I put it all down on paper, precisely and exactly as it occurred, my mind might become easier'),[33] and second, the comforting nature of being able to relate these experiences to those of others through the medium of narrative, denied to the narrator himself by a lack of literary counterparts to his own experience:

If I could only trace one experience similar to mine (as, indeed, I have spent hours and hours browsing over trying to find it) I should feel comforted; but nowhere have I been able to discover the vaguest hint of a resemblance.[34]

The uniqueness of the narrator's experience, on one level the main asset of his story in terms of novelty and literary interest, is a personal disadvantage in dealing with his sense of loss in an inter-war world of shared, institutionalised grief. Ironically, however, the narrator provides exactly this kind of solace to potential readers of his own story: by setting down his unusual tale, he offers readers with similar experiences a foil for their own recollections.

AFFIRMING LIFE: ROMANCE IN A WARTIME SETTING

Romance – particularly of the magazine variety – was easily adapted to a wartime setting, and found the young soldier as useful and popular a protagonist as any pre-war civilian gentleman. So well-suited were romance stories to wartime reading tastes that Keble Howard felt prompted to begin his post-war love story 'Needs Must When Love Drives' (1919) with the words 'In case you are afraid that Romance withdrew to the cupboard on the day the Armistice was signed, I will ask you to read the following story.'[35] His romantic hero is duly an invalided young captain of the British Army, newly returned from the war. Indeed, Ken Gelder notes that although the overall structure of romance fiction is formulaic, the ways and means by which the prescribed happy ending is achieved, and by what characters, may vary considerably.[36] Its mixture of conservative features that provide readers with a comfortable sense of reliability, and of adaptability to seemingly endless new settings, renders romance one of the ideal forms for the narrative configuration of wartime experiences and to reconcile readers with change.[37] Harold Orel, in scrutinising British reading tastes of 1914–18, finds that 'romance, in one or another of its countless disguises, constituted then (as it has for most of this century) the major fraction of reading matter that the public wanted',[38] and stresses in particular its escapist qualities of taking readers away from the subject of war. However, many romance stories offered a different kind of escapism – the relief of fleeing *into* the war, of making it both more bearable and easier to grasp within the framework of well-known generic formulae. More than any other 'popular' genre, romance is founded on the security of formula. Cawelti compares the wish for repetitive, formulaic elements in the readers of popular fiction to the craving of a child for hearing the same story repeated over and over again, indicating that repetition and formulaic structure offer relaxation and security.[39] In times of stress the security and reassurance offered by familiar patterns takes on particular importance, combined with the guaranteed positive outcome that is a staple of romance fiction.[40] Wartime romance seems to meet readers' needs particularly well by offering the chance to rework war-related scenarios and issues into a safe, reassuring format.

The soldier's sweetheart was a recurring figure in magazine fiction, and constituted a concept appealing to men and women alike. For a young woman during the war, 'the cultural context within which she grieved [...] offered multiple narratives designed to console her by glamorising her role as bereaved sweetheart'.[41] Acton notes that female waiting and mourning was 'glamorised and given an elevated status as her emotions are set against the image of combat' in popular magazines.[42] While the notion of a faithful and devoted girlfriend or fiancée at home was reassuring to soldiers absent for long periods of time, the idea of having a soldier-lover appealed to women on the home front because it offered them a chance of indirect participation in the war. Acton observes this attitude in her survey of two popular magazines for working- and lower-middle-class girls and young women, *The Girl's Friend* and *Our Girls*:

Wartime love offers women a role in the 'drama' that is the war: 'At every front there is the drama of fighting; here in Britain there is everywhere proceeding another drama – the drama which is being played out in the hearts and at the lonesome hearthsides of the women who must stay behind.' Women's emotional attachments to men at the front are thus the means by which they are included in the drama even while they are officially excluded from the front.[43]

From as early as December 1914, the *Strand Magazine* published a number of romance stories with a wartime setting that suggested active parts in war for women, such as Richard Bird's 'Little Candles' (April 1916). Governess Dorothy Campion meets Private Charles Tracy on a crowded train, and gives up her seat for him to sleep in to show her gratitude for his service at the front. The pretty governess intrigues Tracy and because she refuses to give him her address he advertises for her in a national paper, but his search for her initially remains fruitless. However, when he returns to England as a subaltern, newly promoted after a few months back at the front and sent home to train recruits, the two meet again owing to a happy coincidence when Tracy knocks on Dorothy's door to remind the family of blackout regulations. 'Little Candles', told by an empathetic third-person narrator in the slightly flowery style of the typical *Strand Magazine* story, contains all the staple elements of romance fiction: hero and heroine meet in an interesting or even peculiar situation, fall in love, are parted by adverse circumstances, but finally manage to overcome the obstacles to their union assisted by the helping hand of fate.

The same formula, altered and somewhat stretching the boundaries of the credible, is repeated in another *Strand Magazine* wartime romance story, 'Scandalous!' by Richard Marsh (August 1916). Young protagonist Ethel Hubert receives a letter from the front, left in an abandoned overcoat and posted on to her by another soldier who found the coat. The letter was written by a young soldier she met just before the war and with whom she had spent some hours walking at the seaside. The young soldier – now a major – is called David Carpenter and confesses his undying love for her in the letter, which he wrote while lying wounded in a trench. Shortly afterwards she receives a communication from Carpenter's lawyers, informing her that he has died and left her £30,000. She is shaken at this discovery and mourns for a man she hardly knew, but presently Carpenter himself turns up at her house alive and well to rectify the mistake, and – as might be expected – they are married within a short time.

One of the more down-to-earth *Strand Magazine* romance stories is W.B. Maxwell's post-war short story 'Joan of Arc' (January 1919), which also constitutes a semi-conscious commentary on the impact of propaganda and particularly the new medium of film on the British public. The story is set in 1917, at a time when the war is in full swing and the military situation of the Allies seems doubtful. Timid housemaid Adelaide is greatly startled when, musing over the poster for a new American recruitment film, 'Joan of Arc', outside the local cinema, she is suddenly invited in by handsome young soldier Dick Budd. Adelaide gains in confidence when she notices his shyness, and encouraged by the stirring film, Adelaide is subsequently determined to do war work and prove herself worthy of Dick. Once she has left her domestic position to the ridicule of her former workmates, however, she is unable to find war-related work, as too many women have already volunteered. She is forced to work as a domestic servant again and at her new employer's house gradually assumes the positions of housemaid, parlour maid and cook, all roles in which she excels. When Dick at last returns on leave and they become engaged, he assures her that, when the war is over and they move to the colonies to make their fortune, her household skills will be invaluable. Maxwell's story has visible traces of the Cinderella fairy-tale motif (the stepsisters replaced by Adelaide's fellow housemaids), but places it in a contemporary context that readers could relate to. The dialogues in the story are deliberately colloquial, imitating everyday conversation in its slightly ungrammatical flow:

And then the young soldier spoke to her.

'Going inside?'

'Beg pardon?' said Adelaide, almost fainting from the suddenness of the surprise attack.

'I passed the remark, whether you were going in to see the show.'

'I wasn't intending,' Adelaide gasped.

'No more was I,' said the soldier; 'that is, not alone. But I don't mind if you don't. Shall us?'[44]

Maxwell's narrator attempts to make the rather speedy agreement between the two more plausible by providing an emotional explanation, presenting it in the light of 'a swiftly evoked mysterious sympathy that made companionship joy, that destroyed bashfulness'.[45] While critical readers are likely to consider a marriage founded on one spontaneous outing to the cinema somewhat risky, the habitual reader of romance fiction rests assured in the knowledge that what appears as a casual and coincidental meeting is nothing less than fate; according to the formulae of the romance genre, the protagonists are usually capable of spotting their ideal soul mate at first sight. The fact that in this story the fateful meeting of the two lovers takes place under wartime conditions adds flavour, as the possibility of Dick's death in action hovers over the story. Compared to similar stories, such as the magazine serial 'Emma Brown' (1914),[46] 'Joan of Arc' is a downright realistic narrative with no undue flights of fancy: while Adelaide meekly searches for war work to be worthy of her soldier-fiancé, eponymous heroine Emma Brown brashly makes her way to Belgium and attacks the Germans in open warfare with a band of boys and old men, accompanied by her aptly named bulldog 'John Bull'.[47] In this rather more unlikely tale, the heroine is likewise compared to Joan of Arc, proving the paradoxical appeal of the warrior-maiden to young Englishwomen during the war, despite the fact that Joan of Arc had, of course, fought against the English and not with them.[48] The versatility and zest with which wartime romance tackled wartime problems confirms what Jean Radford describes as a kind of social or cultural contract between romance writers and their readers, in fulfilment of which writers create texts that meet basic desires of their readership.[49] Great War romance stories fulfil these criteria by combining typical romance patterns with a wartime setting and, as we will see below, confidently tackled deeply unsettling issues such as shell shock or mutilation by embedding them into established patterns.

SOLDIERS' ANXIETIES: SHELL SHOCK, DISABILITY AND REINTEGRATION

The unprecedented death toll of the First World War was an important factor in turning it into the traumatic event of the century, and the psychological impact of actual deaths was amplified by the particular demographic character of those who had died: most casualties occurred amongst the group of males aged twenty to forty.[50] However, the 'Lost Generation' also consisted of those who physically survived but came out of the conflict mentally and/or physically impaired. Society in general and soldiers, their families and friends faced the problem of what long-term effects active service could have on those who served and survived. The lasting influence of disabled – and particularly mentally disabled – ex-servicemen on popular memory of the First World War is visible in the plethora of later writing about shell shock, including modern best-sellers such as Faulks's *Birdsong*, in which the novel's protagonist encounters a shell-shocked First World War veteran still institutionalised decades after the end of the war. Fiona Reid has shrewdly diagnosed the roots of our enduring preoccupation with shell-shocked soldiers, who embody our moral 'lesson' from the war like no others and originate in '[t]he shell-shocked man – often the shell-shocked boy – who was too traumatized to fight' a war that was 'too brutal, too cruel and too futile'.[51]

Of the casualties on the Western Front alone, the majority were injuries, not deaths.[52] Soldiers themselves seemed to prefer a 'clean' death to the lingering evil of disability: Fictional soldier Jim in Florence Barclay's *My Heart's Right There* (1914) tells his young wife, 'So every day I used to pray: "O God, if I'm called upon to die, let it be a bullet, through my heart, swift and clean. But, if I'm to live and go back to Polly, let me get home perfect and entire, wanting nothing."'[53] In *Mud, Blood and Poppycock* (2003), Gordon Corrigan provides statistics relating to those injuries that resulted in permanent disabilities meriting a military pension.[54] The total number of awards, just under 300,000 cases, shows that disabilities of varying severity affected a large group of ex-servicemen after the war, and their overall significance was heightened by the psychological impact of their appearance in society on an unprecedented scale. It must also be borne in mind that all war-related disabilities, particularly mental impairments, were not necessarily accepted as such by the military and civil authorities, and that many veterans who suffered long-term consequences do not appear in these statistics. Deborah Cohen has described in great detail the failure of the British state to adequately recompense veterans, leaving private charitable initiatives to fill the gap.[55] Injured, disabled and disfigured former soldiers had to be reintegrated into a society intent on outliving the trauma of war, and the difficulty of this task is reflected in the war's literature. Rebecca West's novel *The Return of the Soldier* revolves around the return of a shell-shocked army captain, who has forgotten his wife but remembers his sweetheart of twenty years previously. Numerous poems, such as Margaret Postgate Cole's 'The Veteran' and Wilfred Owen's 'Mental Cases' and 'Disabled', depict the despair and hopelessness of the maimed veteran. Short stories of the war form no exception in this regard, and similarly address problems connected with the return of injured and disabled soldiers.

Anxieties were twofold. On the one hand, disabled soldiers themselves were anxious about their reintegration and their chances of living their lives as they had hoped and planned. This prominently included fears of having lost all chances to marry and have a family. On the other hand, families and friends were confronted with the strain of having to welcome back men who were no longer those who had set out to fight, of having to bear cheerfully the care of a lifelong invalid. Gail Braybon vividly evokes the strain on women and children faced with this task:

Many women had to live with men who had been altered profoundly by their experiences, and who, by and large, found it impossible to talk about them [...]. If fathers and husbands had fits of despair and anger, or were woken by nightmares, women had to go on coping, making allowances for moods, and managing with a reduced family income in the case of disability.[56]

Cohen likewise points out the hardships awaiting women married to disabled soldiers, who not only had to care for their husband and often children, but who also frequently had to go out to work in order to supplement the family income.[57] Popular opinion during the war applauded the notion of women taking responsibility for their soldier-husbands and sweethearts. Rather than seeing potential disability as an impediment to committing oneself to a soldier, many women seem to have regarded it as their welcome duty to care for a man injured in the service for his country. At least hypothetically speaking, marriage to a wounded soldier was the most desirable way for a woman to participate in the war effort and do her bit. Carol Acton quotes such sentiments from a serialised romance for working girls, 'Bridegroom at the War':

> It's better to get married to your sweetheart even if you have a bit to bear and help carry one another's burdens. I think the lasses are right who are marrying their sweethearts before they let them go off to the war. Maybe they'll never come back, and maybe they'll come back sadly wounded; then it's the wife that's the one to tend and comfort them.[58]

It goes without saying that women whose husbands returned from the war physically or mentally impaired found their position rather less glamorous and heart-warming than suggested in magazine fiction. Even educated young women such as Vera Brittain, however, could see the attraction of binding themselves to an injured veteran as a means of patriotic sacrifice. In a letter to Roland Leighton of 10 September 1915, Brittain comments approvingly on a personal advert in *The Times* in which a lady whose fiancé has been killed in the war offers to marry any disabled officer (class distinctions quite obviously very much intact). Brittain, initially startled at the idea, seems nevertheless convinced of its feasibility:

> The man, she thinks, being blind or maimed for life, will not have much opportunity of falling in love with anyone and even if he does will not be able to say so. But he will need a perpetual nurse, and she if married to him can do more for him than an ordinary nurse and will perhaps find some relief for her sorrow in devoting her life to him. [...] It is purely a business arrangement, with an element of self-sacrifice which redeems it from utter sordidness. Quite an idea, isn't it?[59]

Brittain herself later contemplated marriage to a friend blinded in the war, but was prevented from carrying out this plan by the man's death.

As a contrast to these sentiments, Mary Borden's 'The Beach' addresses the lasting and incalculable effect that injuries sustained in war could have on marital relationships. The subconscious reflections of Borden's disabled young veteran do not bode well for his future relationship to his wife:

> He loved her. He hated her. He was afraid of her. He did not want her to be kind to him. He could never touch her again and he was tied to her. He was rotting and he was tied to her perfection. He had no power over her but the power of infecting her with his corruption. He could never make her happy. He could only make her suffer. His one luxury now was jealousy of her perfection, and his one delight would be to give in to the temptation to make her suffer. He could only reach her that way. It would be his revenge on the war.[60]

The young soldier feels himself irreversibly cut off from his wife by his war experience and the visible traces it has left on his body. The power relationship in their marriage has been overthrown for good, and he feels keenly, if subconsciously, that he is no longer able to fulfil the traditionally active male role. His wife in turn suffers not because she feels incapable to adjust to his physical shortcomings, but because of his emotional withdrawal and changed character: "'I must love him, now more than ever, but where is he?' She looked around as if to find the man he once had been.'[61] Ariela Freedman points out that the intimate and yet impersonal nature of the story renders it more universal: 'The man and woman are unnamed, outlined only abstractly, and could stand in for any wartime couple' in a similar predicament.[62]

A small number of modernist responses such as Borden's aside, romance generally appears to be the most important subgenre to tackle issues like injury and anxieties about reintegration. As Jane Potter notes, the presence of the war-wounded made it a necessity to refashion 'attitudes attached to physical disability and disfigurement' for men who had suffered these in the service of their country,[63] and romance fiction is at the forefront of this adjustment. Love and marriage are shown, albeit somewhat simplistically, as antidotes to the negative effects of war.[64] Annie Edith Jameson's 'Pie' (1917) for instance features a maimed soldier protagonist who finds a faithful companion in the girl he loves. Billeted in a Yorkshire village, shy and unremarkable Private Jim Ashton falls in love with a pretty farmer's daughter. She bakes him fruit pies and walks out with him good-naturedly, showing him no more attention than she shows to other young soldiers, and pointedly avoids a private interview with him on the last night of his leave to forestall any attempts on Ashton's part to propose. When Ashton returns a few months later with his right hand amputated and a keen sense that his disability has put an end to any romantic aspirations he might have harboured, however, the girl's friendly but non-committal attitude has changed. Rather than waiting for a proposal from the downcast young veteran, she proposes herself. Ashton is initially reluctant to believe in the sincerity of her feelings, as he fears that she may be acting out of pity rather than genuine romantic interest:

He drew away from her, though he was all a-quiver with her sweetness and nearness; and because he was still weak from his wound, his own voice shook a little.
  'It's very good of you!' he said. 'But I don't want – sistering.'
She pressed nearer to him, between laughing and crying.
  'And I don't want to be a sister. Can't you see that?'[65]

Ashton is reassured when the young woman explains her feelings, claiming that she feels that if they are to be thought of as one body and soul,

she can feel she herself has also given a hand for England. His injury sets
him apart from the other young men who are courting her: 'Every time
I look at you I shall think that you and I are one, Jim; and that *I* gave
my right hand for England.'[66] His sacrifice, however unwillingly made,
secures Ashton the marital bliss he might otherwise not have obtained.
The somewhat surprising change of heart on the part of Jim Ashton's new
fiancée, worrying as it might seem, is no stand-alone fictional incident. In
Berta Ruck's story 'Infant in Arms', from the best-selling collection *Khaki
and Kisses* (1915), a formerly spurned lover finds himself proposed to by a
previously disdainful young lady, who explains her altered views by saying: 'Oh, can't you understand that this has made everything different?
You're just twice as much of a man, now that you'll have to get on with
one leg, as you were when you were dancing and fooling about on two.'[67]
'Pie' and similar stories capture an optimistic and largely propagandistic
mood of reassurance visible not only in romantic fiction. Jessie Pope's 'The
Beau Ideal' (1915) describes in short, racy lines the transformation of a
young girl's taste in men. Where she preferred classical symmetry of feature before the war, her wartime taste is marked by admiration for bodily
sacrifice:

> The lad who troth with Rose would plight,
> Nor apprehend rejection,
> Must be in shabby khaki dight
> To compass her affection.
> Who buys her an engagement ring
> And finds her kind and kissing,
> Must have one member in a sling
> Or, preferably, missing.[68]

Although the injury is more severe in Morley Roberts's love story 'The
Man Who Lost His Likeness', a *Strand Magazine* romance published in
the Christmas number for 1916, an injured soldier also finds healing and
solace in the love of a good woman. Formerly a handsome young officer,
protagonist Harry Singleton returns from the front with shell shock and
a badly scarred face, and as a consequence loses his fiancée Rose because
she cannot bear to become the wife of a disfigured man. Figuratively
speaking Singleton has also (at least temporarily) lost his identity, as old
acquaintances and even his former lover no longer recognise him, and he
has to rebuild his identity around his new appearance. Shattered by Rose's
renunciation as much as by his war experiences, Singleton is invited to
his doctor's country house to recuperate, and there meets beautiful young
Joan Chester. Joan is blind and immediately taken with Singleton's voice

and charisma. The blind girl and the disfigured veteran fall in love, complementing their physical shortcomings, and in the end Singleton even feels capable of forgiving his former bride, who comes to him repentant just as he has confessed his love to Joan. The archaic and somewhat stilted language used by the story's protagonists is both a common feature of early twentieth-century popular romance fiction, and expressive of the author's attempt to do justice to a grave subject. Patriotic reverence informs the narrative style of the story, as in the following excerpt:

So wisdom and love worked about Harry Singleton, and Henshaw told him he was busy getting well, and thereby working for his country, though he never so much as heard again any disastrous sound of war. The younger man was glad to think this might be true. For the woman he had loved became gradually as much a dream as the battles in enduring, faithful France. [...]

'So you've come, Joan!'

And she answered with less boldness than her wont: –

'Yes, dear sir, for the night is beautiful, and the dew in the open brings a sweet scent out of the grass, and your stars are shining'.[69]

Singleton's concomitant mental condition is described in some detail: he finds it hard to face strangers and familiar people alike, afraid that they might be disgusted at his disfigured face; he is scared of open spaces, has problems concentrating and at the same time suffers from insomnia and nightmares, all classic symptoms of shell shock. These symptoms are soothed by the peace and quiet of the doctor's country house and the healing influence of Joan's presence:

He was renewing himself faster than he thought. His nights were no longer a recurring drama of hideous inability to meet and avert disaster – dreams in which actual horror, once faced with courage, became a fantastic mixture of reality and sick imagination that froze his blood and woke him sweating ice. These hours returned less often; they moderated their intensity, and he no longer looked forward with apprehension to the hours of sleep. He began to set himself tasks and found it possible to read and keep his attention on his book.[70]

Joan manages to reassure Singleton about his altered appearance with a statement similar to the sentiments voiced by Private Ashton's lover in 'Pie', if more dramatically phrased: When Joan asks for permission to touch Singleton's face and thus 'see' him, she sweeps aside his worries that she might find him hideous by exclaiming indignantly 'A soldier's scars are badges of honour [...] and better than medals. Oh, I shall not mind, but like you all the better for them.'[71] Unlike Rose, Joan rises to the challenge of recognising that true beauty lies within – admittedly made easier for her by the fact that she cannot see – and, in accordance with the conventions of romance fiction, shows herself to be a worthy partner for Singleton. 'The Man Who Lost His Likeness', like 'Pie', taps in on very real concerns. Deborah Cohen observes in her study of disabled ex-servicemen that 'Nurses in military hospitals reported that many wounded soldiers dreaded the once-longed-for reunions with sweethearts. They did not know how their loved ones would respond to their injuries. To "take on" a severely disabled man, a woman had to be "brave".'[72] As feared by the fictional veteran Singleton, his pre-war lover is not ready to take him on, but he is fortunate to find a brave woman prepared to deal with his injuries.

As Singleton's fictional case illustrates, physical disabilities and disfiguring injuries are only the more visible, tangible effects war could have on the lives of former soldiers and their families. The effect of war on veterans' mental health was in many ways a more disturbing problem than physical injuries. Cases of shell shock made up the second-largest group amongst ex-servicemen awarded a pension, constituting nine per cent of the total number.[73] Although fewer texts deal with mental injuries than with the war's physical effects on soldiers' bodies, there are a number of short stories that tackle shell shock in various ways. Wilson Macnair's *Strand Magazine* story 'On Record' (1918) documents the extensive research devoted to a condition that had never before affected such high numbers of servicemen and particularly officers. Macnair's fictional Captain Roland, a young officer of the Royal Army Medical Corps, is shown to treat patients struck dumb by shell shock by means of recording their voices with a special noiseless phonograph of his own invention while he questions them under hypnosis. He then wakes them and plays them the recording to make them realise that the problem is solely psychosomatic and not caused by any physical defect. He feels flattered when he is visited by eminent medical man Sir Ebenezer Vase, who promises him fame under his patronage, but this feeling soon changes to outrage when he discovers that Vase has published an article and is going to lecture on Roland's invention without giving him any credit. Fortunately, he finds he has accidentally recorded his conversation with Vase, and is able to prove Vase's fraud at the next meeting of the Royal Association of Medicine. While the focus of the story is the audacious fraud and Roland's imaginative outwitting of the dastardly Vase, the story also gives a detailed description of the 'cure' of a (fictional) case of mutism, and illustrates how prominent and familiar a topic shell shock was at the time.

While Macnair's story takes the form of crime fiction, comic treatment of shell shock is also not at all unusual in First World War short stories.

Aumonier's 'The Kidnapped "General"' (1923) features an embedded narrative that is told by a formerly successful writer who had returned from the war suffering from shell shock, and the revelation of his condition is the story's twist in the tail. The frame narrator and his friend, who meet the shell-shocked writer on a walking trip through the countryside, subsequently learn from a local innkeeper that the story they have just heard is pure fabrication, the work of an ingenious and amiable madman. The shell-shocked writer lives in a woodland clearing in a converted London General motorbus. The curiosity of the two friends is aroused by his unusual habitation, and they are only too willing to listen to the man's story about how the bus came to be his house. His story turns out to be a tall tale about a disappointed First World War veteran working as a bus driver, who, when he is about to be made redundant, kidnaps a bus full of stockbrokers and financiers to elope with his fiancée. As they later find out, the owner of the converted motorbus had served in a motorbus unit on the Western Front during the war, and returned shell-shocked and confused:

D'you remember during the first weeks of the war they sent a whole lot of London motor buses out to help transport the troops? Well, Mr Ormeroyd was a skilful shuvver, and he volunteered, and got the billet to drive one of these buses. I don't rightly know the details. He was only out there six weeks. There was some awful incident – I believe he was the only one of a company saved – he on his old battered bus. There was a score of them buses, men and drivers, and all blown to pieces. It was somewhere in Belgium. He got away back to the lines. But – well, it's a kind of – what do you call it? – you know, got on his nerves, never thinks of anything else.[74]

A case of severe trauma is here reduced to a trivial diagnosis of 'nerves', yet the consequences of Ormeroyd's illness are described as fairly serious. He has fled to the seclusion of the countryside to live in a bus resembling the one in which he was nearly killed, and is unable to write anything or invent any stories that are not in some way related to this reminder of his traumatic experience at the front.[75] The innkeeper and the local population appear to think that Ormeroyd is on the mend, and rely on the healing powers of a quiet, rural lifestyle: 'They say it is better for him to live like he does – a kind of rest-cure. He's getting better. They say he'll get all right in time. He's got money and his health is otherwise middlin' good'.[76] Partly for eugenicist reasons, as Reid observes, 'British medical and political authorities perceived the countryside in general to be healthier and more morally wholesome than the urban environment', as there was widespread worry about the 'degenerate' males produced by urban confinement and industrial labour.[77] This ties in with the tendency to stress the beneficial effects of country living on mentally injured soldiers promoted in Aumonier's story.

Although this possibility is never explicitly spelled out in the story, Ormeroyd's compulsion to tell stories that centre around his bus may also be seen as self-therapy; therapeutic re-writings of his own story (he usually assigns himself the role of one of the protagonists) that help him come to terms with his real experiences.[78] The innkeeper's main indicator for Ormeroyd's improving mental health is in fact the quality of Ormeroyd's stories: 'His stories get better, you know. I've noticed it.'[79] At the same time, Aumonier's story serves to domesticate and render less threatening the phenomenon of the shell-shocked soldier whose ailment is so hard to understand to the outsider. Ormeroyd's condition may be hard to comprehend – the innkeeper is struggling to describe it in the quote above – but he is 'a very nice fellow' and shown to be perfectly integrated into the rural community of the small Buckinghamshire village where he has 'plenty of friends'.[80]

Where Aumonier's story portrays the shell-shocked veteran in a benevolent light familiar to us, other contemporary stories take a more sinister approach. Fiona Reid reminds us that the 'figure of the shell-shocked soldier who would not or could not fight sits uneasily alongside [...] mentally broken men' who 'did not just display anti-war symptoms', but 'were violent to their comrades [...] and mistreated their wives or mothers'.[81] Sapper's disturbing short story 'The Death Grip' (1916) shows us such a violent 'mental case': his protagonist, the virile and courageous Captain Hugh Latimer, sustains a head injury whilst single-handedly keeping a German bombing-party at bay during an attack on a German trench, winning a V.C. He is not killed and outwardly recovers, but becomes increasingly restless and aggressive, and is eventually taken away to an asylum when he attempts to strangle both his friend and his wife in their sleep. The narrator is one of Latimer's closest friends and traces the sinister changes in the wounded officer from the front to the near-fatal incident. Although Sapper's narrator links Latimer's altered personality and descent into madness exclusively with the physical trauma of his brain injury, the descriptions he receives of Latimer's condition from the latter's wife read like familiar symptoms of shell shock:

Hugh doesn't seem able to sleep. [...] He is terribly restless, and at times dreadfully irritable. He doesn't seem to have any pain in his head, which is a comfort. But I'm not quite easy about him, Ginger. The other evening I was sitting opposite him in the study, and suddenly something compelled me to look at him.

I have never seen anything like the look in his eyes. He was staring at the fire, and his right hand was opening and shutting like a bird's talon.[82]

Latimer's behaviour is seen as 'utterly unlike' him, and he has spells of amnesia, forgetting his odd behaviour in a manner similar to many shell-shock victims.[83] As such, the character of the brain-damaged Latimer offers a point of identification for those affected by violent nervous disorders as a result of their loved ones' war service.

Stories that treat shell shock at a greater distance from the war also tend to take a negative rather than a light-hearted stance. Two excellent examples are Winifred Holtby's 'Such a Wonderful Evening!' (1934) and Aldington's 'The Case of Lieutenant Hall' (1930). Holtby's 'Such a Wonderful Evening!' provides a perspective on shell shock that is both female- and civilian-oriented. Here, a young woman encounters a shell-shocked veteran during a visit to York Tattoo and returns home with the fervent wish that her fiancé will never have to become a soldier. Joanna Bourke notes how even years after the end of the war familiar sights such as a butcher's shop could trigger a recurrence of nightmares or attacks in the victims of shell shock.[84] Holtby's depiction of the fictional veteran's breakdown when faced with a mock execution that is part of the military display is given in some detail; he screams and falls into a fit that renders those around him intensely uncomfortable:

The little man in the shabby raincoat, sitting just in front of Jessie, sprang to his feet, shrieking. It was not a loud shriek – a sickening, choking anguish.

Jessie screamed too, then clung to Herbert.

'It's all right.' 'Take him away.' 'It's a fit.' 'What is it?' From all the neighbouring seats came an uneasy stir of questioning.[85]

The man's escort, a complacent middle-aged woman, merely explains that he has been shell-shocked in the war, and leaves the onlookers to draw their own conclusions. The glamour and reward of soldierly life are here put into question, and long-term consequences of warfare are shown without any glossing of heroism. Holtby contrasts painfully the colourful and stirring display of the military parade with the unglamorous, pathetic figure of the shell-shocked veteran, the 'gallant and splendid tumult, filling the air with courage rendered audible' juxtaposed with the 'little man in the shabby raincoat' who eventually collapses in terror.[86] Holtby's story is not without sympathy for the situation of the shell-shocked man's escort either, relating her unwillingness to tend to her agitated charge to the fact that she 'had so few treats in her drab anxious life' and noting flatly that the war, even years later, 'still had power to frustrate [her pleasure]'.[87]

Aldington's story, on the other hand, adopts the perspective of the archetypal 'disillusioned' ex-serviceman, and has no room for sympathy with civilian war victims. 'The Case of Lieutenant Hall' consists of the fictional diary entries of Henry William Hall between November 1918 and March 1919, and is rounded off by a coroner's report published after Hall has committed suicide. The diary entries document Hall's progressive decline, from the Armistice through his time as a member of the occupational army in Belgium, to his 'demobbed' life in London. While Aldington clearly intended the story as scathing critique of the treatment veterans received on their return – the report on Hall's suicide contains a cynical warning to other veterans not to expect special treatment and to embrace their duty to cope with civilian life after demobilisation – Hall evidently also suffers from a severe form of shell shock. Almost from the beginning, he is tortured by nightmares, lack of sleep, and visions of a dead German soldier until he feels he can bear life no longer. His nightmares are caused mostly by guilt and horror of himself, harking back to an incident on the Somme in 1916 when, clearing out a trench, he had shot three unarmed Germans and bayoneted a fourth in the back. Like Singleton in 'The Man Who Lost His Likeness', he suffers from insomnia and a lack of concentration ('I find it very difficult to think consecutively these days'),[88] and his nightmares gradually develop into full-blown hallucinations:

Of course, I tell myself it's all nerves, but that German is certainly a curious phenomenon. [...] It may be a delusion, but it's real enough to me. I don't see how I can go on living with the constant haunting of that spectral face. If I walk up to it, the damn thing disappears; I turn around, and there it is on the other side of the room. When I read or write I can *feel* it behind me. I keep the electric light on all night now, even when I fall asleep – it's awful to wake up in the dark.[89]

In an embittered and cynical yet curiously analytical tone, Hall documents his own mental decline. Writing in this case fails to be therapeutic, and Hall's decline culminates in his suicide when the pressure of guilt, memories and frustration with his overall situation reaches an insurmountable pitch. The fictional character Hall is modelled to some extent on actual cases of veterans suffering from shell shock or war neurosis. Bourke describes cases of ex-servicemen afflicted by guilt after the war, mostly connected with the killing of unarmed enemy soldiers. Like fictional Lieutenant Hall, real-life soldier Arthur Hubbard was tormented by his killing of three unarmed Germans and relived the deed in nightmares and daydreams.[90] As Bourke also notes,

[T]he men who fought in twentieth-century conflicts were civilians first, and servicemen only by historical mishap. These men were passionately engaged in elaborating ways of justifying killing in wartime, and most were eager to assume moral responsibility for their bloody deeds. As sentient humans, they insisted upon bearing a share of responsibility for their own actions.[91]

This responsibility could result in a mental breakdown as described by Aldington. Aldington's fictional account of a shell-shock victim's case is also in keeping with Bourke's observation that neurasthenic symptoms of shell shock were generally worsened by unfavourable circumstances, such as a lack of family support and the bad economic climate of the 1920s that did not allow ex-servicemen to easily return to work.[92]

The issue of shell-shocked veterans and their problems with reintegrating into society could also be written – and read – in a more oblique manner. Neville Brand's story 'The Returned' (1932) constitutes the perfect allegory for post-war fears surrounding mentally disabled veterans as a problem that haunted the living and simply would not go away. In 'The Returned', set during the war, a mysterious stranger begins to magically resurrect fallen soldiers. Men previously killed in action suddenly reappear and rejoin their units in an eerie, silent, half-asleep state. Their advent spreads fear among the men who knew them before they died, as well as causing endless administrative trouble: wives have remarried and are now faced with charges for bigamy, pensions have already been awarded and casualty lists become useless. The returned men are eventually transferred to a concentration camp so as to give the authorities time to decide what to do with them. Morale among the men in line sinks, since they are all more afraid of being resurrected to a strange half-life than they were before of being killed: 'There was something hideous in the prospect of being called back to walk among your comrades, feared, untouched – among them, but no longer of them.'[93] The image of the resurrected soldiers as pariahs, feared and ostracised, also shows remarkable parallels to the situation of severely shell-shocked or disabled soldiers, who in many ways felt set apart from society and were often viewed uneasily by former friends and strangers alike. Brand's mysterious stranger, when found and arrested, is taken charge of by a general, who wants him to recall to life his only son, recently killed at the front. The stranger first seems inclined to comply, but when he realises that the general intends to send the young man back into the line, he refuses.

The Stranger glanced over his shoulder and his eyes were clouded and troubled.

'You want him back because you love him?'

'He is my only son.'

'And you wish to give him back happiness – the wind and the rain and the sunlight and the years that were due to him?'

'Yes, and I wish to give him back his career – his work that is not finished –'

The Stranger had risen to his feet; he stood facing the general and his whole frame shuddered. Beads of sweat stood out on how [sic] brow.

'You mean that you would send him back again to kill?' he cried. 'Are you so dull that you cannot understand? My work – my calling back – do you imagine it was ever meant for that? ... If that is your fancy, I have finished!'[94]

When the army decides to send all of the returned men back into active service, they rebel and have to be shot by British guns, suggesting a rather less benevolent treatment of disabled veterans than most other texts dealing with either shell shock or physical disability. In Brand's story, the returned soldier is interpreted in the sinister context of a ghost story, and as we will see in Chapter 6, Brand's depiction of soldiers haunting civilians is not an isolated case. Shell shock and the psychological after-effects of war certainly continued to haunt inter-war and post-war society. Whereas this chapter has shown how short stories were instrumental in addressing various effects of war – death, injury and psychological damage – the next chapter takes a closer look at the moral dimension of war as reflected in its short fiction and investigates how short stories deal with the ideological underpinning of war.

CHAPTER 5

Narrative Rehearsals of Moral and Ideological Alternatives

MORAL QUANDARIES: ETHICAL (RE-)ASSESSMENTS OF WARFARE

As a war that confronted the British public to an unprecedented extent with soldiers' deaths and injuries and had a more immediate effect on civilian life (through rationing and the presence of Belgian refugees amongst others) than any war Britain had waged previously, the First World War was also a war with a pronounced moral dimension. While some stories show the psychological damage done by war and military training, other stories investigate the effects of the war on the state of the British nation. Yet other writers use the genre to explore the difficult moral choices faced by individuals in extreme situations in which ordinary, civilian values seem suspended or subdued. Finally, the war's potential to reform men and turn them into soldiers is interesting in the light of how writers as well as politicians justified the war. Joanna Bourke draws on various historical sources, such as John T. MacCurdy's textbook *War Neuroses* (1918), to show that '[d]espite the unique frightfulness associated with modern, technology-driven warfare, it was widely accepted that the "abnormal" men were those who were repelled by wartime violence'.[1] By inference, a 'real' man was aggressive and tough, capable of witnessing and inflicting death,[2] whereas anyone to whom these criteria did not apply had to be cured of essentially being too nice. This view echoes anxieties about the degeneration of Britain's manhood that informed the pre-war invasion literature discussed below. War was seen as 'the supreme test of manliness' and only through the 'unselfish service in the name of a higher ideal' could one hope for reform.[3] The hope for a revitalisation of British manhood is duly reflected in the short fiction of the Great War, and reformed masculinity is presented as one of the positive side effects of war. Its treatment, however, is often humorous, notwithstanding the more serious subtext.

A representative example of a short story portraying a young man transformed by his service for his country is Eden Phillpotts's 'A Touch of "Fearfulness"' (1917). In this tale, set in the fictional village of St. Tid in Cornwall, the young farmer Amos volunteers at the start of the war despite his peaceful temper: 'There was plenty of laughter when we heard gentle Amos was going to the war – a chap, mind you, that even shirked sport.'⁴ He enlists against the wish of his fiancée Lucy, who fears he will disgrace himself (and, by proxy, her) at the front, and that she may lose him. In Amos's absence, the dastardly gamekeeper Jacob persuades Lucy to break off her engagement. When Amos returns on leave with the rank of a sergeant and about to receive a Distinguished Conduct Medal, he takes this news calmly. His friends find him very much changed for the better – still amiable, but hardier and manlier in physique and mentality. Amos confronts Jacob in the public house and humiliates him by frogmarching him to Lucy's house and berating him for his slacking. Lucy realises her mistake and marries Amos before his leave is up while Jacob slinks away in disgrace. The soldier Amos is shown to be what a man ought to be: firm yet gentle, powerful yet in control, assertive and just, and the narrator closes his story with a positive outlook on a future shaped by men like Amos:

And if he's spared to the finish and takes up his Uncle Matthew's farm when the time comes, Amos Barton will be a power of good among us; for though the war's brought out his manhood, it haven't altered his nature, and he'll always be gentle to the weak and kind to the humble, and thoughtful for his fellow man and woman. Because he's built so.⁵

The passage quoted above strikingly reflects Jessica Meyer's observations on male identities during World War I. In her study *Men of War*, Meyer investigates self-description and self-definition of British servicemen through their war experience in letters, diaries and memoirs, and distinguishes between two core identities adopted by these veterans: the heroic identity of the virile soldier and the domestic one of 'good sons, husbands and fathers, as both protector and provider'.⁶ The narrator's evaluation of Amos focuses on both his new and old identities, the heroic and the domestic, and not only assures readers that the war has had a beneficial effect on the young protagonist, but simultaneously tries to convey to the reader a reassurance that men like Amos will not be harmed by their war service. As seen in Chapter 4, by 1917 there was certainly a general awareness of the damage war could inflict on soldiers' psyches as well as their bodies, and the narrator's parting words in 'A Touch of "Fearfulness"' seem designed to alleviate fears that promising young men would return altered beyond recognition.

In a similar vein, the *Strand Magazine* story 'Albert's Return' (1919) by Edgar Jepson portrays a demure young man who is rendered more assertive and manly by his war service. Albert Appleton is initially described as 'a weedy youth'[7] with no discernible physical or intellectual merits. As such, he is an embarrassment to his socially aspiring family, particularly compared to his successful elder brother Frederick. Albert's conscription consequently leaves his family comparatively unmoved, with the exception of his mother. He is sent to Mesopotamia, holds out despite wounds and severe illness, comforts his mother by sending cheerful letters, and slowly but steadily rises to the rank of sergeant. When he returns, his improvement is initially noted only by his mother and by his brother's fiancée Annie, a simple working-class girl patronised profusely by the rest of the family. Albert and Annie inevitably fall in love and begin to resist the social pretensions of the family. In the end, Albert finds work as bailiff for an army friend, the Honourable Alexander Sarratt, who had served with Albert as a private, and Annie renounces Frederick to marry Albert. This short story stresses both positive changes wrought by the war on the class system – Albert's close friendship to a peer due to their mutual experiences is a clear breaching of class boundaries – and the beneficial effect of war on the returned soldier: Albert looks 'so much more alive' than his civilian brother, and Annie finds him very different to her mental image, 'taller and smarter, and his eyes were very blue in his tanned face'.[8] Most of all, however, Albert has become assertive and capable of standing up to his older brother, who wants him to begin work straight away rather than take a much-needed break in the family home: '"Well, I'm going to take all the rest I want," said Albert, slowly and firmly. "As for hanging about home, there wouldn't be any home to hang about, if I and the chaps like me hadn't fought for it".'[9] The moral of the story is that Albert has benefited from the war's ability to 'cure British society of the physical degeneracy of the middle classes',[10] heralded by Edwardian commentators as the salvation of the British nation.

A naval version of the moral reformation plot is Taffrail's adventure story 'The Bad Hat' (1929). Taffrail – the pen name of H.T. Dorling – wrote a large number of naval tales set during the war, and in the case of this story, set in 1915, outlines the transformation of a confirmed good-for-nothing seaman into a war hero. Lazy and careless Charles Whitlock, an uneducated Cockney, has been causing trouble ever since his taking up post on a British cruiser. His particular nemesis is Petty Officer Burton, whom he insults when asked to clean up his mess, and vows to punish for reporting him to the captain. When the ship encounters a German battle cruiser, however, Whitlock proves his mettle as a fighter and demonstrates that he is capable of genuine bravery. Despite being severely injured himself, Whitlock remains at his gun post and risks his life to put out a fire that might cause the entire deck to explode, saving Petty Officer Burton and others from certain death:

He did not at the time understand the gravity of the situation; he only thought of saving life; and tottering to his feet, swaying like a drunken man, he made for the pile of blazing ammunition. The effort hurt him hideously, but he gritted his teeth and forced himself along [...] at last it was done and he might sit down on the deck. He was breathless and faint with pain. 'Thank Gawd!' he muttered thankfully.[11]

In the moment of danger, the cynical, good-for-nothing Whitlock discovers his humane impulses and surprises himself by his actions. As a result of his bravery, the German cruiser is sunk, Whitlock is promoted, awarded the Conspicuous Gallantry Medal, and he and Burton become friends.

The positive effect of war as depicted in fiction was not, however, restricted to men. In Florence Barclay's *My Heart's Right There* (1914), even in its earliest stages the war serves to inspire selfless determination in the story's heroine Polly. The young mother is married to a professional soldier, who returns home on leave injured after the retreat of Mons. Her fears and worries, initially centred on her own family, soon turn into a more general spirit of moral reform:

A sudden sense of calm came to Polly. [...] If this war has already served to turn our mind's eye away from the contemplation of our own particular stew – however savoury – to the great essentials of life; if it has begun to give us a wider, a more extensive, outlook, not bounded by our own particular horizon, but by our knowledge of the needs of others; if it has done this for us, in our own individual lives, which, after all, go to make up the great whole of national life – then already we see a gleam of the eternal good which is going to work out from this apparently intolerable evil.[12]

This insight is clearly presented as the story's proverbial silver lining. Fictional Polly thus illustrates the notion that war, precisely through its acknowledged horrors, has the power to reinforce selfless and sacrificial impulses and engender consideration for others as well as positive sentiments such as endurance, patience and human solidarity.

On the flipside of the coin, there were also very real apprehensions that the war would spoil and brutalise young men. An inter-war story by I.A.R. Wylie, 'All Dressed Up', shows the potentially fatal psychological effects of an enforced transformation from civilian to soldier. During the last months of the war, a battalion of conscripts are subjected to military training. All men in this battalion suffer from physical defects that had previously led to their repeated rejection for active service, and they find it almost impossible to transform into soldiers. One of the men, Cobham, soon succumbs to despair: he has had to give up his job, fears he may have lost his girlfriend, and his only desire is to be able to make sense of the months of suffering in training camp by engaging in actual combat before his death. The battalion is hurried to the front in November 1918, but the Armistice is announced just as they are preparing to go into action for the first time. Frustrated and horrified that his ordeal has been pointless, Cobham loses his head and assaults one of his fellow soldiers, an attack resulting in the tragic and meaningless death of both men. His desperate anticipation of fulfilling the role he has been trained for against his nature is captured in the following passage:

Cobham tried to remember all he had ever learnt about machine-guns. No frontal attack. You wormed round them. On all sides. And then – bayonet work. Or, better still, a couple of well-planted grenades that would knock the crew clean out.

No more throwing into emptiness. Next time he took his aim it would be at men. His bayonet would go home into live flesh. He would know at last how it really felt...[13]

This fictional incident is not completely divorced from reality, given that as a result of the largely passive role of infantry soldiers in trench warfare, 'Medical Officers at the front were forced to recognize that more men broke down in war because they were *not* allowed to kill than collapsed under the strain of killing.'[14] Wylie's protagonist has been forcibly transformed into a soldier and is then denied the fulfilment of that role, leading to his brief but fatal mental breakdown. Cobham and the other men in his company, hit by the news of the Armistice and frustrated in their fearful yearning for a soldier's death, attack each other like wild beasts released from a cage:

It happened. It exploded. The pent-up force was released – at last. Cobham, with his free hand on Cuffy's throat, felt it break in him like an abscess. It broke over him in a crushing wave of men's bodies – of beating, bruising hands and feet. He went down under it. [...] He couldn't let go. He didn't want to. He'd got to choke the life out of someone – someone who'd done him out of something. [...]

Something went out of him. He collapsed – emptied.[15]

Wylie's story disturbingly portrays a transformation that has gone wrong because it has passed the mark. Given that especially during the early stages of the war the transformation of civilians into soldiers was generally considered to be a beneficial process, Wylie breaks with a powerful taboo in showing its downside. Her depiction of brutalised conscripts, however, tallies with anecdotal evidence from war correspondent Philip

Gibbs's account in *Realities of War* (1920), recalling a 'conversation with a Bantam soldier on the Somme in 1916', who holds forth about his desire to mutilate German soldiers and the likely after-effects of the war: '"Oh," said that five foot hero, "there will be a lot of murder after this bloody war. What's human life? What's the value of one man's throat? We're trained up as murderers – I don't dislike it, mind you – and after the war we shan't get out of the habit of it. It'll come nat'ral like!"'[16]

Short stories exploring the moral and physical effects of the war, however, are only part of the picture, as an even greater number of stories explore its ethical dilemmas. As Ricoeur observes of the ethical dimension of narrative, war stories can function as a laboratory in which authors can question or affirm war experiences by concentrating on individual acts and sentiments. Both during and after the war, short-story writers engaged in exploring the moral ambiguities inherent in armed conflict. Wylie's fictional study of the effects of military training on the human psyche is just one example of a critical voice which attempted to show the downsides of the 'war to end all wars' next to its widely propagated humane aims. One of the earliest stories to seize upon moral quandaries inherent in the waging of a 'just' war is Conrad's 'The Tale' discussed above. Where Conrad's approach is in deadly earnest, however, moral dilemmas are discussed with more humour, but not lacking in essential seriousness, in Sapper's wartime short stories. Always narrated by an amiably sarcastic career officer, Sapper's stories repeatedly entertain through their treatment of seemingly impossible coincidences that call into question basic human values. In 'The Fatal Second' (1916), a young officer promises his fiancée, Patricia, to protect her younger brother, Jack, at the front. Instead of being able to save him, however, the officer has to shoot Jack himself because he threatens to fall behind during an attack. Unable to be truthful to Patricia regarding her brother's cowardice or to marry her without telling her that he is his killer, the principled young officer returns to the front and deliberately sacrifices his life in saving a wounded man. His situation is the more tragic because shooting his friend and future brother-in-law is a strategic decision made for the good of the regiment that could arguably have been avoided. In a perverse coincidence, the scenario had previously been discussed by Patricia and her fiancé in a purely hypothetical argument. The young woman had argued in favour of personal responsibility and humanity, opposing her fiancé's conception of soldierly duty:

'But the awful thing, Jerry,' said Pat quietly, 'is that you would never know whether it had been necessary or not. It might not have spread; he might have answered to your voice – oh! a thousand things might have happened.'

'It's not worth the risk, dear. One man's life is not worth the risk. It's a risk you just dare not take. It may mean everything – it may mean failure – it may mean disgrace'.[17]

In this case, personal duty stands pitted against duty towards one's country, and whichever path the young officer chooses, he will necessarily fail either his fiancée or his country. His only solution to this ethical conundrum is sacrificial suicide.

Larger issues such as conscription or court-martial decisions and their impact on the individual were also scrutinised in First World War short stories. The issue of conscientious objection, perhaps surprisingly, hardly features in popular Great War short stories even after the signing of the Armistice, and if it does, is treated in a negative light. Given that there are at least some texts that address this sensitive topic – first and foremost Rose Allatini's novel *Despised and Rejected* (1918) – one suspects that the reason for the relative absence of pacifists and conscientious objectors in World War I short fiction is at least partially linked to issues of publication. Only very few liberally minded publishers (such as Allatini's publisher, C.W. Daniel) were willing to risk an 'unpatriotic' novel, and controversial short stories could only hope for publication in magazines that supported the pacifist cause, such as the *Labour Leader* and the *Tribunal*, the latter established in 1916 as the official weekly paper of the No-Conscription Fellowship. Because such stories voiced a minority opinion, popular periodicals such as the *Strand Magazine* would not have considered them for publication, and even the *English Review* was too supportive of the British war effort to publish openly pacifist material. Given that *Despised and Rejected* was 'banned shortly after publication and the publisher [...] prosecuted under the terms of the Defence of the Realm Act',[18] it is not surprising that sales-conscious magazine editors steered clear of such material.

Patriotic sentiment among authors as well as publishers also contributed to the comparative dearth of popular pacifist writing. Although John Galsworthy was a liberal-minded and compassionate man, his letters show little understanding for pacifists and conscientious objectors:

I was never for a moment a pacifist in this war. From the first, like the ordinary human being that I am, I felt that we could not stomach the invasion of Belgium and had to fight; and I knew that if we once began to fight, we had to go on to the bitter end. You will not find any word written by me of a pacifist nature in relation to *this war*.[19]

In his story 'The Peace Meeting', written in 1917 and collected alongside other war stories in *Tatterdemalion* (1920), those opposed to the war are given short shrift. The story focuses on two pacifists, very different in character, who attend a peace meeting in a church. One of them, Colin Wilderstock, is a feeble elderly gentleman who begins to support the peace movement only when he feels that the death toll of the war is rising too high, but is shown to half-consciously resent his own weakness. The other, John Rudstock, is a vigorous middle-aged man who opposes the war purely for the sake of opposition. A crowd of outraged soldiers soon break up the peace meeting. Although they behave violently, Galsworthy portrays them as rough but upstanding patriots who spare the ladies, and have the sympathies of both the police and Wilderstock on their side. While Wilderstock is portrayed as well-meaning but misguided, Rudstock is shown unsympathetically as an anti-social troublemaker. Having just fought the disruptive soldiers by hurling chairs at them and dealing out punches, Galsworthy has Rudstock claim somewhat unconvincingly, 'I came, as you know, because I don't believe in opposing force by force. At the next peace meeting we hold I shall make that plainer.'[20]

The reluctance on the part of popular short-story writers even after the war to vindicate conscientious objection may in part derive from a sense of continuing respect for soldierly sacrifice, which served to taint those as cowards who had chosen to spend the war in prison. In his account of conscientious objection during World War I, the journalist Will Ellsworth-Jones reports that even as late as 2002 public opinion on conscientious objection was by no means unanimously sympathetic. When English Heritage established a memorial garden for sixteen conscientious objectors imprisoned in Richmond Castle during the war, local residents opposed the idea: '"Why should we have a living memorial to sixteen people who refused to fight for their country?" asked one town councillor, while a retired major who lived in the town said the commemoration of these "cowards" showed a "twisted sense of values"'.[21] Outside the sympathetic circles of the No-Conscription Fellowship and some Christian and socialist organisations, conscientious objectors continued to be represented in negative terms, ranging from effeminate coward to degenerate criminal.[22]

The most notorious bone of contention after the war was that of retrospectively justifying court-martial executions. While desertion in general continued to be regarded, uneasily, as a cowardly act meriting stern punishment, it was also increasingly felt that the particular circumstances of individual cases ought to be taken into consideration. In the mounting anti-war climate, the death sentence for desertion became a political issue between liberals and pacifists on the one hand and military and conservative forces on the other. A debate in the House of Commons, reported in *The Times* on 30 March 1927, reflects these altered post-war views on desertion. A Labour MP had 'moved a new clause to abolish the death penalty in the class of cases which involve cowardice and desertion on active service', arguing that in 'the conditions of modern warfare it was just a chance whether a man came out of an engagement to be decorated for bravery or shot for cowardice'.[23] The question of whether or not the death penalty was appropriate was not, claimed the MP, 'a military question to be decided by Army opinion, but a humane one to be decided by a knowledge of human nature' – thus arguing from the same standpoint as the young woman in Sapper's 'The Fatal Second'. The MP's suggestion was seconded by a fellow Labour MP, who further claimed that 'there was general agreement that cowardice on the battlefield was due to nervous failure', rendering overly harsh penalties an injustice towards a sick man. This argument draws attention to altered attitudes towards bravery and manliness after the war, and the centrality of shell shock as a new psychological phenomenon. Shell shock as a mitigating circumstance for breaches of military law was a particularly difficult subject, as psychological symptoms were hard to determine objectively, and shell shock must have been a tempting excuse for unacceptable behaviour even to those who were not suffering from any genuine mental impairments.[24] As might be expected, the Labour MP's proposal was opposed by a lieutenant-colonel of the British army, who felt that the death penalty was a crucial instrument in maintaining army discipline. His objections echo in the words of military historian Corrigan, who argues against the myth of unjust court-martial executions during the Great War by stressing the necessity and use of military law in upholding discipline and ensuring the functioning of the army.[25] Corrigan points out that while the death penalty was a possible consequence of desertion, it was dealt out sparingly and the majority of men sentenced to death were subsequently pardoned, with only 346 out of several million British soldiers actually executed, thirty-seven of whom were convicted for murder, 266 for desertion and only eighteen for cowardice.[26]

Those few short stories that deal with the issue of desertion, however, tend to work on the assumption that a death sentence once issued will be carried out regardless of the circumstances. Popular author Alfred Noyes penned a dramatic renunciation of the death penalty for deserters in his post-war short story 'Court-Martial' (1924). Its protagonist is 35-year-old office clerk George Mason, married with a young son, who enlists in autumn 1914 and initially makes a good recruit despite his thoroughly civilian mindset. Mason realises the inhumanity of the war when, going up to the frontline to attack, his company is ordered to let a soldier drown in a mud hole so as not to be delayed and again when he is splattered by the blood of a comrade killed right next to him. Mason suffers a nervous breakdown, falls behind and decides without considering the consequences to go back and try to save the man in the mud hole. Unsuccessful in this endeavour (the man is already dead), Mason still feels he has to escape from the war machine and manages to hide for four weeks before being caught. He is sentenced to be shot for desertion, but feels comforted in his last hours by an encounter with the A.P.M.[27] of his battalion who understands that Mason is neither a coward nor a scoundrel, but simply an ordinary civilian whose nerves have given way and who is now 'unjustly' punished for it. Noyes strategically opens his story by informing the reader of Mason's pre-existing nervous disposition, stemming back to early childhood. Mason is also described as physically inferior: 'Mr. Mason's undernourished physique hardly suggested a war-like disposition. He stood about five feet four inches in his socks. He had the round shoulders and narrow chest of a confirmed desk-worker; and he had to be very careful about catching cold.'[28]

The recruiting sergeant who convinces Mason to join up encourages him to take up a military life for the benefit to his health, and Mason enlists out of conscientiousness and a readiness to oblige. His time in the army seems unreal to the homesick Mason, and he stumbles into desertion almost by chance: 'He hardly realised this phantasmagoric quality of his life until he found himself – one might almost say awoke and found himself a prisoner, not of the enemy, but of his own countrymen.'[29] He is tried and sentenced for an offence that, as the narrator puts it, 'had no legal existence in civil life; but, in the Army, was a serious crime and punishable with death'.[30] Since Mason remains a civilian in thoughts and habits, his perception of his actions and those of martial law clash irreconcilably:

> All through the trial, he was conscious that everyone was doing his best to be fair and to give him every chance of acquittal, if he could only somehow prove that he had lived up to a standard that had never been his own. He could not even express this idea, of course, in his defence. He merely became eloquent in describing his motives, and the description was quite enough to condemn him in the eyes of those alien judges. [...]
>
> The difficulty was that Private Mason was not really a soldier, but a civilian in khaki, and that he and his judges moved in absolutely different worlds.[31]

Mason's predicament is reminiscent of the so-called cultural-patterning model used by Eric Leed, namely the fact that 'restraints upon aggression learned in the process of socialization are not purely external rules and inhibitions that can be left behind with civilian clothes. If restraints upon aggression are truly learned, they become constituent elements in the personality of the citizen-soldier.'[32]

Noyes's narrator is sympathetic to Mason, whose 'failure' he presents not simply as cowardice, but as the clash of two irreconcilable mindsets. The army is presented as an efficient system with its own rules and regulations, which are regrettably too inflexible to accommodate the particulars of Mason's case and cannot afford to spare him lest a host of Masons abandon their post. Mason's A.P.M. is used as the only mouthpiece of direct criticism when he deplores at length the shooting of 'one 'o the pluckiest little volunteers' he has known.[33] In the officer's opinion, Mason's is a case of nervous breakdown and should have been treated as such. The narrator reinforces this diagnosis by establishing clear narrative links between Mason's desertion and a traumatic childhood experience, which is repeated in the moment of doubt and indecision at the front that leads to his desertion ('he felt as helpless as the child in the dark garden when the ghost clutched him by the hair').[34] He is also described as 'shaking uncontrollably from head to foot' after he has been sprayed with the blood of his comrade and subsequently stumbles into a destroyed trench full of body parts.[35] Noyes's story also speaks on behalf of those readers who had to live with the shame of their dead husband or son's perceived cowardice, and acknowledges that their experience of loss might differ from the officially sanctioned and commemorated death in action. Noyes's fictional presentation of Mason's case noticeably tallies with the idea that congenital nervous conditions were the most likely factor leading to mental breakdown in soldiers.[36] However, the particular circumstances of Mason's desertion serve to justify his offence in the eyes of a civilian readership not simply because shell shock had become an accepted medical condition, but also because of the immediate cause of his breakdown. By the mid-1920s, the figure of the soldier drowning in mud had become a notorious and haunting image that recurs time and again in descriptions of the front, particularly in connection with the battle of Passchendaele.[37] Mason's desertion is thus turned into an event readers could relate to by aligning themselves with the protagonist's humanity in the face of the inhumanity of the war.

Stories about deserters were for the most part consigned to the cultural archive of the war rather than incorporated in its working memory, but recent attempts to include formerly marginalised groups such as deserters or conscientious objectors in the popular consciousness of the Great War may result in a resurfacing of these accounts. It is worth noting, however, that leniency towards those who failed the test of military pressure tends to be restricted to the demonstrably 'innocent', the underage, mentally unstable or frail. This was visible as recently as 2001, when the Shot at Dawn Memorial designed by Andy de Comyn was unveiled in the National Memorial Arboretum in Staffordshire. The memorial is modelled on an underage deserter, implying that desertion was a matter of conscience or breakdown rather than an act of cowardice or self-interest.[38]

ESPIONAGE, THE ENEMY AND HOME-FRONT ANXIETIES

If writing about conscientious objection and deviant behaviour in their own ranks posed challenges for British writers addressing the war, writing about the enemy certainly did, too. Despite assumptions that British writing of the period, particularly in the popular press, uniformly condemned Germany, literary depictions of Germans throughout the war and in the inter-war period can be surprisingly nuanced. Generally speaking, First World War short stories addressing specifically the subject of Germans and Germany fall into two broad categories. While one presents Germans as a threat, the other, smaller group empathises with Germans, particularly those living in Britain who were adversely affected by the war between their country of origin and their adopted country. The two groups of stories adopt different popular forms as the most conducive to their message: while the spy thriller seems to have been the medium of choice for stories condemning Germans, sympathetic tales tended to adopt the melodramatic mode. Spy stories allowed not only for an open voicing of anxieties with the safety buffer of fictionality, they also served to alleviate these fears by portraying the ultimate futility of German attempts at sabotage and infiltration. Not least of all, they gave readers a sense of participation in the war effort. By constant vigilance, these stories suggested, every man and woman could do his or her bit even without leaving British soil or taking up munitions-making. More humanitarian concerns about naturalised Germans in Britain, on the other hand, were voiced by John Galsworthy and others and employed a melodramatic mode as a matter of course. The familiar sentimentality of melodrama would have guaranteed their stories a greater appeal and strove to elicit sympathy even from readers still under the influence of wartime propagandist representations of German 'frightfulness'.

Spy thrillers were largely a wartime phenomenon, although they continued in the inter-war period subject to gradual modifications. The spy craze that swept through Britain following the outbreak of the war and that led, among other things, to the retirement of Lord Louis of Battenberg (later Mountbatten) as First Sea Lord on 27 October 1914, has been amply documented.[39] These sentiments stand in close relation to a climate of general hysteria and suspicion towards France and Germany rampant in the latter decades of the nineteenth and early years of the twentieth century, made visible most tellingly in the 'invasion literature' of the pre-war decades. The term invasion literature broadly refers to fiction addressing the state of the nation and alleged threats of a foreign invasion of the British Isles as a consequence of decay in British moral and physical stamina. The best-known examples of this kind of invasion fiction are probably William le Queux's *The Great War in England in 1897* (1894) and Erskine Childers's *The Riddle of the Sands* (1903), both part of a surprisingly long-lived trend originating in the aftermath of the Franco-Prussian war of 1870.[40] Readers were encouraged to believe in the omnipresence of German spies, with an abundance of spy novels 'reflecting and reinforcing the belief that the country was beset by agents of the Kaiser'.[41] These invasion novels and stories sought to promote the values of patriotic sacrifice and courage by showing British masculinity to be under threat. Their depiction of daring action and traditional male virtues echoes in many stories and novels written during and after the First World War, such as Ernest Raymond's *Tell England* or Sapper's war stories. Fired by idealism (in Raymond's case), or grit and determination (in Sapper's case), the fictional heroes of these texts face up to hardships and death with a fitting degree of courage and stoicism, putting their country first.

Given literary precedents and the general political climate of the decade before the war, it is not surprising that fears of German espionage and sabotage surfaced in a great number of popular war stories. Under conditions of war, heroes and villains are particularly easy to come by, and although Great War spy stories for the most part require a great deal of good faith from their intended readers, audiences were prepared for such exuberance by their familiarity with pre-war spy tales. Popular spy stories reflect complex anxieties on the part of primarily civilian audiences: obvious worries about national security, a sense of being shut out from the main action of the war and the wish to actively help the war effort when one could not join the army, as well as concerns about the British capability to win the war against an opponent seen as both ruthless and efficient. At the same time, other short stories betray a humorous awareness of the absurdity of some anti-espionage measures.

The vast majority of wartime spy stories repeat formulaic patterns. The basic plot is simple, but allows for a great deal of variation: a German spy, or agent in German pay, attempts to sabotage the British war effort. Thanks to the patriotic alertness of a British citizen, frequently aided by the clumsiness of the spy's disguise, the enemy is discovered and arrested and catastrophe averted. Not infrequently, the same author would produce several stories written to the same successful formula. Best-selling *Strand Magazine* writer Harold Steevens published two spy stories during the war that closely resemble each other in their set-up: 'The Sentry Post at Cowman's Curl' (1915) and 'Schmitt's Pigeons' (1916). Both stories feature a female heroine who saves her country from grave danger, catering to an audience thrilled by the prospect of active participation in the war. The plots of both stories appear hair-raisingly contrived to the modern reader, but Steevens takes great care to supply sufficient detail to make his stories appear at least within the realm of the possible, and at any rate seeks to cater to a desire for involvement more than realistic expectations. In 'Schmitt's Pigeons', the courageous wife of a naval officer, Mrs. Gondula Egerton, exposes one Hans Kultur Schmitt as a spy, a naturalised German-British subject who lives in England under the name of Andrew Graham Malcomson. Travelling to a Northern port to meet her husband, Mrs. Egerton shares a railway carriage with Schmitt, and her suspicions are aroused by the unusually large number of sandwiches Schmitt eats. While Schmitt visits the restroom, she checks his picnic basket and discovers two messenger pigeons. Mrs. Egerton alerts the guards on the train, the spy is arrested and, we are told, subsequently commits suicide in prison. It turns out that he had been signalling to the German air force in preparation for a raid which fails because the investigating Mrs. Egerton accidentally exchanged the birds and the wrong message was sent.

Steevens's style in 'Schmitt's Pigeons' is sparse and matter-of-fact, resembling the language of news reports, attempting to invest the story with an element of reality. 'The Sentry Post at Cowman's Curl', on the other hand, borrows elements of conventional romance and combines them with its spy plot. Young New Army soldier Roland saves beautiful Claudine Dorrington from being run over by a train while he is on sentry duty along the rail track. As might be expected, they fall in love, and Claudine begins to visit Roland at his level-crossing with flasks of coffee. Before long she in turn is able to save his life: one Professor Blinkhorn, a lodger in Claudine's house, turns out to be the German spy and saboteur Blinckhörnstein. Blinckhörnstein attempts to kill Roland and explode the rail tracks but is prevented by Claudine, who pours hot coffee in the saboteur's face, enabling Roland to overpower him. In light of the general spy hysteria of 1914–18, one can only suppose that the notion of a German

spy with the middle name 'Culture' signalling from a train using hom-
ing pigeons, or of a pretty girl thwarting a saboteur with a flask of coffee,
would have seemed if not entirely plausible, then at least possible. Given
that pre-war literature such as Jerome K. Jerome's fictional account of a
cycling tour through the Black Forest, *Three Men on the Bummel* (1900) or
Katherine Mansfield's first collection of short stories, *In a German Pension*
(1911), described Germans as either obsessively consuming or talking
about food, it is perhaps not surprising that the spy in 'Schmitt's Pigeons'
is discovered because he eats too many sandwiches.[42] Despite the claims
of exasperated reviewers such as Harold Child, who observed that 'most
authors of spy-stories load their tales up with wild doings in which no
one can believe, and which would have the effect (if they had any effect)
of persuading one that there are no German spies in England',[43] the public was evidently entertained by the vast array of somewhat improbable
spy stories. In adult and juvenile fiction alike, German spies are usually,
as Krista Cowman observes, portrayed as simultaneously dangerous and
pathetic, exposing themselves by exclaiming 'Lieber Himmel!' or expressing patriotic sentiments that fit ill with their assumed disguise.[44] These
fictional portrayals are mirrored in popular artwork such as the Schmidt
the Spy cartoons by Alfred Leete (1882–1933), first published in the weekly
London Opinion and later collected in Leete's book *Schmidt the Spy and his
Messages to Berlin* (1916). Schmidt, who is dispatched to Britain in a crate
of Dutch cheese and proceeds to bumble and blunder in the best fashion
of magazine spies, assumes a range of wildly comic disguises that never
quite hide his telltale walrus moustache, misinterprets everything he sees
and finally ends up in a British prison camp.

Compared to Steevens's spy tales, Arthur Conan Doyle's treatment
of the espionage subject is both more serious and more politicised.
Doyle, too old for active service, put his writing at the disposal of the
War Propaganda Bureau, alongside a wide and disparate range of writers
including other well-known authors such as J.M. Barrie, Arnold Bennett,
John Galsworthy, Thomas Hardy, Rudyard Kipling and H.G. Wells.[45]
Other writers, such as Ford Madox Ford, produced anti-German writing
independent of a government commission. Conan Doyle resuscitated once
more his most enduringly popular literary character, Sherlock Holmes, in
moral support of the war effort.[46] Unlike almost all other Sherlock Holmes
tales, 'His Last Bow' is not narrated by Watson as a first-person narrator,
but by a largely neutral third-person narrator, who increases the mystery
and suspense of the story by leaving its readers in the dark as to the real
identity of Sherlock Holmes until the very last. The plot is simple yet

effective and takes place exclusively in and around the country house of German agent Ambassador Von Bork, head of a network of German spies operating in Britain prior to the outbreak of the war. On 2 August 1914, when Von Bork is about to leave the country, he finds himself fooled and arrested by Holmes. In order to convict Von Bork for his illegal activities, Holmes has assumed the disguise of Altamont, an Irish-American patriot recruited by Von Bork as an agent for Germany. The real German spy may here be tricked by the mastermind of the famous detective, but unlike Steevens's Schmitt, Von Bork is no bumbling idiot and certainly not an object of derision. He is intelligent, methodical and has successfully deceived the British political establishment. His crucial mistake, however, lies in underestimating British determination and resourcefulness, visible in his derisive comments to the secretary of the German legation:

Von Bork laughed.

'They are not very hard to deceive,' he remarked. 'A more docile, simple folk could not be imagined.'

'I don't know about that,' said the other thoughtfully. 'They have strange limits and one must learn to observe them. It is that surface simplicity of theirs which makes a trap for the stranger. One's first impression is that they are entirely soft. Then one comes suddenly upon something very hard, and you know that you have reached the limit [...]. They have, for example, their insular conventions which *must* be observed.'

'Meaning, "good form" and that sort of thing?' Von Bork sighed, as one who had suffered much.[47]

Doyle has Holmes himself describe the English mentality in a similar, if more positive vein: 'The Englishman is a patient creature, but at present his temper is a little inflamed and it would be as well not to try him too far.'[48] Conan Doyle uses his villain and hero alike as mouthpieces for his own political convictions, as when Von Bork talks about the British lack of preparation for war in 1914, claiming that 'as far as the essentials go – the storage of munitions, the preparation for submarine attack, the arrangements for making high explosives – nothing is prepared'.[49] From the retrospective of 1917, Doyle can criticise previous British unpreparedness, while at the same time showing through Holmes's triumph over the arrogant Von Bork that British pluck and ingenuity may yet triumph. While Doyle's narrative technique and more sophisticated ways of building up suspense by playing on the shared ignorance of reader and characters alike distinguish 'His Last Bow' from the spy stories discussed above, its basic plot – evil spy tricked and overpowered by resourceful patriot – corresponds to that of less elaborate spy tales.

Inter-war stories continued the popularity of espionage themes, but once wartime spy hysteria subsided, spy stories of the late 1920s took an altogether different stance on espionage. Empathy and belated understanding for the former enemy characterise John Buchan's 'The Loathly Opposite' (1928).[50] The narrator of this story – who had worked as a code-breaker during the latter stages of the war – had encountered a particularly pernicious code during the last months of the war. Although he eventually succeeded in cracking it, he had not been able to stop wondering about the true identity of his opposite number on the German side, who answers to the code name Reinmar. After the war, the narrator falls ill and is eventually referred to Dr Christoph, a German doctor with a small sanatorium in Saxony. Christoph manages to cure him, and on the last evening of his stay the narrator discovers the truth about the doctor: Christoph turns out to be the mysterious Reinmar, and his code name is the name of his young son, who has died of the effects of wartime malnutrition. In response to an altered political climate, and in sharp contrast to Buchan's wartime spy novels, this story shows the enemy as humanised and deserving of sympathy: '[Dr Christoph] sat staring beyond me, so small and lonely, that I could have howled. I put my hand on his shoulder and stammered some platitude about being sorry.'[51] Another particularly successful example of inter-war spy fiction are the stories collected in W.S. Maugham's *Ashenden, Or, The British Agent*. First published in 1928, this volume was reprinted twice each in 1928 and 1929, once each in 1931, 1934, 1938, twice again in 1948 and 1951, once in 1950 and in 1956, and its anti-heroic stance was praised as the first example of realistic spy fiction.[52] All stories are loosely based on Maugham's own experiences working abroad for the secret service during the war. Their popularity may partly be explained by their claim to authenticity, as well as the popular appeal of their author. Maugham's agent Ashenden frequently finds himself in situations where he has to suppress natural feelings of sympathy and compassion in order to do his job, and counter-espionage and the thwarting of enemy plans are here no longer presented as straightforward patriotic acts. Rather, they are an ambiguous business resulting in conflicts of sympathy and humanity with patriotic duty.

Before the gradual shift in attitude towards Germany, the Great War had largely been rationalised by and for the British public as a righteous struggle for the values of civilisation and humanity against a foe portrayed as either dangerous or outright inhuman, a line of argument centring in particular on the cause of invaded Belgium, but also on the potential threat of invasion that permeated pre-war invasion fiction. This was not simply the result of brainwashing propaganda, and it echoed similar sentiments in Germany, where hatred for the 'traitor' England was running high.[53] German political and military decisions, such as unlimited submarine warfare and the sinking of the *Lusitania*, the introduction of poison gas, the destruction of historic buildings and cultural artefacts in Belgium and France or the execution of Nurse Cavell facilitated the exploitation of anti-German sentiments in British propaganda. The Bryce report (or Report of the Committee on Alleged German Outrages), was an inquiry into German war crimes in Belgium and France commissioned by the British government in early 1915, and published shortly after the sinking of the *Lusitania*. Despite post-war criticism of the report's embellishments, German war crimes were most certainly perpetrated, and the effect of the Bryce Report on British and international public opinion was profound. It lent official confirmation to any rumours of rape, murder and mutilation committed by the German army in the occupied territories and helped to convince the public of the justness of Britain's participation in the war. Apart from such official sources of atrocity propaganda, word-of-mouth propaganda contributed to a negative image of the enemy and justification of the war effort in terms of German 'frightfulness'.[54]

Amongst those short-story writers foremost in highlighting German 'frightfulness' and justifying the British war effort was Frederick Britten Austin, whose stories almost unfailingly portray the German enemy as inhuman and cruel. A particularly sensational choice of subject is visible in Britten Austin's 'A Problem in Reprisals' (1919), one of several similarly themed stories published in the *Strand Magazine* shortly after the end of the war. The story is set in a German village occupied by a French battalion just after the end of the war, much to the dismay of its inhabitants:

The scared faces of slatternly women, obsequiously gesturing the mud-stained French soldiers into occupation of their cottages, turned to look anxiously at them as they passed, in evident apprehension of the order which should let loose a vengeful destruction only too probable to their uneasy consciences.[55]

The rhetoric is as obvious as it is inflammatory: German women are 'slatternly' and their consciences fraught, in complete disregard of the fact that the majority of the German population felt Germany had been justified in declaring war. In contrast to his unflattering description of the defeated enemy, Britten Austin depicts the French soldiers as behaving decently towards the defeated Germans. The battalion-commander, his captain and medical officer are billeted with a pretty young war widow, in whose house the doctor finds a porcelain clock that he had been given by his wife, lost in German-occupied Cambrai during the war. He realises that he is in the house of the man who in all likelihood killed his wife. His method of verifying his suspicion is deeply implausible and builds on Britten Austin's interest in parapsychological phenomena. To gain certainty, the French doctor calls in his landlady and places her under deep hypnosis, then uses the porcelain clock as a channelling device that allows the hypnotised woman to 'see' and describe the terrible events in the doctor's house. The young widow suffers terribly under what she is made to witness: her husband's attempt to rape the doctor's wife and the wife's suicide. Ultimately, however, the French officer decides to make her forget what she has seen despite his thirst for retribution. The question of revenge and reparation is clearly the prominent issue addressed by this story. Britten Austin was only one of the many authors who, once the conflict had ended, 'found it remarkably difficult to forget the hymn of hatred they had espoused during the war',[56] and more sympathetic stories have to be read also as a response to hatemongering tales on both sides.

There is some evidence of light-hearted criticism of the widespread anti-German hysteria, such as Blanche Wills Chandler's 'Our Catch' (1917). The narrator of this story, fifteen-year-old Patricia, and her twelve-year-old brother Bimfield are trying to aid the war effort in their own way. Unfortunately, they fail at everything they attempt: they spoil the food for the soldiers at the local Soldiers' Institute, cause a traffic accident while carrying messages for the Red Cross and hit their rich uncle with a sandbag thrown out of a window to test its quality. Depressed by these numerous failures, they are determined to catch a spy described in the local newspaper. When they spot a man who seems to fit the description, they follow him around trying to trick him into betraying himself, and finally pounce on him in an attempted arrest, only to find that he is a British general on vacation. Mortified and severely disappointed, the two children apologise, but the general is amused rather than angry and, sensing their disappointment, explains to them that at least their escapades have afforded his men at the front something to laugh about. The children's efforts at exposing the 'spy' are comical indeed, and seize upon many clichés about how a German spy might inadvertently give away his identity: young Bimfield tries to provoke a reaction by playing 'God Save The King' over and over on his mouth-organ (unsurprisingly, the 'spy' reacts with signs of exasperation, which the children take as a sign of his abhorrence for the British national anthem rather than disgust at the boy's deficient musical talents), and the narrator takes the general's whistling of a piece by Wagner as the ultimate proof of his identity:

In the meantime he was sloping off behind a bunker humming a tune as he went. The air was familiar to me. I'd had to practise one beastly bar five hundred times over, the term before the war. I grabbed Bim by the arm.

'Lohengrin!' I whispered.

'How much?' said Bim.

'A rotten piece of music chock-full of sharps and flats written by a pig of a German.'

Bim's eyes blazed. 'Come on,' he said, and we sprinted over the green. [57]

Besides their entertainment value, these fictional exploits can also be seen as a humorous caution not to see danger where there is none.

Another category of stories offers a more serious critical stance on the First World War spy craze and its darker aspects, most importantly the wartime internment of British citizens who were naturalised Germans. While the idea of ordinary citizens on the lookout for spies on their way to work may appear comical, the general climate of hysteria and mistrust had a palpably negative effect on Germans living in Britain, even those who had acquired British citizenship or were married to British subjects. By mid-1915, 19,000 male Germans had already been interned, and many more were to be repatriated with their families, while London's East End witnessed anti-German riots and looting. D.H. Lawrence and his German wife, Frieda von Richthofen (a distant cousin of German flying ace Manfred von Richthofen) are a prominent example of the persecution suffered by Germans living in Britain at the time, who experienced drastic curtailments of their personal freedom. [58]

Galsworthy wrote a number of stories about the plight of Germans in Britain during the war. This was most likely due to his personal circumstances: Galsworthy's sister Lilian was married to the Bavarian painter Georg Sauter, who – much to the writer's indignation – was interned during the war. Galsworthy's 'The Bright Side', written in 1919, is a scathing denunciation of such blanket security measures. It is the story of Max Gerhardt, a German craftsman who has lived and worked in London for twenty-five years and has been married to an Englishwoman for twenty. The father of three children finds himself helplessly enveloped by the anti-German sentiment that spreads in England after the outbreak of the war. Mostly from the perspective of his wife Dora, the reader is shown how the family are borne down by Mr Gerhardt's internment and the many little cruelties and humiliations they are subjected to even by friends and neighbours. On Mr Gerhardt's eventual return home after the end of the war he is a broken man, crushed by the weight of the injustice done to him, and the family's happiness is ruined for good. This is a particularly sentimental story, dwelling at length on the moral superiority of its protagonists to highlight the injustice done to them. Mr Gerhardt is described as a 'harmless, busy little man',[59] a kind father and loving husband, always ready to help others, as is his gentle Cockney wife Dora. In 'The Bright Side', Galsworthy also voices criticism of hatemongering in the British press, describing the dismay of the story's Anglo-German protagonists at finding themselves reviled in the newspapers:

Reading their papers – a daily and a weekly, in which they had as much implicit faith as a million other readers – they were soon duly horrified by the reports therein of 'Hun' atrocities; so horrified that they would express their condemnation of the Kaiser and his militarism as freely as if they had been British subjects. It was, therefore, with an uneasy surprise that they began to find these papers talking of 'the Huns at large in our midst,' of 'spies,' and the national danger of 'nourishing such vipers.' They were deeply conscious of not being 'vipers,' and such sayings began to awaken in both their breasts a humble sense of injustice, as it were.[60]

Despite its sentimentality, 'The Bright Side' is expressive of real moral outrage, and founded largely on valid observation of the plight of Anglo-Germans during the war.[61]

Galsworthy was not the only writer with popular appeal to portray Germans sympathetically during or just after the war: Alec Waugh's 'An Autumn Gathering' (1918) follows the plight of two young German lovers, Pieter and Gretchen, whose hopes of a shared future are shattered when Pieter is killed on the Somme. His last letter to Gretchen is found by a young English officer, whom it prompts to reflect on the cruelty of a war that destroys an entire generation of passionate and hopeful young people. Flora Annie Steel's 'Sunrise' (1914) is a short sentimental tale about three soldiers – one French, one German, one British – who find themselves sheltering in the ruins of a Belgian village church in November 1914. Although unable to communicate with each other, they bond in their desire to help each other. The wounded French and British soldiers attend to the dying German, and all three show each other photographs of their little sons. They are brought even closer together when they are joined by a young Flemish boy, who reminds each of them of his own son.

Both Waugh and Steel qualify their sympathetic portrayal of the enemy by creating German protagonists who are placed in an impeccable moral position that allows readers to empathise with them without having to compromise their patriotic sentiment. Where Galsworthy's Anglo-German Gerhardt family is redeemed from any accusations of 'frightfulness' by long years in Britain and a kindly and selfless disposition, Waugh's German lovers are exonerated by their extreme youth, which Waugh emphasises from the start of his story:

They were both very young. Gretchen, dark and slim, with her hair still falling like troubled waters about her neck, was only seventeen, and Pieter was hardly three years older. But he already bore the burden of manhood, the burden that the day demanded of every man whether he willed it or not; on his shoulders were the epaulettes of a lieutenant, and the hour of love was charged with the sorrow of parting.[62]

The parting of the two lovers is rendered with poignant pathos, filled with evil foreboding of Pieter's death:

'Oh, Gretchen, Gretchen,' he cried, 'I love you, I love you so terribly! I can't do without you!'
'We're going to be wonderfully happy afterwards, Pieter.'
Very tenderly he folded her into his arms and kissed the pathetic, trembling mouth. 'If they let us,' he said softly, 'if they let us.'[63]

The tragedy of Pieter's death is presented to the reader, ultimately, through the eyes of the young British officer who reads Pieter's final letter, and whose response guides that of the reader: 'Very still and quiet he sat, reading the unfinished letter to Gretchen. For he was young, and he was a lover, and beneath the abrupt awkward sentences he knew how strong a flame had burnt.'[64] Steel's German soldier is similarly redeemed by his fatal wounds and his tenderness towards the Flemish boy as the father of a young son:

Johan the German's wistful eyes were all he could place at the service of the little lad, until as the pitiful wailing would not cease, a trembling hand pointed waveringly to a haversack, and once again the unwritten unspoken word brought comprehension. The little Flamand munching away contentedly at a concentrated German sausage ration gave his name shyly with a smile as 'Jan-pi' ou' Jan.'[65]

Steel manages to highlight the similarities between the three soldiers without exculpating the German army per se (the three men are called Jean, John and Johan respectively), and lays great emphasis on the power of compassion, in which the British soldier takes the lead. The German is rendered safe as an object of compassion by his near-dead state, but also shown to be compassionate himself when he gives the little Flamand his rations. The tone of all three stories is decidedly sentimental and the diction deliberately archaic with a somewhat flowery effect. However, it is precisely this sentimentality that allows their authors to humanise their

German protagonists and give them appeal for a wider audience accustomed to fictional Germans who were merciless killers or cold-hearted saboteurs.

These stories significantly predate the relenting of public opinion towards Germany and Germans that characterised the second half of the 1920s and, as we have seen, sympathise with Germans only with certain qualifications. Fictional accounts of the former enemy aided the gradual relenting of British public opinion towards Germany considerably: Geoffrey Moss's short-story collection *Defeat* (1924) is one example of popular writing that paved the way for at least temporary reconciliation. The eponymous short story 'Defeat' is narrated by an English war veteran who reports the story of his friendship with Graf Hasso von Koekritz and the latter's tragic death. Koekritz is a German nobleman with a long military career. Their acquaintance had been conceived in pre-war Brussels, interrupted by the war for over a decade, and is finally revived in a Rhenish industrial town between the wars under French occupation. The story describes some of the complications of the occupation and the feelings in defeated Germany, particularly for the returned military who face a complete breakdown of their careers. Von Koekritz, who has joined the security police as a 'Green Policeman', is beaten to death by Rhenish separatists after having been deliberately disarmed and rendered defenceless by the French occupational force. Moss's story not only condemns the French as vindictive, deliberately humiliating an already beaten enemy, it also stresses older bonds between Prussia and England and the internationalism of the old military elite: 'A Koekritz served Carlos Quinto in Italy: one fought under Marlborough, several under Frederick the Great. A Koekritz fell at Austerlitz, another at Waterloo.'[66] Indeed, von Koekritz is shown to be indistinguishable from an English gentleman, with a keen sense of fair play that prompts him to make allowances even for what is presented as the mean-spirited policies of the French occupational force, an interest in hunting, horses and good company, and cordial international friendships. His horrible end, battered to death by an unruly mob before the eyes of the narrator and a company of French soldiers who refuse to interfere, is described with pathos and in great detail, and directs the reader's sympathies unambiguously towards Germany while condemning the former ally France:

Presently the noise decreased: the rain of blows slackened and ceased. The circle widened. Some of the troopers who had now dismounted drew near and joined it. In the centre at their feet lay a limp form in a faded green jacket. For a moment they stood silent. Then the tension slackened, congratulations were exchanged, and the French and their agents shook hands over the body which they had vanquished.[67]

EXPRESSING WAR AND VIOLENCE

Even during the war, German brutality was not the only form of violence writers addressed. A range of short stories written for a variety of audiences explore the violence of war, including a large proportion of Sapper's war fiction, or Wylie's intriguing analysis of pent-up soldierly aggression in 'All Dressed Up'. Violence was an ambiguous issue in that it was at once necessary in terms of defending one's country, and reviled when engaged in by the enemy. Those writing about the war were consequently faced not only with the question of how to portray violence but also how to distinguish between violence as physical courage and as depraved brutality. In the majority of short stories, violence as brutality or sadism – as opposed to 'clean' manly violence – is with few exceptions ascribed only to the enemy, most poignantly so in Britten Austin's tales depicting Germans as both ruthless and cruel. If employed by British protagonists, on the other hand, violence tended to be violence of retribution.

Like Wylie, Mary Borden or D.H. Lawrence, Herbert Read's war writing explored the effect of violence on the mind as well as the body and looked beyond violent action at the motivations, fears and consciousness behind it. In Read's stories, violence is no longer ascribed purely to the agency of the enemy: rather, the condition of war itself engenders brutality, even in those who are ostensibly fighting for a just cause. Many post-war disillusioned texts share with the canonised (anti-)war poems of the trench poets their depiction of soldiers as victims, not perpetrators, in blatant disregard of the fact that, as Bourke has pointed out, '[t]he characteristic act of men at war is not dying, it is killing'.[68] Herbert Read's war writing, by contrast – like his poem 'The Happy Warrior' – depicts soldiers who are both agents and objects of violence. His war stories are characterised by sometimes visibly strained attempts at finding new means to express perceptions of violence and its effects, employing modernist techniques with varying degrees of success.

In Read's story 'Killed in Action' (1919), British officer Danvers (whose first name or rank we never learn) is a victim of the circumstances and of his own mental breakdown in battle conditions. The title is eminently ironic in Fussell's sense of contrasting expectation with reality, in that it quotes one of the standard euphemistic phrases of Great War parlance that could encompass such a wide range of deaths as to be comfortingly vague.[69] In this case, Danvers actually kills himself in a moment of intense fatigue and world-weariness in the aftermath of battle. At the outset of the story, we encounter Danvers in the squalid conditions of a frontline dugout, cold, uncomfortable, dirty and tired, barely able to take control of his own body: 'His teeth chattered and he couldn't stop them. Involuntary shivers passed down his body.'[70] Danvers and his battalion are caught in a German counter-attack and ordered to retaliate. They are routed by German forces, and almost all of the men are killed. Danvers himself survives and lives to witness the destruction of his men and fellow officers only to break down and shoot himself in the face once the fighting is over. Read's soldier protagonist in 'Killed in Action' can be seen as closely linked with that of Aldington's story of the same title, which focuses on the bitter rivalry between two enlisted men in the other ranks. One of the protagonists takes advantage of the chaotic aftermath of the first day of the Battle of the Somme and kills his rival in a flurry of rage with a German revolver he had found and kept hidden weeks before.[71] Both stories thus subvert in different ways readers' expectations raised by the story title as to their plot and their depiction of the soldier.

However, Read clearly strives to de-glorify the figure of the British soldier without vilifying him. Danvers is no storybook hero: he summons his courage with a sip of rum,[72] experiences intense fear under bombardment[73] and in the heat of fighting he unconsciously urinates into his breeches.[74] Yet he is no coward or weakling either; he carries on regardless and performs satisfactorily what he is instructed to do. Danvers is shown as largely reduced to physical reaction to the war. His actions are dictated by his body, not his mind, into which we gain insight through passages of free indirect discourse interspersed with seemingly neutral description:

There was an infernal babbling of machine-guns on the right. The Boche must be in sight there. If so, the barrage would be lifting. Our barrage was damned poor. Eugh! Dudd! A great heavy ball of blood shot to his gullet as he drew his body taut to receive the expected detonation. The thing furrowed the ground not two yards from his feet. Harmless enough. But God! What a fright. Did he duck? Well, it was only natural.[75]

His fear mounts to a pitch where the tension becomes so unbearable that it paradoxically seems impossible *not* to die, and Danvers forms an almost involuntary resolution to seek out death if death fails to seek out him: 'He jumped up suddenly, facing the enemy. A wild energy blazed in every gesture. "Fire, damn you, fire! Kill me, you bloody swine." No answer. A man coughed somewhere.'[76] Failing to make the enemy kill him, Danvers kills himself. The act of his suicide is described as a violent struggle rather than a merciful release, and Danvers is as much a victim of the violence of war as if a German had pulled the trigger:

A sudden snap and nothing else. A misfire. His eyes opened wide with the agony of a sudden unleashed tension of will. His strained hands trembled. His parched throat emitted a scream.

He stared and screamed at the six neat black holes before his face. Unconsciously he was again squeezing the trigger. The hammer moved back, gaping with its one black tooth. [...] The night, hitherto secretly stealing towards him, made a sudden leap to devour his life with blackness and annihilation.[77]

In his attempts to render Danvers's surroundings, Read employs frequent personification and a variety of domestic similes. His metaphors are often mixed under the pressure of describing the violence of the scene: a bombed and ruined wood is compared to 'an old broken comb against the skyline',[78] the forlornness and scattering of a battalion of charging soldiers likened to the equally mundane image of 'flies crawling across a side of bacon in a grocer's shop'.[79] The landscape, to Danvers's violent disgust, is 'riven and violated; a wide glabrous desolation; a black diseased scab, erupted and pustulous',[80] a pestilential vista in which war is the disease that has ravaged the body of the land. The battlefield immediately after the end of a barrage is again described in anthropomorphic terms: 'A strange but blessed stillness came over the scene, as though the guns had vomited themselves to death' – the guns, instruments of death, have become animated beings, set to kill and now perished themselves from the violence of their efforts.[81] The dead, on the other hand, are de-humanised, such as Danvers's fellow officer and friend Flint, who is killed next to Danvers in the British counter-attack. At the very moment Flint is making what would appear to be a heroic gesture – brandishing his revolver and spurring on his men to follow him – he is shot in the face: 'A bullet hit him in the snout. He fell down, sniggering blood, dying. Danvers glanced at him. Poor devil. Must go on.'[82] In but a moment soldier-hero Flint is dehumanised, as the reference to his 'snout' suggests, and his death is robbed of all tragic grandeur through the nature of his wound, which makes it seem as if he is dying with an immature snigger on his face. As in a linguistic equivalent to shell shock, Read's language appears disjointed, strained and fragmented. His short sentences, often incomplete, are clearly meant to mirror the hasty thought and speech of his protagonist, whose own perceptions alternate with outside descriptions: 'Wedge. Conic wedge. Red conic wedge of pain – it entered between his contracted eyebrows, and there was slowly, decisively driven in by the hovering power of despair.'[83] Passages such as this appear somewhat laboured, but illustrate the writer's struggle for adequate literary expression.

Read is exceptional in the sense that he attempts to reconcile the endeavour to provide a truthful record – shared by many less experimental war writers – with the use of modern(ist) literary techniques. Compared to the majority of stories here discussed, most of which are popular magazine fiction, Read and a small number of avant-garde and/or modernist writers such as Wyndham Lewis, Richard Aldington and Mary Borden experimented with new ways of narrating their war experience. The majority of short-story writers, however, chose to address the war within a framework of established genre conventions. As suggested, this use of established patterns benefited readers and writers alike who look to fictional war stories for the means of comparing and evaluating their own experiences of the war in its many theatres and facets, whereas Read certainly aimed to startle and unsettle more than to console and explain. Nevertheless, work such as Read's contributes to the large body of short narratives available to readers as potential narrative foils for their own war experiences. As the need for such narrative models changed, however, short stories began to engage with the First World War in different ways. The final chapter of this book will scrutinise how post-war writers of short fiction continued to address the war up to the present, with a view to both subject matter and form.

CHAPTER 6

Commemorative Narratives and Post-War Stories

In the decades after the end of World War II, fiction continued to deal with the First World War but described a steady trajectory from emotional involvement with the war to an increasingly abstract interest in the psychology of grief, the remembrance and changing perceptions of the war, or the war as an historical event. Gradually and inevitably, as readers' and writers' horizon of expectations changed, short stories, like other war writing, adopted new perspectives on the First World War. These new perspectives often resulted in a rejection of the commonplaces and discourses of earlier war stories, but they also promoted an evolving mythology of the war as a futile tragedy of the waterlogged Western Front trenches. As a consequence, although these later stories continue to address the war, their treatment of the war's experience differs from earlier accounts in both subject matter and form. While the inter-war years in Britain witnessed the publication of many now canonical texts about the Great War, the publication of First World War-related short stories dropped significantly after 1945. Nevertheless, references to the earlier war continued from the inter-war period into the post-war era. During the Second World War, the 'trench poets' of the Great War remained an important reference point for young war writers, and the experience of the earlier war was similarly used in many prose texts as a foil or precedent for narratives of the later conflict. Although this did not happen with the same frequency as during the inter-war period, especially writers with first-hand experiences of the Great War still continued to address these experiences in their fiction.

Stories dealing with the subject of loss and mourning were of continuing social importance in inter-war Britain, and endured even after the end of the Second World War. These mourning stories illustrate perfectly how both the nature and purpose of First World War-related fiction changed as a result of the Second World War and evolved further in the wake of the pacifist movement associated with the Vietnam War and Campaign for Nuclear Disarmament from the 1960s onwards. Carol Acton notes a distinct connection between mourning discourses of the First and Second Word Wars in particular, claiming that, in 1939, 'British emotional response necessarily merges with a still raw memory of the First World War, the legacy of that war informing the way the Second World War is received and responded to at the emotional level', and that 'bereavement discourses in the Second World War were necessarily informed by private experiences of the first'.[1] This merging of experiences of grief and trauma is also evident in short stories addressing the First World War. Mourning and loss did not cease to be important topics after the end of the war, as the inter-war period in particular was marked by both personal and institutional attempts to come to terms with the war dead and establish patterns of remembrance. The building of war cemeteries in France, Belgium and other theatres of war overseas; the erection of the cenotaph in Whitehall and a plethora of war memorials in towns and villages across Britain; the institutionalisation of the two-minute silence, Armistice Day and then Remembrance Sunday, have been scrutinised at length by scholars such as Samuel Hynes, Jay Winter and Dan Todman. Like writing in other genres, inter-war short stories also tackled this sensitive subject.

For one thing, we can see a continuation of the motif of spiritual solace in short stories such as Jeffery Farnol's 'The Great Silence' (1940). This story consists of a dialogue between grizzled and disfigured veteran George and a sympathetic passer-by, in the course of which George comes to realise that there is more to be hoped for than his earthly existence has to offer. Set on Armistice Day a good decade after the end of the war, veteran-protagonist George describes the misery and squalor of his lonely life and his longing for his former comrade Tommy. The stereotypically named everyman Tommy was killed in the latter stages of the war and, George feels, has left his friend behind in a cold and unsympathetic world. Talking to a kindly stranger, George reminisces about Tommy, and when he is suddenly taken fatally ill, he dies in the happy certainty that he will be rejoining his dead friend. Although George, with the post-war bitterness of the invalided veteran, has previously scorned the institution of the Two-Minute Silence as hollow and pointless, he is reconciled to the loss of his friend at the moment of his own death. A vision of Tommy come to meet him eases the passage for him, and 'this pale, bitterly scarred visage that had been George's was transfigured by a radiance, a serene dignity it had never held in life, the look of those that shall not grow old, for George had marched away with his young comrade Tom into that Great Silence where no age can be'.[2] The echo of Binyon's 'For the Fallen' in this passage is not coincidental; the sentiment of the poem is consciously embedded in the story. The sympathetic stranger, seeking to convince George of the value of the Two-Minute Silence, slightly misquotes Binyon's lines 'They shall not grow old as we that are left grow old: / Age shall not weary them, nor the years condemn'.[3] These lines are proven right when George is faced with the unscathed, youthful vision of his dead comrade.

Other stories, however, move in rather unexpected directions when exploring grief and mourning and point towards problems in coming to terms with the legacy of the war beyond the (comparatively speaking) straightforward grieving for lost relatives and friends. Winifred Holtby's story 'The Casualty List' – written in 1932 and first collected in Holtby's *Truth is Not Sober* (1934) – offers an inter-war treatment of grief with an emphasis on the complexity of emotions connected with loss and death. On Armistice Day 1928, after a visit to the theatre to see R.C. Sherriff's then brand-new play *Journey's End*, Mrs Lancing, an elderly married woman, remembers her anxiety during the war over not having a son to send to the front. Her feelings echo wartime propaganda and reflect the omnipresent nature of public, institutionalised grief and commemoration:

[S]he had always hated to feel out of anything – of the best set in town, or the Hospital Ball, or the craze for roller-skating – or even the war. [...] Those Wonderful Mothers who Gave their Sons held an immense moral advantage over the ordinary women who only coped with a sugar shortage and the servant problem, and the regulations about darkening windows. When Nellie Goodson's only son was killed, she had felt almost envious, of the boy for his Glorious End, of the mother for her honourable grief. Her sin had always been to covet honour.[4]

Even though she is not directly affected by loss, Mrs Lancing is enveloped in an all-pervasive culture of remembrance. She, too, finds consolation in the lines of Binyon's 'For the Fallen', which allow her to think of herself as fighting her own war against time and death, left behind by those whose privilege it was to die in the Great War: 'We who are left grow old, thought Mrs. Lancing. The years condemn us. We fall in a war with Time which knows no armistice.'[5] Holtby renders Mrs Lancing's pompous self-awareness and egocentricity subtly yet strikingly, and the sentiments voiced by fictional Mrs Lancing reflect a feeling that many real-life survivors of the war experienced equally keenly. Roy Fuller's post-World

War II poem 'Epitaph for Soldiers' addresses the poet's 'terror for survival in peacetime':

> Incredibly I lasted out a war,
> Survived the unnatural, enormous danger
> Of each enormous day. And so befell
> A peril more enormous and still stranger:
> The death by nature, chanceless, credible[6]

Fuller's surviving soldier, like Holtby's elderly housewife, realises that surviving a war does not make one immortal; that natural death, unlike death in battle, is ultimately impossible to evade. Mourning for the war dead takes on an element of envy because, in a certain sense, the dead of the war are immortalised where the civilian dead merely fade into nothingness. While dead soldiers are given memorials and (for the first time ever in the First World War) perpetuity in sepulchre, the likes of Mrs Lancing will have to be content with a private burial and a headstone that will in due course have to make way for new graves.[7]

Richard Aldington wrote extensively of his combat and frontline experience, both in his novel *Death of a Hero* (1929) and in his subsequent collection of short stories, *Roads to Glory* (1930). The novel was begun just after the war but abandoned for almost a decade until Aldington decided to finish the project whilst settled in France.[8] The short-story collection in many ways forms an afterthought to the novel, addressing various issues that presumably continued to niggle and that Aldington could not accommodate in the longer work; they were written and prepared for publication in the summer of 1929.[9] Although he waited to be called up and conscripted under the Military Service Act in 1916, Aldington came to identify strongly with his fellow officers and soldiers and was profoundly affected by his time at the front. In a letter to Amy Lowell on 23 August 1916, D.H. Lawrence 'diagnosed' Aldington even before his war service had actually begun, saying of him that 'I can tell that the glamour is getting hold of him: the 'now we're all men together' business, the kind of love that was between Achilles and Patroclus.'[10] Cy Fox describes Aldington as an 'infantryman who emerged in a state of shock and moral outrage'[11] and most of the writer's war fiction is devoted to descriptions of the devastating effects of war on the soldiers' psyche, on its blighting impact on their personal lives and careers. While most of Aldington's disillusioned short stories about the war, such as 'The Case of Lieutenant Hall', adopt a straightforward narrative style and are primarily concerned with placing blame for soldiers' suffering on politicians and dignitaries, other stories stand out both by dint of their more experimental style and their slightly different focus. In 'Farewell to Memories', conscious processes of mourning and remembrance are at the centre of attention.

'Farewell to Memories' relates the Great War experience of Private Brandon, a sensitive young volunteer thrown in with men whom Aldington portrays as brutalised characters. Descriptions of events witnessed at the front are interspersed with the protagonist's retrospective reflections on the war. Brandon undergoes the stereotypical hardships of a middle-class, white-collar civilian such as Aldington himself, suddenly faced with what he considers as inhuman discipline, lack of comfort and danger in the trenches. That this depiction is not the universally valid representation of the war experience of civilians-turned-soldiers has been demonstrated by Janet Watson, who shows that whereas artistic middle- and upper-class volunteers such as Aldington or Sassoon viewed their time in the military as 'service' to their country and responded with much greater disillusionment to the taxing conditions of war, working-class volunteers in particular frequently took a more practical approach to their war service and regarded it as another job to be done.[12] After the war, too, the majority of veterans may have been enraged at the insufficiency of state measures for compensation, but they were not as bitter and negatively disposed towards the public as Aldington and other 'disenchanted' writers suggest. As Deborah Cohen points out, the 'figure of the disgruntled ex-serviceman aptly conveyed literary modernism's alienation from the post-war world, but it tells us much less about veterans' perceptions more generally'.[13] The intellectual Brandon suffers most from his feeling of being degraded to a mere war tool and from the loss of faith in what he had previously believed to be the meaning of life his war service induces in him:

The crash of shells, the tearing whine of bullets seemed to beat into him misery and despair and grief. The very thought of hope became intolerable, and he despised himself for ever having been deluded by the vain shows of life, sneered at himself because he had once cared for intelligence and beauty.[14]

From Brandon's point of view, the reader learns about the loss of his friends in the unit, one of whom dies while the others are transferred elsewhere. We are given descriptions of his experience of a gas attack, and of the Armistice which, when it finally comes, finds Brandon a mere machine: 'Brandon stared out the window [of the train taking him back to England], still wearing his full equipment, with his rifle mechanically clutched between his knees.'[15] His overwhelming feeling is of regret and mourning for the dead. He sits, unable to stop crying, and sees before his inner eye 'only the lines upon lines upon lines of crosses'.[16] The first-person retrospective voice of the later Brandon concludes the story questioning whether the survivors really are the luckier ones, in an ironic twist of the gladiators' salute, *morituri te salutamus*: 'Lost, terrible, silent comrades, we, who might have died, salute you.'[17] 'Farewell to Memories' is not simply a disillusioned attack on the internal enemy, the general staff and politicians that came to be regarded as the main culprits of the war; it is also a study of human reactions to the strain of war. The structure of Aldington's story ensures that we are always given both immediate perceptions in the third-person narrator's interpretation of Brandon's state of mind, thoughts and feelings, and Brandon's own later reflections, refining and adding to the initial impressions. The tendency of the retrospective voice is to lyricize the experience, to rephrase it in more elegiac tones, reflecting the transformation of spontaneous grief into a more formalised sense of mourning, as in Aldington's variation on the gladiators' salute in the final lines of the story. The retrospective sections also represent a cementing of the war's myth of futility and disillusionment.

Detailed descriptions of stereotypical features of the war in Aldington's stories – the sense of disillusionment and betrayal, the mechanised horror and stagnation of trench warfare, the hardships of the soldiers' lives in the trenches and focus on the Western Front – locate them safely and unmistakably in a First World War context and make them compatible with the mythology of the war that shapes and informs the canon of Great War literature. At the same time, their pacifist agenda endows them with a universally pacifist message that transcends this particular war. Fictional Brandon wants his own horrific war experiences to set an example that may prevent future wars; his (and Aldington's) declared aim is to make sure their sufferings are not repeated with new protagonists. As such, Aldington's war stories support post-war pacifism and conform perfectly to the emerging mythology of the war. Indeed, many anthologies of First World War prose, as we have seen, include a mandatory piece by Aldington, although this is often an excerpt from his better-known novel *Death of a Hero* rather than a short story. The main interest that Aldington's war fiction holds for editors and publishers after 1945 is its reinforcement of the disillusioned Great War myth and the author's status as a veteran able to supply readers with an 'authentic' depiction of the war. While his short stories served Aldington as a means of venting a veteran's anger and frustration during the inter-war years and arguably offered other veterans a chance of identifying themselves and their own experiences in his semi-autobiographical fiction, these stories subsequently take on a different function as an illustration of the master narrative of the war as wasteful, futile and damaging to the individual participant.

Stories written about mourning that were published during and after the Second World War take yet another stance on the issue. Writers sometimes addressed old losses after 1945 because the trauma of loss had been rekindled by the war just witnessed or had been threatened with smothering or superseding. However, the temporal distance between the post-war world and loss experienced during the First World War could also lead to a certain extent of repression and willed forgetfulness, particularly in cases where the author of a story had first-hand experience of the war. These may make a renewal of grief all the more acute. Frances Bellerby is one such writer who chooses mourning as her subject in the aftermath of the Second World War, both mourning for the dead and mourning for a way of life irrevocably lost. In her short story 'The Green Cupboard' (1952), childhood grief has turned into adult grief, long suppressed and seemingly forgotten. Nathalie Blondel has characterised Bellerby as a writer whose works are haunted by the Great War long after the end of its successor. Bellerby's fiction, Blondel argues, is so compelling because it shows '[how the] fragile interwoven cloth of respectable English life sometimes veils but often cannot protect the bereaved [...] whose lives have been broken by their sense of loss. People live double lives: they interact with the living whilst dwelling in memories of the dead.'[18] Bellerby, who was born in 1899 and lived through both world wars, lost her only brother in the First World War. According to Blondel, as late as 1970, Bellerby stresses that 'far from diminishing, the experience of [her brother's] death "goes on happening", and her writing reflects the way in which the past does not disappear but remains in the minds of those who remember, who cannot help but remember'.[19]

Next to well-known figures such as Kipling, Blunden and Sassoon, Bellerby is perhaps the most strident example of a writer who could not let go of the First World War as a subject, even beyond the next war. Most of Bellerby's fiction was published during and after the Second World War, but in its majority it is informed by the First World War and her personal experience of loss. World War II is to a great extent ignored; it pales into insignificance because it cannot inflict the same wounds. Bellerby's story 'The Green Cupboard' is narrated by a middle-aged woman from a post-war perspective. The eponymous cupboard of this story is a curiously mundane symbol of loss and the repression of grief. Originally the cupboard had been a cheerful apple green, but it was repainted black after the narrator's father abandoned the family, the first in a series of traumatic events in the narrator's childhood forty years previously. This series culminated in the death at the Western Front of a favourite uncle and replacement father figure. It is a casual remark made by a visiting child that prompts the narrator to acknowledge the altered appearance of the cupboard, and her own repressed feelings of grief. She realises that she had continued to think of the black cupboard as green

[b]ecause of the passionate intensity of my desire to move life back to the time when the cupboard was still green. [...] I saw clearly that the re-painting of that cupboard symbolised for me the change which I had never, in spite of all pretence, ceased to blame and deplore. I had been at-home [sic] in life before the re-painting of the green cupboard. But ever since then I had been a homesick stranger.[20]

The black coat of paint thus symbolises to the narrator the most traumatic events of her life which time and a second war have enabled her to push out of her consciousness: the abandoning by her father, her mother's gradual slide into mental illness, the death of a close family friend and the death of her mother's brother in the First World War. Even at a distance of almost forty years, the narrator perceives this last death as an irreparable loss. Having previously been abandoned by her father, her uncle's death had been devastating and can only be repressed and lived with, not forgotten or lived down, as the narrator observes: 'Oh, but we were broken. Each in our different way. Each unmendable. Time never mends. I am thankful, really, to have learnt at least that one lesson so early in life.'[21] Early disillusionment is naturally at best a cold comfort, and loss and death have had a permanent, blighting effect on the narrator's life. She has attempted to keep the damage in check by suppressing her grief across several decades, spanning a second war that could no longer take any loved ones away from her. Repression has been her protection; only now has it been stripped away from her, and she finds herself confronted once more with the consequences of a war that seemed at a safe distance. Speaking in terms of mourning processes, the protagonist of 'The Green Cupboard' has failed to progress through the different stages of mourning and has attempted to ignore all emotions connected with her loss altogether – as it turns out, in vain.

Another of Bellerby's short stories, 'Winter Afternoon' (1952), turns the impact of war and grief around: another chance encounter offers an old woman the opportunity to reconcile herself with the loss of her son in the First World War. Three girls have stayed on in an Evacuee's Hostel in the countryside because they have nowhere else to go.[22] Sent out on an errand, the girls are invited in for tea by old Annie Jasper. During the ensuing conversation, it transpires that Mrs Jasper's oldest son Gerald was 'killed in 1917, in the war which was to his mother the whole of War'.[23] Mrs Jasper tells the girls about her son as he was before the war, and experiences a strange sense of peace and reconciliation with her loss:

'Tell us some more,' urged June.

The old woman started off again with a promptness that showed she could have gone on for hours, and that, indeed, she often had gone on thus, in her mind, for hours. No need to choose words. They'd every one of them been chosen years and years ago, and here they were. [...] Unaware of any discovery or re-discovery, yet she was moved by an emotion whose existence she had forgotten long ago, an emotion of such peace, gentle safety, and complete at-homeness, as she had neither experienced nor hoped to experience since that day in 1917 when War had splintered her brittle world.[24]

The chance encounter of the children in need of human contact and the old woman in need of a sympathetic audience at least partially heals a grief as yet unvoiced. The old woman has, as Blondel puts it, interacted with those around her, including her remaining children, and yet been caught up in inescapable, painful memories of her dead son; only the encounter with the evacuee girls – themselves victims of the war – helps her merge the two and bring together the two parts of her life, the visible and the hidden. While suppressed feelings may result in a renewal of trauma when finally broken into, as in Bellerby's first story, 'The Green Cupboard', the venting of reminiscences bottled up for years has a beneficial effect in 'Winter Afternoon'. Unlike novels, short stories need to establish links between the two wars without lengthy panoramic views of the war and inter-war years, but they nevertheless use family and generational con- frontations as well as flashbacks as similar means to establish continuity, such as a father-son-relationship suddenly altered in the wake of a new war in Arthur Calder-Marshall's 'Before the War' (discussed in detail later in this chapter), or indeed the mental journey of 'The Green Cupboard' narrator back into her own childhood. Personal memories serve as a link between the experiences of the two wars and create the opportunity to fictionally deal with both.[25]

Elizabeth Bowen, like Bellerby, was born in 1899 and experienced the First World War as a teenager. In her short story 'The Demon Lover' (1945) she offers a study of suppressed trauma that is renewed in the midst of the Second World War.[26] Bowen did not lose any close relatives during the war, but had been badly affected by the death of her mother from cancer in 1912. Her later husband, Alan Cameron, had been gassed in the war, but survived to be awarded the Military Cross. Like Bellerby's stories, 'The Demon Lover' focuses on the trauma of the First World War continuing into the Second. First published in October 1945, the story's protagonist is again middle-aged, in this case a married woman. Mrs Drover returns to her London house during the Blitz to collect possessions for her family, who have taken refuge from the bombs in the country. In her empty house, she is suddenly confronted with her past through a ghostly letter from her former fiancé, who was to the best of her knowledge killed twenty-five years previously in the summer of 1916. The letter reminds Mrs Drover of a meeting arranged at parting, an uncanny promise extracted from her by a possessive young soldier not to forget him, and to be prepared for his return. The sudden memory of her youthful engagement, entered into rashly and hardly regretted when it ended, immediately transports Mrs Drover back to a past beyond the current war, which only moments before had been such threatening reality. Now the threat of real bombs is replaced by the threat of this phantom from her past. Mrs Drover has failed to grieve for her erstwhile fiancé, and suddenly his disappearance in the earlier war catches up with her – quite literally – with a vengeance. Mrs Drover attempts to flee from the ghostly rendezvous she had agreed to unwittingly decades earlier, but she finds herself abducted by the spectre from her past, which makes off with her in a taxi. The story ends on the unsettling note of a screaming woman driven off into the unknown, and the previous conflict, long buried underneath years of married life and family routine, has violently caught up with the protagonist across the divide of the later war. Despite the threatening tone of her story, Bowen did not consider it an expression of danger as much as a means of acknowledging the impact of war on the psyche: if Mrs Drover's vision of her former fiancé come back to abduct her is a hallucination, it is an example of hallucinations that are 'an unconscious, instinctive, saving resort on the part of the characters: life, mechanized by the controls of wartime, and emotionally torn and impoverished by changes, had to complete itself in *some* way'.[27] Though unpleasant, Mrs Drover's surreal encounter at least shakes her out of a draining routine and allows her an outlet for suppressed fears, as well as a chance to acknowledge that these current fears are linked to older fears carried over from the First World War.

Bellerby and Bowen are writers who, as adults, experienced both the First and Second World War. Their stories testify to the fact that both writers, like most of their contemporaries, saw the two wars as connected not merely historically, but emotionally, in that the later war recalled memories and emotions connected with the earlier conflict.[28] Although these two stories constitute only a tiny selection, they allow us to trace the profound impact of the earlier war continuing through its successor. Grief, loss and trauma encountered in the First World War, buried and suppressed emotions, are shown to find ways of resurfacing during and after the Second World War. Whether they have been renewed, buried or assuaged by the Second World War, they do not lose their hold on those who experienced two world wars in their lifetime, in many cases reliving as adults what they believed they had left behind in their youth, and indeed on those whose memories of the war were merely inherited. These short stories testify to the fact that, far from obliterating it, the Second World War has strengthened the impact of the Great War on British consciousness to this day. Indeed, Jay Winter has suggested that many socio-political upheavals commonly attributed to the impact of the First World War were only effective in the aftermath of the Second, particularly the breakdown of a traditional language of mourning and remembrance. Winter argues that because the traditional expressions of the inter-war years had been designed to heal, warn and prevent a repetition of war, it was only when, in the wake of another war, these aims were seen to have clearly failed that the traditional languages of grief and their 'message of hope' were finally devalued.[29]

Initially, short stories that continued to address the First World War into and beyond its successor may be described as an effort 'to dwell [...] in the aftermath of the Great War',[30] to hold on to personal memories and losses. Dan Todman observes that up to the late 1960s, the war 'was still an event in family memory as well as family history'.[31] The change traceable in later stories addressing the Great War, stories written by those who had no personal experience of the conflict, pertains to their outlook on the war and the use it is put to: rather than offering narrative models for actual memories and experiences, later literary commentators on the war engage with issues of remembrance and historicity, or make use of the war as a defining event in British popular consciousness that can serve numerous purposes as a plot intensifier, reference point or metaphor for futility. A range of approaches to the war are conflated in Julian Barnes's short story 'Evermore', first published in the *New Yorker* in 1995. 'Evermore' addresses the fear of losing the legitimacy for one's mourning, but also constitutes a fictional commentary on the evolution of the war's remembrance and the impact of the intervening Second World War on its place in popular consciousness. In this story, Barnes as an observer with no personal memories of the war shows us an elderly woman who persistently grieves for a brother killed in the Great War. Barnes's fictional Miss Moss feels that the Second World War jeopardises her mourning and her remembrance of the lost brother: 'She hated Hitler's war for diminishing the memory of the Great War, for allotting it a number, the mere first among two.'[32] The dead of the Second World War she sees as obstructing her own dead, the brother she has chosen to mourn indefinitely. Even memorials for those who died between 1939 and 1945 offend her: 'They blocked the view, these deaths and these dates; they demanded attention by their recency. She refused, she refused.'[33]

'Evermore' addresses the issue of mourning and remembrance in a more remote, self-conscious manner and can be read as a detached sociological and psychological study of mourning rather than an attempt to interpret and alleviate grief for a readership still caught up in the emotions that accompany bereavement.[34] Set at the end of the twentieth century, this short story presents mourning no longer as spontaneous emotion, but as a duty and mission, a carefully cultivated set of rituals. Miss Moss, the elderly Anglo-Jewish protagonist of the story, has retired from her work as assistant editor and still travels annually to the cemeteries of the Western Front in a ritualised pilgrimage for her brother Sam.[35] She always carries with her his three last field postcards and tours a set number of cemeteries and memorials:

[H]er routine remained almost immutable. She would drive to Dover and take a night ferry, riding the Channel in the blackout alongside burly lorry-drivers. It saved money, and meant she was always in France for daybreak. No Morning Dawns… He must have seen each daybreak and wondered if that was the date they would put on his stone… Then she would follow the N43 to St-Omer, to Aire and Lillers, where she usually took a croissant and *thé à l'anglaise*.[36]

Once more we encounter a conscious use of the remembrance motif used in Binyon's 'For the Fallen', the hour of daybreak as the moment for ritualised remembering. Barnes also comments overtly on the development of grief and mourning that is depicted more indirectly in Mansfield's 'The Fly' and points out the comfort inherent in a sense of community:

At first, back then, the commonality of grief had helped: wives, mothers, comrades, an array of brass hats, and a bugler amid gassy morning mist which the feeble November sun had failed to burn away. Later, remembering Sam had changed: it became work, continuity; instead of anguish and glory, there was fierce unreasonableness, both about his death and her commemoration of it.[37]

As is the case with the protagonist of Mansfield's 'The Fly', grief and mourning turn into a conscious effort. 'Evermore' not only relates its protagonist's routines, but also her musings on grief, mourning, remembrance and the possibility of a collective memory of the war. These are stipulated in particular by the great monument for the missing at Thiepval. Miss Moss disapproves of its intimidating scope, and the story derives its title from her reflections on the inscription 'EVERMORE', which she thinks ought to be spelled in two words to give it more symbolic weight.[38] Her abhorrence of Thiepval as a memorial for those missing and without a known resting place and her relief that her own dead brother has a grave of his own that she can visit correspond to what has been described as the importance of burial rites, to a sense of '*obligation* to the corpse' whose absence leads to states of extreme distress when there are no remains to be buried.[39] Miss Moss's pilgrimages are shown to have commenced immediately after the war, and we are also told that, just after the war, she decided to marry her fiancé Denis despite his shell shock, only to deliver him back to his sisters two years later to devote her life entirely to mourning for her own brother. Rather than attempting to forget and move on with her life, Barnes's mourning sister clings to grief as if it were a professional occupation, in defiance of the fact that life and history move on. Barnes's story rehearses a scenario that might have grown out of an earlier mourning story such as Redman's 'The Enduring Image': Miss Moss is a wry and somewhat disturbing take on the bereaved sweetheart who lives on and refuses to shift her loyalties from the dead to the living.

ALTERED OBJECTIVES: POST-WAR SHORT STORIES ADDRESSING THE GREAT WAR

Prolonged grief and mourning were not the only issue that continued to be addressed through short fiction into the inter- and post-war world. As another war approached, writers of fiction picked up on the uneasy sense that recent history was about to repeat itself. In Arthur Calder-Marshall's short story 'Before the War' (1941), set on the eve of the Second World War, the young English narrator is training to be a soldier. He takes his fiancée, Esther, to see his invalid father, Mr Burrows, in a nursing home for First World War veterans. Mr Burrows lost both his legs in the Great War and suffered terrible, disfiguring injuries to his face, which are described in some detail:

Every time you saw him it was a fresh shock. When you go away, you kid yourself it can't be as bad as you saw it was. Luckily he was asleep. When his eyes are closed, I don't have to think he's human, with thoughts in his brain and emotions like me. What I fear are his eyes, like caged ferrets in his ravaged head, the life shooting from the setting of graft skin. You see his face isn't a human colour. It's white here and red there and the wrinkles aren't the lines that come from laughing or worry. They've got as much expression as the skin of a stale mushroom.

Mum said Dad in his day was jolly and strong. But I could never believe it from what the war left of him.[40]

Fictional Mr Burrows functions as a living reminder of the potentially devastating effects of war. He has been confined to the nursing home ever since his return from the war – not an unusual case in real life, as nursing homes such as the Star and Garter Home for Disabled Sailors and Soldiers were still caring for veterans in the 1930s and 1940s and beyond, having nursed almost 2,000 severely disabled veterans by 1936.[41] Mr Burrows's son, who had so far never been very attached to a parent he scarcely knew, begins to feel more strongly for his father as he himself is about to fight in the next war, and he is greatly concerned about his fiancée's disdainful attitude towards all kinds of unpleasantness and physical suffering. Esther agrees to accompany him to the nursing home primarily because it is hosting a fundraising rally for the Voluntary Aid Detachment service in the presence of a member of the Royal family, and the young couple nearly have a row when, for financial reasons, Esther refuses to get married straight away. When the young narrator goes to see his father by himself, father and son talk freely about the young man's anxiety about the coming war and the father's motivation for fighting in the last war. Mr Burrows senses his son's fears and tries to convince him that, in order to live the life he hopes for, he too will have to fight:

'You came out of it worse than most,' I said, 'what do *you* think? [...] [T]he war – what you were fighting for – was it worth it?'

'What I was fighting for?' [sic] That was worth it,' Dad said. 'But we never got it. To do away with the old gang, with greed and corruption and profiteering and each chap pitted against another. We said we'd chuck out the old gang when we got home. But I was out of it and the others found when they got back, everything had been settled years before in these secret treaties. When they tried to change things, the old gang beat them. That's why you've got to fight again, son.'

'But I don't want to fight, Dad,' I said, for the first time in my life seeing him as the man of his eyes instead of the mutilation of his flesh. 'I want to live in peace and marry Esther and do a job and enjoy myself evenings.'

'I know, son,' he said, taking my hand, 'but to do it, whoever Esther may be, you'll have to fight [...]'.[42]

Before the war is also after the war, and father and son experience a moment of closeness only when the younger man is forced into a situation that makes him understand his father's thoughts and motivations. Such a sudden closeness and mutual understanding, achieved only when the son finally finds himself in a position to understand the father's war experiences by facing a war of his own, are a recurrent element in inter- and post-war fiction.[43] The moment of understanding between father and son in this case is quickly broken up: Esther unexpectedly joins her fiancé and sees Mr Burrows for the first time; unprepared for the sight, she runs away in shock. However, the young soldier finds that, far from breaking off their engagement, as he feared she would, Esther is suddenly prepared to get married immediately because she has realised how much is at stake. Her change of heart is described by the narrator as an almost epiphanic moment: 'I thought I knew her face and its expressions, but this was new, was what her face was meant to be, if you understand. She leaned over and spoke into my ear. "When's the soonest we can get married?" she asked'.[44] Although the narrator, who comments freely and in a self-aware manner on his own thoughts and feelings, does not explicitly voice it, the fear of his being similarly mutilated permeates the story, and this fear of what the near future may have in store for them brings father and son closer and convinces Esther to consent to a hasty marriage. Calder-Marshall's depiction of the disabled Great War veteran tallies with inter-war reportage in magazines and newspapers. Deborah Cohen notes that '[by] the 1920s, the smiling bed-case had replaced the "human wreckage" in representations of the disabled. It was in a large measure wishful thinking, a reassuring portrait for the generous British public.'[45] In Calder-Marshall's story, the reassurance is twofold. Not only is the general public assured of the veterans' continued gratefulness and good humour in the face of adversity, the story also seeks to alleviate the fears of those who may be called upon to repeat a similar sacrifice.

Fictional echoes of the war such as Bellerby's, Bowen's and Calder-Marshall's stories aside, it is not without reason that most studies of First World War literature and poetry restrict themselves largely to texts published up to the early 1930s. There is not only a decided break in publication around 1935, with a dramatic falling-off of publications relating to the First World War once the prospect of the next war came into focus, but also a shift in the nature of those texts still published. During the war itself and in the decade following it, the target audiences of magazines that published the majority of Great War short stories had a particular interest in these stories, based on their first-hand experience of the war and the necessity to use fictional accounts of the war as a means of exploring their own narratives of the war, their validity and implications. We have seen that war stories, particularly those stories published in popular magazines, offered a plethora of different war narratives that successfully addressed personal concerns and anxieties owing to their topicality, their easily accessible style, and their use of familiar jargon and reassuring generic patterns. Although these stories made every bid to be accessible to wartime audiences and readers just after the war, they could not matter in the same way to a readership with no personal memories of the war. This category includes a generation of readers who had experienced the war as children or very young adults and consequently had no share in certain key experiences. These readers turned to war literature to find out more about a conflict that their parents or brothers might be reluctant to talk about, to 'penetrate the silence'[46] of their elders, but they no longer relied on these stories for evaluation or confirmation of their own experiences. As the aspect of narrative configuration ceased to be of primary importance, fewer stories were written about the First World War, and their agenda altered significantly, with a much stronger focus than before on their relation to the myth and memory of the war and the question of authenticity.

The majority of wartime and inter-war stories do not conform to the current myth of the war, as most of them fail to condemn it, or are set in places and situations not widely commemorated as part of the war's Western Front-based myth. These stories are brief, fictional glimpses of wartime and inter-war life that do not offer either the contemplative scope of a war novel, the eyewitness (if not always historically accurate) authenticity of a war memoir, or the overarching pathos and pacifist sentiment of the canonised trench poetry. On the other hand, post-war short stories about the First World War gradually move away from the function of narrative configuration to a critical engagement with the war's memory and/ or implicit commentary on its impact as a defining historical event of the twentieth century. Where the majority of earlier war stories made heavy use of established literary formulae to provide reassurance and familiar frameworks of understanding, post-war stories are also less indebted to particular subgenres than wartime and inter-war stories. Post-war short stories addressing the war moved into less standardised narrative territory, and this development, gradual but pronounced, reflects changes in readers' and writers' aims and expectations concerning retellings of the First World War. Jay Winter speaks of a second-generation memory emerging in the 1970s and 1980s. While, he claims, '[w]ar and mourning are also at its core', the trajectory of this second surge in remembering the war 'differed sharply from that of the first memory boom. For many reasons, the balance of creation, adaptation, and circulation in producing the second wave of concern about memory was entirely different from the earlier case.'[47] Winter notes the considerable time lag between the end of the Second World War and this second boom, which he explains by a slow and gradual shift from an interpretation of the war as heroic resistance to an interest in survivors as witnesses and victims.[48] In Winter's opinion, the second memory boom is at its core essentially moral in nature, centring on the aspect of victimisation and the avoidance of war altogether,[49] and this is an evaluation that is certainly backed up by the tenor of war-story anthologies.

Like Winter, Barbara Korte and others argue that there are certain 'cumulative phases' in British remembrance of the war during which the cultural memory of the conflict was boosted and the event remembered and commemorated with particular intensity. As the first of these phases of intense commemoration they identify the late 1920s and early 1930s, corresponding to the original war-books boom; followed by a second such phase beginning in the 1960s and attributed to the influence of the pacifist movement and the Campaign for Nuclear Disarmament. While the most iconic text of this commemorative period is Joan Littlewood's bitingly satirical Theatre Workshop play *Oh, What a Lovely War!* (1963 [1965]), an excellent though little-known short-story example of this phase is Robert Graves's story 'Christmas Truce'. 'Christmas Truce' was first published in the *Saturday Evening Post* on 15 December 1962 under the title 'Wave No Banners' and reveals changing social attitudes towards the First World War in its frame narrative. The story is an account of the unofficial Christmas truce between German and British soldiers on the Western Front in 1914, told by a grandfather to his grandson from a post-war perspective. The grandson, whose father has died in the Second World War, wants his veteran grandfather to march in a 'Ban the Bomb' rally, which the narrator refuses to do, as he believes that only nuclear arms will prevent another war. There is a visible focus on the horrors and futility of war in the fictional veteran's conviction that war must be avoided at all costs, a conviction that has ironically survived in the aftermath of a second war that was demonstrably fought to remove a murderous, totalitarian regime. At the same time, Graves's story arguably contributed to the formation of one particular aspect of the Great War myth, the notion that Allied and German soldiers bore each other no genuine malice and, given a choice by warmongering generals and politicians, would have preferred to be friends. Naturally, this view has to be put into perspective. Although stories such as Graves's and a variety of other fictional and eyewitness accounts are not factually untrue, in the sense that the Christmas truce(s) of 1914 did happen, the peaceful meeting described in 'Christmas Truce' is only part of the picture. While many soldiers were happy to fraternise with the enemy at this early stage of the war, others were reportedly not willing to tolerate such behaviour, and the latter years of the war saw no successful repetition of the Christmas truce. It is not surprising, however, that the notion of the inherent comradeship and connection between soldiers on all sides of the divide came to the fore at a time when the pacifist movement harnessed First World War narratives to emphasise the destructive nature and futility of war more generally, and when blame for the war's losses was increasingly placed on the shoulders of a military establishment that had previously been hero-worshipped and respected. In his increasingly irritated attempts to persuade the old man to join his rally, the narrator's grandson in 'Christmas Truce' exclaims '*you* didn't hate the Germans even when you were fighting them',[50] trying and failing to impress a universal brotherhood of men on his grandfather. The older man reminds his idealistic grandson, however, that even in 1914 the truce was not universal even along the Western Front, and by December 1915 the 'gentlemanly spirit' had largely been replaced by 'patriotism and [...] hatred of "the Teuton foe"'.[51]

Robert Westall's autobiographical short story 'The Making of Me' (1989) provides a fascinating example of a post-war story that not only engages with the First World War as a key event of the twentieth century, but also uses narrative fiction to explore immediate family history in relation to the war. Addressing an audience of young adults, Westall describes his childhood relationship to his paternal grandfather, a shell-shocked World War I veteran whose gas-impaired lungs, violent outbursts and intemperate habits inspire the young boy with awe. Westall's description of his grandfather combines a variety of features that have become stereotypical of the damaged First World War veteran, including a sensitivity to loud noises, spells of disorientation and hallucination and a latent guilty conscience for an act of violence during the war, but also a tendency to violence and alcoholism shown to be linked to his war experiences:

But the Great War had done for him. [...] Nana always had to be careful with the big black kettle she kept simmering on the hob to make a cup of tea. If it was allowed to boil, the lid would begin to rattle, making exactly the same noise as a distant machine-gun. And that would be enough to send him off into one of his 'dos', when he would imagine he was back in the hell of the trenches and would shout despairing orders, and I would be sent out for a walk till one of his powders settled him.

They said he had killed an Austrian soldier in a bayonet fight and taken his cap badge. [...] When Granda was *really* bad, he thought the dead Austrian had come back for his badge.[52]

At the same time, the story also reveals less traumatic aspects of the war, when Westall's grandfather recalls the wartime routine of playing cards in the trenches and the camaraderie in his Tyneside regiment. His continued use of dead comrades' shaving articles '[t]o remember them by'[53] is mirrored by the presence of his own photograph, in uniform, on his grandson's desk decades later. The love of objects linking the present with the past that the story promotes – grandfather and grandchild ultimately bond over a selection of old memorabilia saved up by the older man in a wooden trunk – emphasises a connectedness with the past and a recognition of its impact on the present. 'The Making of Me' in this respect is particularly intriguing as it combines a retrospective narrative from a 1980s perspective with a story set in the mid-1930s, encompassing two different phases in the war's remembrance.

A third phase in the development of the popular memory of the war can be identified as starting in the early 1990s, and this was accompanied by its own war books boom. Short stories representative of this most recent phase illustrate the change in agenda and expectations that results from their greater temporal distance from the actual historical event. While producers and audiences of commemorative texts in the first phase had some degree of personal memory of the war, the second and third phases differ in that the majority of readers and writers no longer had their own experience of the war with which to compare its fictional representation. Consequently, the texts produced in the second war books boom of the late 1980s to the early twenty-first century are entirely dependent on and reflective of previous fictional representations of the Great War, and in most cases – such as Sebastian Faulks's novel *Birdsong* (recently adapted for television by the BBC), or Anne Perry's short story 'Heroes' discussed below – recycle well-worn tropes.[54]

The relatively few texts addressing the first World War that were published between the end of the Second World War and the 'revival' of writing about the First World War in the 1970s and 1980s (marked by Susan Hill's novel *Strange Meeting* [1971]), such as Bellerby's short stories discussed previously, are documents of continued trauma and part of the cultural archive of the war only. These stories focus on personal experience carried over from the Great War and do not usually engage with official practices of remembrance or the myth of the war. By contrast, more recent stories dealing with the First World War often make a conscious bid to engage with the myth of the Great War, in a manner similar to Pat Barker's *Regeneration* trilogy. Examples of such more recent short stories about the First World War besides Westall's autobiographical tale are Anne Perry's 'Heroes' (2000), Robert Grossmith's ghost story 'Company' (1989), and Julian Barnes's 'Evermore' (1995). Of these three stories, 'Company' has the most impressive (and unusual) publication history, as it first appeared in the *Spectator* in December 1989 and was subsequently included in two anthologies of short stories, *Best English Short Stories 2* (1990) and the *Minerva Book of Short Stories 3* (1991). Anne Perry's 'Heroes', on the other hand, appeared in a specialised anthology of crime fiction, *Murder & Obsession* (2000), edited by crime-fiction expert Otto Penzler and clearly aimed at Perry's usual audience of readers with a specialised interest in murder mysteries and historical detective fiction. Barnes's 'Evermore' first appeared in the *New Yorker*, but was subsequently collected and published in one of the writer's own story collections, *Cross Channel* (1996).

Perry's self-contained story 'Heroes' recreates the world of the Western Front trenches as a setting for its detective plot and features military chaplain Father Joseph, the protagonist of her ongoing series of popular historical crime novels set on the Western Front. In the short story, Joseph is prompted to investigate the case of a dead soldier, Private Ashton, who allegedly panicked in no man's land during a patrol and whose body was returned to the trenches by his captain. Joseph's suspicions are aroused by a general consensus among Private Ashton's friends that he was a courageous, level-headed man unlikely to panic and by a closer investigation of his wounds. It turns out that Captain Holt, who had claimed he tried to rescue Ashton, was in fact the one who panicked and shot his subordinate to cover up his own failure. Instead of turning Holt over to the military police, however, Joseph makes him return to no man's land to try and eliminate a German sniper as a means of making amends for his crime that will save his face and spare his family's feelings. Perry's story has all the trappings of a Great War front-line story, and is visibly concerned with creating a 'realistic' image of the front-line trenches. The Western Front in itself is the dominant setting in the war's popular memory, but Perry litters her fictional trenches with rats, mud, machine-gun bullets and stoical Tommies in a clear attempt to make her story conform to the mythology of the war, repeating and condensing stereotypical images as instantly recognisable temporal and cultural markers:

It was a little after six when [Joseph] reached the firing trench beyond whose sandbag parapet lay no-man's-land with its four or five hundred yards of mud, barbed wire, and shell holes. Half a dozen burnt tree stumps looked in the sudden flares like men. [...] More star shells went up, lighting the ground, the jagged scars of the trenches black, the men on the fire steps with rifles on their shoulders illuminated for a few, blinding moments. Sniper shots rang out.[55]

Such a description of an almost iconic landscape of suffering, well-known to readers through images and texts republished consistently for decades, draws the reader into a setting that is familiar and alien at the same time. Maunder for instance observes how Rosenberg's 'Break of Day in the Trenches' (1916) epitomises our understanding of World War I, and stresses the centrality of poetic war-scapes like Rosenberg's to our cultural perception of the war, noting that through continued teaching of First World War poetry in schools '[t]he images contained in Rosenberg's verse are familiar to most of us'.[56] In Perry's case, Rosenberg's poetic description of the trenches is turned into easily recognisable prose. As Todman observes, descriptions of battlefield gore and squalor are used as 'key historical signposts. They let the audience know that they were reading a book about the First World War. Mud and horror were a requirement, allowing readers quickly to situate themselves in a shared sense of the past.'[57] Perry's story is but one example of popular fiction emulating the classic, disillusioned narratives of the war and blending them with generic features of the detective or adventure genres. Simon Morden's 'Brilliant Things' (2004), a supernatural tale in which a soldier on the Western Front finds a magic wish-fulfilling gem, strives to achieve the same effect. Stories such as Julian Barnes's 'Evermore', on the other hand, engage with that mythology by questioning it and interrogating motivations for continued remembrance.

Where these more recent stories about the Great War do not engage directly with the Great War myth, they tend to refer back to the Great War as an increasingly distant, if recurring, memory and discuss the experience of its impact rather than the experience of war itself, often from the perspective of a generation with no first-hand personal recollections of the war, and in the majority of cases no experience of the Second World War, either. Robert Grossmith's 'Company' is a powerful emblem of our relationship to the war as an historical event and part of its readers' cultural memory. In Grossmith's story, the lonely ghost of a young soldier killed by gas poisoning in the First World War still haunts the house in which he was born and died, long after even his niece has died an old woman. When a family with a young daughter, Angela, move in, he tries to befriend the girl, but she is scared of him and eventually (and tragically) falls to her death from a window when he approaches her to apologize and take his farewell. Memory is the undercurrent that flows through the story: not satisfied with the 'vaporous' world of spirits, the soldier's ghost feels that 'it was the memories that held him, the memories he subsisted on, like a diet of ersatz foodstuffs, knowing he would never taste real nourishment again'.[58] His attempt to swap memories for interaction with the world of the living by befriending the new tenants' young daughter ends in her disastrous death, and he feels forced to finally leave the house because he fears he will otherwise be 'haunted by the ghost of her memory, by the permanent presence of her absence from the family where she belonged'.[59] Although the story contains almost no explicit reference to the First World War other than in relation to the ghost soldier's death, an implicit commentary can be found in the ghost's tormented feelings relating to Angela's death, that '[the] thought of all those unlived years, those untested experiences, would pursue him like a life sentence, a death sentence, through eternity'.[60] Although he is thinking of the girl he has inadvertently caused to fall to her death, the words also apply to the ghost soldier himself, since he died 'not yet a man'[61] and is now left with the only option of letting go of even his shadowy, vicarious existence in favour of complete dissolution. There is no way for him to connect with the world of the living anymore; the child Angela is frightened of him and does not understand him because she cannot relate to his predicament. She even fails to recognise him for what he is, a Great War veteran: '"Why do you wear those funny army clothes? You don't look like a proper soldier."'[62] Her inability to place him may be read as another implicit commentary on the war, in that it exposes the temporal distance between his former present and hers, which makes a healthy, living recognition of the past impossible and leaves us with only a faint, lingering echo. Despite the continuing interest in the First World War in Britain and beyond, manifest in a revival of remembrance rituals, academic research and popular publications, the war's centenaries mark its final entrance into historicity rather than lived history. To enable a continued meaningful engagement with its legacy, its half-forgotten stories, representing glimpses into a personal experience of the war, are becoming more important than ever: as Grossmith's story suggests, the experience of the Great War may have paled into a ghostly memory, but this memory continues to haunt us.

Notes

INTRODUCTION

1 Samuel Hynes, *A War Imagined: The First World War and English Culture* (London: Pimlico, 1992), p. x.

2 Dominic Hibberd, *The First World War* (Basingstoke: Macmillan, 1990), p. 3.

3 Andrew Maunder (ed.), *British Literature of World War I*. Vol. I: The Short Story and the Novella (London: Chatto & Pickering, 2011), p. xlvii.

4 Dan Todman, *The Great War: Myth and Memory* (London: Hambledon, 2005), p. 17.

5 Both Carol Acton and Penny Summerfield note the importance of popular narratives to both the individual experience of war and subsequent expressions of that experience. See Acton, ' Best Boys and Aching Hearts: The Rhetoric of Romance as Social Control in Wartime Magazines for Young Women', *British Popular Culture and the First World War*, ed. Jessica Meyer (Leiden: Brill, 2008), pp. 173–93; and Penny Summerfield, *Reconstructing Women's Wartime Lives: Discourse and Subjectivity in Oral Histories of the Second World War* (Manchester: Manchester UP, 1998).

6 Maunder (ed.), *British Literature of World War I*, p. xxvii.

7 Christopher Martin refers to Pope as 'the crude recruiting versifier of the *Daily Mail*, who was so detested by Wilfred Owen', in 'British Prose Writing of the First World War', *Critical Survey* 2.2 (1990), pp. 137–143; 138.

8 See Acton's essay 'Best Boys and Aching Hearts'.

9 Michael Paris, *Over the Top: The Great War and Juvenile Literature in Britain* (Westport, CO: Praeger, 2004).

10 Paul March-Russell, *The Short Story: An Introduction* (Edinburgh: Edinburgh University Press, 2009), p. 112.

11 See for example Santanu Das's excellent edited collection *Race, Empire and First World War Writing* (Cambridge: Cambridge University Press, 2011).

12 Das (ed.), *Race, Empire and First World War Writing*, p. 7; quoting from *Evidence, History and the Great War: Historians and the Impact of 1914–18*, ed. Gail Braybon (New York: Berghahn, 2003), p. 28.

13 There are a few exceptions in the form of stories that explicitly address the participation of non-white troops, such as Alfred Ollivant's rather patronising prose sketch about a visit to a military field hospital for colonial soldiers, 'The Indian Hospital' (1916).

14 Dominic Head, *The Modernist Short Story: A Study in Theory and Practice* (Cambridge: Cambridge University Press, 1992), p. x.

15 For two particularly pragmatic approaches to defining the short story, see Norman Friedman, 'Recent Short Story Theories: Problems in Definition', *Short Story Theory at a Crossroads*, eds. Susan Lohafer and Jo Ellyn Clarey (Baton Rouge: Louisiana State UP, 1989); and Helmut Bonheim, *The Narrative Modes: Techniques of the Short Story* (Cambridge, MA: Brewer, 1992).

CHAPTER I. CANON, GENRE, EXPERIENCE, AND THE IMPLIED READER

1 Todman, *The Great War*, p. 132.

2 Todman, *The Great War*, p. 29.

3 See for example Michael Paris, *The First World War and Popular Cinema: 1914 to the Present* (Edinburgh: Edinburgh University Press, 1999), p. 53; Victoria Stewart, '"War Memoirs of the Dead": Writing and Remembrance in the First World War', *Literature and History* 14.2 (2005), p. 50; Todman, *The Great War*, pp. 141–5.

4 For a discussion of the diversity of Great War poetry and its narrowing down to a male, combatant perspective, see Hynes, *A War Imagined*, particularly chapter 2, 'The Arts Enlist'; Sarah Cole, *Modernism, Male Friendship, and the First World War* (Cambridge: Cambridge University Press, 2003); as well as Nosheen Khan, *Women's Poetry of the First World War* (New York: Harvester, 1988).

5 See Dominic Hibberd and John Onions (eds.), *Poetry of the Great War: An Anthology* (Basingstoke: Macmillan, 1986), p. 1.

6 Martin Stephen states with some justification that popular conceptions of the home front were established almost entirely by the negative descriptions of ignorant women and pompous old men to be found in Sassoon's poetry. See Martin Stephen (ed.), *Never Such Innocence: A New Anthology of Great War Verse* (London: Buchan & Enright, 1988), p. 262.

7 Edna Longley, 'The Great War, History, and the English Lyric', *The Cambridge Companion to the Literature of the First World War*, ed. Vincent Sherry (Cambridge: Cambridge University Press, 2000), p. 57.

8 Ibid. This anthology is a selection of war poems through the ages, from classical Greek epitaphs to modern poetry of the first Gulf War, accompanied by an afterword by Andrew Motion. Motion identifies the poets of the First World War (naming in particular Wilfred Owen, Siegfried Sassoon, Ivor Gurney and Isaac Rosenberg), whose poems make up a considerable portion of the volume, as the first true anti-war poets who 'not only questioned the purpose of war, but also challenged previous poetic orthodoxies'. Andrew Motion, Afterword, *101 Poems against War*, eds. Matthew Hollis and Paul Keegan (London: Faber, 2003), p. 135.

9 Longley, 'The Great War, History, and the English Lyric', p. 60.

10 Todman, *The Great War*, p. 165.

11 Esther MacCallum-Stewart, "'If they ask us why we died": Children's Literature and the First World War, 1970–2005', *The Lion and the Unicorn* 31.2 (2007), p. 179.

12 Hynes, *A War Imagined*, p. 28.

13 For a brief overview of some anthologies of Great War poetry, see Longley, 'The Great War, History, and the English Lyric', pp. 58–9.

14 For a discussion of inter-war middlebrow fiction and its attempts at healing and consolation, see Rosa Maria Bracco, *Merchants of Hope: British Middlebrow Writers and the First World War; 1919–1939* (Providence: Berg, 1993).

15 Mary Cadogan and Patricia Craig, *Women and Children First: The Fiction of Two World Wars* (London: Gollancz, 1978), p. 88.

16 Bracco, *Merchants of Hope*, p. 11; George Simmers, 'Military Fictions: Stories about Soldiers, 1914–1930', PhD thesis, Oxford Brookes University (2009), pp. 124–5.

17 Michael Paris, *Warrior Nation: Images of War in British Popular Culture, 1850–2000* (London: Reaktion, 2000), p. 82; and *Over the Top*, p. 18.

18 Paris, *Over The Top*, p. 40.

19 Paris, *Warrior Nation*, chapter 5; Paris, *Over the Top*, p. 158.

20 The findings of a 2003 survey of short story reading habits and publication, carried out by the British Council, confirm that publishers and readers alike prefer short story collections by established authors. For a summary of the report, see March-Russell, *The Short Story*, pp. 49–51.

21 John Rodden, 'Canonization and the Curriculum: George Orwell in the Anglo-American Classroom', *REAL: The Yearbook of Research in English and American Literature* 7 (1990), p. 230.

22 Aleida and Jan Assmann define cultural memory as an institutionalised memory made up of key events and artefacts relevant to a given group or society. See Jan Assmann, 'Communicative and Cultural Memory', *Cultural Memory Studies: An International and Interdisciplinary Handbook*, eds. Astrid Erll and Ansgar Nünning (Berlin: de Gruyter, 2008), pp. 110–11.

23 See Aleida Assmann, 'Vier Formen des Gedächtnisses' ['Four Forms of Memory'], *Erwägen Wissen Ethik* 13.2 (2002), p. 189; and 'Canon and Archive', *Cultural Memory Studies*, eds. Erll and Nünning, p. 99.

24 Aleida Assmann, 'Funktionsgedächtnis und Speichergedächtnis – Zwei Modi der Erinnerung', ['Working Memory and Reference Memory – Two Modes of Remembering'] *Generation und Gedächtnis: Erinnerungen und kollektive Identitäten*, eds. Kristin Platt and Mihran Dabag (Opladen: Leske und Budrich, 1995), p. 178.

25 Assmann, 'Canon and Archive', p. 99.

26 See Assmann, 'Vier Formen', p. 189.

27 See Assmann, 'Funktionsgedächtnis', p. 182.

28 Assmann, 'Funktionsgedächtnis', p. 185.

29 Assmann, 'Canon and Archive', p. 104–5.

30 Samuel Hynes, *The Soldiers' Tale: Bearing Witness to Modern War* (New York: Allen Lane, 1997), p. xiii.

31 Although Ricoeur had previously considered the importance of narrativity in his three-volume study *Time and Narrative* (1983–85), it is only in *Oneself as Another* that he focuses on narrative not solely concerning its bearings on human perceptions of time, but regarding its 'contribution to the constitution of the self'. Paul Ricoeur, *Oneself as Another* (Chicago: University of Chicago Press, 1992), p. 114.

32 Ibid., p. 114.

33 Ibid., p. 115.

34 Ibid., p. 117.

35 Ibid., p. 140.

36 Ibid., p. 142.

37 See the introduction, titled 'A Gap in History', of Hynes, *A War Imagined*.

38 Ricoeur, *Oneself as Another*, p. 147.

39 Ibid., p. 158.

40 Ibid., p. 162.

41 W. David Hall, *Paul Ricoeur and the Poetic Imperative: The Creative Tension between Love and Justice* (Albany, NY: State University of New York Press, 2007), pp. 42–3.

42 Hans Robert Jauss, *Toward an Aesthetic of Reception*, transl. Timothy Bahti, intro. Paul de Man (Minneapolis: University of Minnesota Press, 1982), p. 12.

43 Elizabeth Bowen, *The Mulberry Tree: Writings of Elizabeth Bowen*, ed. Hermione Lee (London: Virago, 1986), p. 97.

44 Jane Potter, *Boys in Khaki, Girls in Print: Women's Literary Responses to the Great War 1914–1918* (Oxford: Oxford University Press, 2005), p. 149.

45 Michael Roper, 'Re-Remembering the Soldier Hero: The Psychic and Social Construction of Memory in Personal Narratives of the Great War', *History Workshop Journal* 50 (Autumn 2000), p. 184.

46 See also Barbara Korte, Ralf Schneider and Claudia Sternberg, *Der Erste Weltkrieg und die Mediendiskurse der Erinnerung in Großbritannien: Autobiographie – Roman – Film (1919–1999)* (Würzburg: Königshausen & Neumann, 2005), pp. 17–18.

47 See Kate McLoughlin, *Authoring War: The Literary Representation of War from the Iliad to Iraq* (Cambridge: Cambridge University Press, 2011), pp. 1–2.

48 Cyril Falls, *War Books: A Critical Guide* (London: Peter Davies, 1930), p. xiv.

49 Falls, *War Books*, p. 294. This particular instance of criticism was levelled against Remarque and his novel *All Quiet on the Western Front*. In other instances, Falls commends a war book because it 'reveals the truth' (p. 296), because it shows us 'the authentic British infantrymen' (p. 292), or for its author's 'sincerity and the power with which he described what he had seen' (p. 273).

50 Quoted in Hynes, *The Soldiers' Tale*, p. 16.

51 See Dorothea Flothow, 'Popular Children's Literature and the Memory of the First World War, 1919–1939', *The Lion and the Unicorn* 31.2 (2007), pp. 151–2.

52 Evelyn Cobley, *Representing War: Form and Ideology in First World War Narratives* (Toronto: University of Toronto Press, 1993), p. 6.

53 Cobley, *Representing War*, pp. 10–12; 24–33.

54 Samuel Hynes proposes that 1920s literature and art bear testimony to 'attempts to reconstruct history and values' lost in the gap of the war years. In the process of these attempts the mythology of the war as a war of loss and futility was established through the now canonical prose narratives of the war (Hynes, *A War Imagined*, p. 459). Naturally, this interpretation is based on a fixed idea of what constitutes the truth of war, and feminist critics in particular have shown that it is a limiting and falsifying assumption to restrict authentic war experience exclusively to what happens at the front. Debra Rae Cohen points out how the history of the First World War as it was remembered emerged almost exclusively from the 'soldiers' tales' of the 1920s and for this reason represents an exclusively male perspective. See Debra Rae Cohen, *Remapping the Home Front: Locating Citizenship in British Women's Great War Fiction* (Boston: Northeastern University Press, 2002), p. 2. See also Margaret R. Higonnet (ed.), *Behind the Lines: Gender and the Two World Wars* (New Haven: Yale University Press, 1987); Claire M. Tylee, *The Great War and Women's Consciousness: Images of Militarism and Womanhood in Women's Writings, 1914–64* (Iowa City: University of Iowa Press, 1990); Susan R. Grayzel, *Women's Identities at War: Gender, Motherhood, and Politics in Britain and France during the First World War* (Chapel Hill: University of North Carolina Press, 1999) and Cole, *Modernism, Male Friendship, and the First World War.*

55 Maunder (ed.), *British Literature of World War I*, p. xv.

56 Hynes, *A War Imagined*, p. 459.

57 Teacher Robert Jeffcoate observes that the 'poetry of the First World War has been a staple of the English curriculum' since the 1960s. Robert Jeffcoate, 'Teaching Poetry of the First World War in the Secondary School', *Critical Survey* 2.2 (1990), p. 151.

58 Since April 2012, the national curricula for England, Wales and Northern Ireland have been monitored and are being continually revised by the central Standards and Testing Agency (STA), formerly the Qualifications and Curriculum Development Agency. While these curricula outline core skills and abilities that students have to achieve at the various stages of their education, the range of texts and subjects to be studied are largely defined by the various examination boards and awarding bodies. These texts and subjects thus change regularly and differ depending on which exam board a school subscribes to, making it hard to determine exactly which First World War texts are being studied. Textbooks are more helpful in this respect. Andrew Motion states in the preface to a teaching anthology that the teaching of Great War poetry in school leads to an infusion of the trench poets – and hence the Great War narrative of the Western Front trenches – into the 'national bloodstream', thus acknowledging the predominance of the Western Front and the soldierly perspective of the war. Andrew Motion (ed.), *First World War Poems* (London: Faber, 2003), p. xi.

59 See Niall Ferguson, *The Pity of War* (London: Allen Lane, 1998), p. xxiii.

60 Brian Bond, *The Unquiet Western Front: Britain's Role in Literature and History* (Cambridge: Cambridge University Press, 2002), p. 28.

61 Alisa Miller's study 'Poetry, Politics and Propaganda: Rupert Brooke and the Role of "Patriotic Poetry" in Great Britain, 1914–1918', D.Phil thesis, University of Oxford (2008), outlines the enormous flexibility of Brooke's poetry, reputation and ensuing myth, both in terms of political exploitation, and of altered agendas after the war.

62 Bond, *The Unquiet Western Front*, p. 29.

63 For a definition of popular versus literary texts, see Pierre Bourdieu, *The Field of Cultural Production: Essays on Art and Literature* (Cambridge: Polity, 1993) pp. 82–83; and the introductory chapter to Ken Gelder's *Popular Fiction: The Logics and Practices of a Literary Field* (London: Routledge, 2004).

64 Janet S.K. Watson, *Fighting Different Wars: Experience, Memory, and the First World War in Britain* (Cambridge: Cambridge University Press, 2004), p. 186.

65 Ibid., p. 187.

66 Ibid., pp. 219–60.

67 Ibid., pp. 204; 210.

68 Ibid., p. 215.

69 See Parfitt on John Buchan, Gilbert Frankau and Frederic Manning in *Fiction of the First World War: A Study* (London: Faber, 1988), pp. 20; 70; 90–91.

70 Modris Eksteins, *The Rites of Spring: The Great War and the Birth of the Modern Age* (New York: Mariner-Houghton Mifflin, 2000), p. 210.

71 Hynes, *A War Imagined*, p. xi.

72 Ibid., p. 425.

73 On the suitability of the short story to express the fragmented nature of the modern experience, see for example Barbara Korte, *The Short Story in Britain: A Historical Sketch and Anthology* (Tübingen: Francke, 2003), p. 19. Contemporary voices such as G.K. Chesterton already noted the connection between the 'fleetingness and fragility' of modern life and its representation in short stories: G.K. Chesterton, *Charles Dickens* (London: Methuen, 1906), p. 69, quoted in March-Russell, *The Short Story*, p. 25. Edmund Blunden observed with particular reference to the First World War that '[t]he mind of the soldier on active service was continually beginning a new short story, which had almost always to be broken off without a conclusion'. Edmund Blunden, Introduction. *Great Short Stories of the War: England, France, Germany, America*, ed. H.C. Minchin (London: Eyre & Spottiswoode, 1930), p. ii.

74 J.M. Winter, *Sites of Memory, Sites of Mourning: The Great War in European Cultural History* (Cambridge: Cambridge University Press, 1995), p. 3, and 'The Great War and the Persistence of Tradition: Languages of Grief, Bereavement, and Mourning,' *War, Violence, and the Modern Condition*, ed. Bernd Hüppauf (Berlin: De Gruyter, 1997), p. 39.

75 Jauss, *Toward an Aesthetic of Reception*, p. 30.

76 Stacy Aumonier, Foreword. Michael Joseph, *Short Story Writing for Profit*, 2nd edition (London: Hutchinson, 1923), p. vii.

77 Joseph, *Short Story Writing for Profit*, p. 179.
78 Claire Hanson, *Short Stories and Short Fiction, 1880–1980* (Basingstoke: Macmillan, 1985), p. 55.
79 Ibid., p. 56.
80 Alfred C. Ward, *Aspects of the Modern Short Story: English and American* (London: University of London Press, 1924), p. 17.
81 Ibid., p. 18.
82 Joseph, *Short Story Writing for Profit*, p. xiii.
83 Ibid., p. xiii.
84 Rita Felski, *The Gender of Modernity* (Cambridge, MA: Harvard University Press, 1995), p. 13.
85 Ibid., p. 23.
86 March-Russell, *The Short Story*, p. 25.
87 Chris Hopkins notes the selective processes that led to the exclusion of non-modernist fiction from university curricula. He argues that the neglect of the majority of First World War fiction originates in the fact that innovation was and in many ways still is valued by academic critics as the 'prime literary quality' a text ought to possess, while 'little of the fiction of the war is generally classed as modernist or strikingly radical in its procedures'. See Hopkins, 'Registering War: Modernism, Realism, and the Can(n)on', *Focus on Robert Graves and His Contemporaries* 2.5 (1996), p. 38.
88 Head refutes the idea of short stories being based on the notion of unifying, single effect advocated by Edgar Allan Poe and Brander Matthews, and claims instead that they rely on *dis*unifying devices as the 'seminal features of the literary effects produced in the genre' (Head, *The Modernist Short Story*, p. x) and which show the short story 'through its formal capacities, to be a quintessentially modernist form' (ibid., p. xi).
89 Ibid., p. 2.
90 Hopkins, 'Registering War', p. 38.
91 Nicholas Daly, *Modernism, Romance and the Fin de Siècle: Popular Fiction and British Culture* (Cambridge: Cambridge University Press, 2006), p. 23.
92 Maunder (ed.), *British Literature of World War I*, p. xiv.

CHAPTER 2. THE WAR IN THE MAGAZINES

1 William J. Locke, *Far-Away Stories* (1916. London: John Lane, 1926), p. vii.
2 As March-Russell observes, '[a]lthough magazine circulation has ensured an enduring role for the short story in Europe and the United States, it has also fostered the idea that the form is ephemeral. Magazine stories do not have the same physical or cultural status as fiction published in book form' (March-Russell, *The Short Story*, p. 43).
3 For the analysis in this chapter, roughly twenty specialised war anthologies and more than 100 general story anthologies published between 1914 and the present day were taken into account, including series such as *New Writing* and *Best British Short Stories*. A list of stories and anthologies consulted can be found in the bibliography.

4 See Sabine Buchholz, *Narrative Innovationen in der modernistischen britischen Short Story* (Trier: WVT, 2003), p. 2.

5 March-Russell finds that '[s]ingle-author collections tend to sell or to be borrowed from public libraries if the writer's name is already familiar, usually if s/he is a popular novelist' (March-Russell, *The Short Story*, p. 53).

6 Suzanne Ferguson points to this element of distraction when she says that '[w]hat they come with – other stories or other kinds of printed material – may distract readers from perceiving them as discrete works of art' ('The Rise of the Short Story in the Hierarchy of Genres', *Short Story Theory at a Crossroads*, eds. Susan Lohafer and Jo Ellyn Clarey. Baton Rouge: Louisiana State University Press, 1989, p. 178), and March-Russell argues that a reading of short stories within an anthology potentially 'violates Poe's contention that a short story is to be read as a single and self-sufficient unit' (March-Russell, *The Short Story*, p. 53), given that its impact may be diluted by the reading of another story before and immediately after its perusal.

7 Joseph Conrad, 'The Tale', *Best Short Stories of the War: An Anthology*, ed. and intro. H.M. Tomlinson (New York: Harper, 1931), p. 653.

8 Ibid., p. 653.

9 Ibid., pp. 661–2.

10 Ibid., p. 664.

11 While it is difficult to determine how much exactly Conrad received for 'The Tale' in the absence of archival material, documented payments made to other contributors can give an idea of the sums involved. In 1908, Winston Churchill received £150 per contribution for a series of nine articles. At the same time, Kipling was paid £90 and W.W. Jacobs £110 per short story, which was later raised to £350 as Jacobs's popularity increased. See Reginald Pound, *The Strand Magazine, 1891–1950* (London: Heinemann, 1966), pp. 4; 122.

12 In America, the same anthology was published the following year under the title *Best Short Stories of the War* (1931), introduced by British journalist and writer H.M. Tomlinson.

13 Hanson, *Short Stories and Short Fiction*, p. 11.

14 See Thomas Owen Beachcroft, *The English Short Story* (London: Longmans Green, 1964), p. 35.

15 Mary Louise Pratt, 'The Short Story: The Long and the Short of It', *The New Short Story Theories*, ed. Charles E. May (Athens, OH: Ohio University Press, 1994), p. 110.

16 Bourdieu, *The Field of Cultural Production*, pp. 38–9.

17 Thomas A. Gullason, 'The Short Story: An Underrated Art', *Short Story Theories*, ed. Charles E. May (Athens, OH: Ohio University Press, 1976), p. 18.

18 Valerie Shaw, *The Short Story: A Critical Introduction* (London: Longman, 1995), pp. 2–3.

19 Joseph, *Short Story Writing for Profit*, p. 3.

20 Ibid., p. 2.

21 George Newnes, quoted in A.J.A. Morris, 'Newnes, Sir George, first baronet (1851–1910)', 12 August 2009, *Oxford Dictionary of National Biography*, Oxford

University Press. http://www.oxforddnb.com/view/article/35218. Most biographical information on Newnes is also derived from this article.

22 Potter, *Boys in Khaki*, p. 76.

23 Morris, 'Newnes, Sir George'.

24 For the *Strand Magazine*'s rates of pay see Pound, *The Strand Magazine*, pp. 2; 4–5; 44; 70, 74; 97; 122.

25 Frank Delaney, Introduction. *Short Stories from the 'Strand'*, ed. Geraldine Beare (London: Folio Society, 1992), pp. vii–viii.

26 Of the *Strand Magazine* in the 1890s, Clive Bloom claims that each issue reached 'a general readership of between 300,000 and 500,000, especially so when a new Conan Doyle story appeared'. See Clive Bloom, *Bestsellers: Popular Fiction since 1900* (Basingstoke: Palgrave, 2002), p. 33.

27 Delaney in Beare (ed.), *Short Stories from the 'Strand'*, p. ix.

28 David Miller and Richard Price (eds.), *British Poetry Magazines 1914–2000: A History and Bibliography of 'Little Magazines'* (London: British Library-Oak Knoll, 2006), p. 19.

29 See Martha S. Vogeler, 'Harrison, Austin Frederic (1873–1928)', 5 February 2008, *Oxford Dictionary of National Biography*, Oxford University Press. http://www.oxforddnb.com/view/article/40734. The following biographical information is derived from Martha S. Vogeler, *Austin Harrison and the English Review* (Columbia: University of Missouri Press, 2008).

30 Adrian Gregory, *The Last Great War: British Society and the First World War* (Cambridge: Cambridge University Press, 2008), p. 280.

31 See Paris, *Over the Top*, particularly chapter 1, and Acton, 'Best Boys', pp. 176–7.

32 Vogeler, 'Harrison, Austin Frederic (1873–1928)', p. 80.

33 Vogeler, *Austin Harrison*, pp. 86–7.

34 Pound, *The Strand Magazine*, p. 122.

35 Once at the front, Briggs lives through a series of rather ludicrous adventures involving several miraculous escapes and the single-handed taking of large numbers of German prisoners. Briggs's exploits are faintly reminiscent of Arthur Conan Doyle's 'Brigadier Gerard' stories, which were published in the *Strand Magazine* in the 1890s and 1900s. Like Gerard, Briggs is protagonist and narrator at the same time and is awarded almost as many decorations and commendations as his French precursor. Unlike Gerard, however, he is overly modest rather than exuberantly vain. Marsh's Sam Briggs stories were collected and published posthumously under the title *Sam Briggs, V.C.* by Fisher Unwin in 1916.

36 Da Costa Ricci, a prolific writer of naval stories, is better known under his pseudonym Bartimeus.

37 Although Lawrence published stories in the profitable *Strand Magazine* when he could – always desperately pressed for money during the war years – his admiration and approval were with the *English Review* rather than the *Strand Magazine*. See James T. Boulton, *The Letters of D.H. Lawrence*, Vol. I, *September 1901–May 1913* (Cambridge: Cambridge University Press, 1979), pp. 139–40.

Although his estimation of the *Review* cooled in later years when Harrison refused to print certain stories he considered too 'steaming' even for a Great Adult Review, Lawrence was nevertheless 'willing to have his name on its blue cover for as long as Harrison was its editor' (Vogeler, *Austin Harrison*, p. 168).

38 Delaney in Beare (ed.), *Short Stories from the 'Strand'*, p. xiii.

39 Gelder's main means of distinguishing between what he calls 'popular' and 'literary' fiction are target audience and commercial outlook of a text or its author. Acknowledging the phenomenon of the 'literary bestseller', Gelder considers as works of popular fiction not those texts that sell particularly widely, but those that aim to reach a wide market. The empirical problems inherent in this approach are obvious, as proof of an author's intention is hard to establish, but Gelder attempts to circumvent these difficulties by taking into account criteria such as where a text is published, how it is marketed and whether or not it caters to genre expectations. See Gelder, *Popular Fiction*, chapters 1–3.

40 The change in headlines to more reconstruction-orientated slogans coincides with and was probably influenced by David Lloyd George's creation of a new 'Ministry of Reconstruction' in July 1917. See Rodney Lowe, 'Government', *The First World War in British History*, eds. Stephen Constantine, Maurice W. Kirby and Mary B. Rose (London: Arnold, 1995), p. 36.

41 See *English Review* 70 (September 1914). The articles in question are entitled 'Psychology and Motives' (pp. 233–47) and 'The Task of the Allies' (pp. 248–61) respectively.

42 The striking difference in length may be attributable to Harrison's strict editorial requirements. Martha Vogeler notes that Harrison was frequently criticised for demanding rigorous cuts of his contributors (Vogeler, *Austin Harrison*, p. 80).

43 Carl Krockel, *War Trauma and English Modernism: T.S. Eliot and D.H. Lawrence* (Basingstoke: Palgrave Macmillan, 2011), p. 4.

44 See Timothy Clark, 'Not Seeing the Short Story: A Blind Phenomenology of Reading', *The Oxford Literary Review* 26 (2004), p. 6.

45 Published in four series, in 1939, 1958 (ed. Dan Davin), 1965 (ed. T.S. Dorsch) and 1976 (ed. Roger Sharrock).

46 Humphrey Milford's *Selected English Short Stories* (1927); Ernest Rhys's *English Short Stories from the Fifteenth to the Twentieth Century* (1921, republished 1926); Richard Wilson's *English Short Stories: An Anthology* (1921, republished 1957).

47 See Jane Potter, 'For Country, Conscience and Commerce: Publishers and Publishing, 1914–18', *Publishing in the First World War: Essays in Book History*, eds. Mary Hammond and Shafquat Towheed (Basingstoke: Palgrave Macmillan, 2007), pp. 13–8.

48 See for example Edna Longley on poetry anthologies (Longley, 'The Great War, History, and the English Lyric', pp. 58–9).

49 Walter Wood (ed.), *Soldiers' Stories of the War* (London: Chapman and Hall, 1915), p. v.

50 See Phillip Knightley, *The First Casualty: The War Correspondent as Hero and Myth-maker from the Crimea to Iraq* (Baltimore: Johns Hopkins University Press, 2004), and Barbara Korte, 'Being Engaged: The War Correspondent in British Fiction', *Anglia* 124 (2006), pp. 432–48.

51 Edward James Parrott, *The Path of Glory: Heroic Stories of the Great War* (London: Nelson, 1921), p. 22.

52 The issue of how to deal with the bodies of the many soldiers fallen and interred abroad, and of how to adequately mourn the dead, was of particular momentousness immediately after the war and in the 1920s. For an account of the difficult work of the Commonwealth War Graves Commission see Fabian Arthur Goulstone Ware, *The Immortal Heritage: An Account of the Work and Policy of The Imperial War Graves Commission During Twenty Years, 1917–1937* (Cambridge: Cambridge University Press, 1937), and Julie Summers, *Remembered: The History of the Commonwealth War Graves Commission* (London: Merrell-Commonwealth War Graves Commission, 2007).

53 Junior Allan (ed.), *Humorous Scottish War Stories: Selected from the 'Daily Mail'* (Dundee: Valentine, 1930), p. 3.

54 Wingrove Willson (ed.), *Naval Stories of the Great War* (London: Aldine, 1931), p. 5.

55 A term used as early as 1930 by Cyril Falls in his guide to war fiction (Falls, *War Books*, p. 298).

56 Minchin (ed.), *Great Short Stories of the War*, p. e.

CHAPTER 3. POST-WAR PUBLICATION AND ANTHOLOGISATION

1 See e.g. Bernard Bergonzi, *Heroes' Twilight: A Study of the Literature of the Great War* (London: Constable, 1965), p. 213, and Adrian Barlow, *The Great War in British Literature* (Cambridge: Cambridge University Press, 2000), pp. 44–5.

2 See Vernon Scannell, 'The Great War', *Collected Poems 1950–1993* (London: Robson Books, 1993), pp. 68–9.

3 Todman, *The Great War*, p. 39.

4 Ernest Hemingway (ed.), *Men at War: The Best War Stories of All Time* (New York: Crown, 1942), p. xi.

5 Robert Fox, Introduction. *The Mammoth Book of Modern War Stories*, ed. Jon E. Lewis (London: Robinson, 1993), p. xi.

6 Lewis, *The Mammoth Book of Modern War Stories*, p. xv.

7 Sebastian Faulks, Introduction. *The Vintage Book of War Stories*, eds. Sebastian Faulks and Jörg Hensgen (London: Vintage, 1999), p. xi.

8 Ibid., pp. xii–xiii.

9 Quoted in Hibberd, *The First World War*, p. 169.

10 MacCallum-Stewart, 'Children's Literature and the First World War', p. 182.

11 Eleanor Updale, 'Not a Scratch', *War: Stories of Conflict*, ed. Michael Morpurgo (Basingstoke: Macmillan Children's Books, 2005), p. 161.

12 On the appeal of Captain 'Biggles' Bigglesworth, see Flothow, 'Popular Children's Literature and the Memory of the First World War', p. 153.

13 John L. Foster (ed.), *Twelve War Stories* (Harlow: Longman, 1980), p. iv.

14 Jane Christopher (ed.), *War Stories: Major Writers of the 19th and 20th Centuries* (Harlow: Longman, 1999), p. viii.

15 Ibid., p. viii.

16 First published by Octopus Books in 1983 under the title *Call to Arms*.

17 Jon Glover and Jon Silkin (eds.), *The Penguin Book of First World War Prose* (Harmondsworth: Penguin, 1989), p. 1.

18 Ibid., p. 2.

19 Ibid., p. 11.

20 See in particular the essay 'The Field of Cultural Production, or: The Economic World Reversed', in Bourdieu, *The Field of Cultural Production*, pp. 29–73.

21 Bourdieu, *The Field of Cultural Production*, p. 78.

22 Gelder, *Popular Fiction*, p. 3.

23 John G. Cawelti, *Adventure, Mystery, and Romance: Formula Stories as Art and Popular Culture* (Chicago: University of Chicago Press, 1976), p. 30.

24 Ibid., p. 300.

25 One can assume that at least some of the stories in that volume would have first appeared in a newspaper or periodical, but unfortunately it is in most cases either impractical or impossible to determine when and where a story was first published unless by coincidence. The online *FictionMags Index* (http://www.philsp.com/homeville/FMI/ostart.htm) is an amateur project providing indices for a wide range of popular fiction magazines, which, however, relies on contents lists of book auctioning sites and is consequently incomplete and of limited reliability. A project proposing to compile an *Index to British Popular Fiction Magazines, 1880–1950*, reputedly to be published by the British Library and undertaken by Mike Ashley, appears to be still in the planning stages. Individual indices exist for some magazines – such as Geraldine Beare's *Index to the Strand Magazine, 1891–1950* (1982) – but these cover only a small selection of possible publication outlets.

26 Ben Ray Redman, 'The Enduring Image', *Down in Flames* (New York: Payson & Clarke, 1930), p. 281.

27 See for example Christine Darrohn, '"Blown to Bits!": Katherine Mansfield's "The Garden Party" and the Great War', *Modern Fiction Studies* 44.3 (1998), pp. 513–39.

28 Katherine Mansfield, 'The Fly', *Women, Men and the Great War*, ed. Trudi Tate (Manchester: Manchester University Press, 1995), p. 72.

29 Ibid., p. 70.

30 Ibid.

31 Redman, 'The Enduring Image', p. 269.

32 Winter, *Sites of Memory*, p. 5.

33 Stewart, 'War Memoirs', p. 45.

34 Blanche Wills Chandler, *Tommies Two* (London: Sampson Low, 1917), p. i. Chandler's title emulates the title of Kipling's popular short story collection *Soldiers Three* (1888).

35 Falls commends Montague for his 'valuable quality of being able to display his bitterness and ram home his criticism without ranting', noting that Montague can at times be 'delightfully humorous' (Falls, *War Books*, p. 287).

36 C.E. Montague, 'The First Blood Sweep', *Fiery Particles* (1923. London: Chatto & Windus, 1936), p. 113.

37 David Cannadine, 'War and Death, Grief and Mourning in Modern Britain', *Mirrors of Mortality: Studies in the Social History of Death*, ed. Joachim Whaley (London: Europa, 1981), p. 206.

38 See Daniel Karlin, 'Kipling and the Limits of Healing', *Essays in Criticism: A Quarterly Journal of Literary Criticism* 48.4 (1998), pp. 331–56.

39 Michael C. Kearl, *Endings: A Sociology of Death and Dying* (Oxford: Oxford University Press, 1989), p. 28.

40 Ibid., p. 85.

41 Wyndham Lewis, 'The King of the Trenches', *Unlucky for Pringle: Unpublished and Other Stories* (London: Vision, 1973), p. 60.

42 H.C. McNeile ['Sapper'], 'The Sixth Drunk', *Sapper's War Stories: Collected in One Volume* (London: Hodder & Stoughton, 1932), p. 345.

43 See Jessica Meyer, 'The Tuition of Manhood: "Sapper's" War Stories and the Literature of War', *Publishing in the First World War: Essays in Book History*, eds. Mary Hammond and Shafquat Towheed (Basingstoke: Palgrave Macmillan, 2007), pp. 113–28. Jane Potter notes a similar focus on the 'transformative power' of the war in women's romances and memoirs of the war years, indicating that this was a feature shared by most popular literature of the war; see Jane Potter, '"A Great Purifier": The Great War in Women's Romances and Memoirs 1914–1918', *Women's Fiction and the Great War*, eds. Suzanne Raitt and Trudi Tate (Oxford: Clarendon, 1997), pp. 85–106.

CHAPTER 4. NEGOTIATING DISASTER IN POPULAR FORMS

1 Ricoeur, *Oneself as Another*, p. 162.

2 Carol Acton, *Grief in Wartime: Private Pain, Public Discourse* (Basingstoke: Palgrave Macmillan, 2007), p. 3.

3 Laurence Binyon, 'For the Fallen', *The Penguin Book of First World War Poetry*, ed. George Walter (London: Penguin, 2006), pp. 235–6.

4 See for example Jenny Hockey, Jeanne Katz and Neil Small (eds.), *Grief, Mourning and Death Ritual* (Buckingham: Open University Press, 2001).

5 Todman, *The Great War*, p. 132.

6 Gregory, *The Last Great War*, p. 152. See also Michael Snape, *God and the British Soldier: Religion and the British Army in the First and Second World Wars* (London: Routledge, 2005); and Richard Schweitzer, *The Cross and the Trenches: Religious Faith and Doubt among British and American Great War Soldiers* (Westport, CT: Praeger, 2003).

7 Annie Edith Jameson ['J.E. Buckrose'], 'The Parcel', *War-Time in Our Street: The Story of Some Companies Behind the Firing Line* (London: Hodder & Stoughton, 1917), p. 23.

8 Ibid., p. 24.
9 Ibid., p. 26.
10 Ibid., p. 24.
11 Anne Douglas Sedgwick, 'Hepaticas', *Atlantic Narratives*, ed. Charles Swain Thomas (Boston: Atlantic Monthly Press, 1918), p. 54.
12 John Hartman Morgan ['Centurion'], 'The Lieutenant', *Gentlemen at Arms* (London: Heinemann, 1918), pp. 3–4.
13 Ibid., p. 6.
14 Ibid., p. 11.
15 Stewart, '"War Memoirs"', p. 43.
16 Stacy Aumonier, 'The Brothers', *Love-a-Duck, and Other Stories* (London: Hutchinson, 1921), p. 286.
17 Ibid., p. 280.
18 See Trudi Tate, *Modernism, History and the First World War* (Manchester: Manchester University Press, 1998), pp. 11–14.
19 Ibid., p. 39.
20 See the women visiting Jesus's tomb in Luke 24:1–12.
21 Rudyard Kipling, 'The Gardener', *Debits and Credits* (1926. London: Macmillan, 1949), pp. 413–14.
22 Ibid., p. 406.
23 Jay Winter notes the importance of what might be called war-grave pilgrimages from Britain to the cemeteries of France and Belgium, undertaken by thousands of grieving relatives and friends. He points out that these pilgrimages, 'for many both physically and emotionally difficult', were often undertaken in groups and in the company of fellow sufferers, as is the case with Helen Turrell (Winter, *Sites of Memory*, p. 52).
24 Kipling, 'The Gardener', p. 407.
25 On Kipling's work for the Imperial War Graves Commission, see Karlin, 'Kipling and the Limits of Healing', pp. 334–5; Ware, *The Immortal Heritage*, p. 61; Michael Jubb, 'Rudyard Kipling and the Message of Sympathy to the Relatives of Soldiers Killed in the First World War', *Notes and Queries* 32.3 (Sept. 1985), p. 377; and Steven Trout, 'Christ in Flanders?: Another Look at Rudyard Kipling's "The Gardener"', *Studies in Short Fiction* 35.2 (1998), pp. 169–78. See also Joanna Scutts's excellent article on the interrelation of remembrance, literature and mourning, 'Battlefield Cemeteries, Pilgrimage and Literature after the First World War: The Burial of the Dead', *ELT* 52.4 (2009), pp. 387–416.
26 The boss's visitor in 'The Fly', Old Woodifield, reminds the boss of his son's death because his daughters have just been to France to visit their brother's grave, where they have come across the grave of the boss's son (Mansfield, 'The Fly', pp. 69–70)
27 Kipling, 'The Gardener', p. 414.
28 See for example Jane Potter, 'The Great War Poets', *The Blackwell Companion to the Bible in Literature*, ed. Rebecca Lemon, Emma Mason, Jonathan Roberts, and Christopher Rowland (Oxford: Wiley-Blackwell, 2009), pp. 681–95.

29 Snape, *God and the British Soldier*, p. 20.

30 Richard Aldington, 'Of Unsound Mind', *Roads to Glory* (1930. Freeport, NY: Books for Libraries Press, 1970), p. 123.

31 Ibid., p. 127.

32 Arthur Walter Wells, '"Chanson Triste"', *Best Short Stories of 1925*, ed. Edward J. O'Brien (London: Jonathan Cape, 1925), p. 239. The story was first published in the *English Review* in November 1924.

33 Wells, '"Chanson Triste"', p. 239.

34 Ibid., p. 240.

35 Keble Howard, 'Needs Must when Love Drives', *Strand Magazine* 57 (April 1919), p. 312.

36 Gelder, *Popular Fiction*, p. 45.

37 Nicholas Daly reads romance fiction within a British context as a 'form of narrative theory of social change', particularly for a middle-class audience (Daly, *Modernism, Romance and the* Fin de Siècle, p. 5).

38 Harold Orel, *Popular Fiction in England, 1914–1918* (New York: Harvester Wheatsheaf, 1992), p. 19.

39 Cawelti, *Adventure, Mystery, and Romance*, pp. 1–2.

40 'Much of the artistry of formulaic literature involves the creator's ability to plunge us into a believable kind of excitement while, at the same time, confirming our confidence that in the formulaic world things always work out as we want them to' (Cawelti, *Adventure, Mystery, and Romance*, p. 16).

41 Acton, *Grief in Wartime*, p. 18.

42 Ibid.

43 The quote refers to 'War-Time Weddings', *The Girl's Friend* (9 January 1915), p. 611; quoted in Acton, 'Best Boys', p. 181.

44 W.B. Maxwell, 'Joan of Arc', *Strand Magazine* 57 (January 1919), p. 59.

45 Ibid., p. 60.

46 Serialised in *The Girls' Reader* from October to December 1914 and discussed in depth by Jane Potter in *Boys in Khaki*, pp. 77–81.

47 Ibid.

48 It is interesting to note in this context that Joan of Arc had been adopted as the 'patron saint' of the women's suffrage movement before the war, and was thus a familiar role model to evoke. However, like the majority of suffrage campaigners, she seems to have taken on a more patriotic and less subversive role during the war. See Angela K. Smith, *Suffrage Discourse in Britain during the First World War* (Aldershot: Ashgate, 2005), p. 3.

49 Backing the idea that romance offered not simply fantastical escapism but realistic scenarios that nevertheless allow reprieve from the mundane, Radford also argues that romance frequently constitutes a mixture of both the real and the ideal. See Jean Radford, *The Progress of Romance: The Politics of Popular Fiction* (London: Routledge & Kegan Paul, 1986), pp. 8–12.

50 Cannadine, 'War and Death, Grief and Mourning in Modern Britain', p. 200.

51 Fiona Reid, *Broken Men: Shell Shock, Treatment and Recovery in Britain 1914–1930* (London: Continuum, 2010), p. 1.

52 Gail Braybon points out the much higher proportion of wounds and disabilities over deaths in 'Women and the War', *The First World War in British History*, eds. Stephen Constantine, Maurice W. Kirby and Mary B. Rose (London: Arnold, 1995), p. 165.

53 Florence Barclay, *My Heart's Right There* (London: G.P. Putnam's Sons, 1914). Quoted from Maunder (ed.), *British Literature of World War I*, p. 19.

54 Gordon Corrigan, *Mud, Blood and Poppycock: Britain and the First World War* (London: Cassell, 2003), p. 62.

55 See Deborah Cohen, *The War Come Home* (Berkeley: University of California Press, 2001).

56 Braybon, 'Women and the War', p. 165.

57 Cohen, *The War Come Home*, p. 107.

58 The quote is from 'Bridegroom at the War', *The Girl's Friend* (8 January 1916), p. 563; quoted in Acton, 'Best Boys', p. 187.

59 Vera Brittain, *Testament of Youth: An Autobiographical Study of the Years 1900–1925*, ed. Mark Bostridge (1933. London: Virago, 2004), p. 312.

60 Mary Borden, 'The Beach', *The Forbidden Zone* (London: Heinemann, 1929), p. 48.

61 Borden, 'The Beach', p. 49.

62 Ariela Freedman, 'Mary Borden's *Forbidden Zone*: Women's Writing from No-Man's-Land', *Modernism/Modernity* 9.1 (2002), p. 118.

63 Potter, *Boys in Khaki*, p. 91.

64 Sharon Ouditt and Deborah Cohen both note the importance of romantic love as a life-affirming and ordering force for lives affected by the war and the anxiety of disabled veterans to find a partner. Peter Leese also lists marriage and family support as a vital factor in facilitating veterans' reintegration. See Sharon Ouditt, *Fighting Forces, Writing Women: Identity and Ideology in the First World War* (London: Routledge, 1994), p. 89; Cohen, *The War Come Home*, p. 106; Peter Leese, 'Problems Returning Home: The British Psychological Casualties of the Great War', *The Historical Journal* 40.4 (1997), p. 1060.

65 Annie Edith Jameson ['J.E. Buckrose'], 'Pie', *War-Time in Our Street: The Story of Some Companies Behind the Firing Line* (London: Hodder & Stoughton, 1917), p. 50.

66 Ibid., p. 51.

67 Berta Ruck, 'Infant in Arms', *Khaki and Kisses* (London: Hutchinson, 1915), p. 15, quoted in Potter, *Boys in Khaki*, p. 102.

68 Jessie Pope, 'The Beau Ideal', *More War Poems* (London: Grant Richards, 1915), p. 43.

69 Morley Roberts, 'The Man Who Lost His Likeness', *Strand Magazine* 52 (December 1916), p. 692.

70 Ibid., p. 687.

71 Ibid., p. 691.

72 Cohen, *The War Come Home*, p. 106.

73 See Leese, 'Problems Returning Home', p. 1058, and George L. Mosse, 'Shell-Shock as a Social Disease', *Journal of Contemporary History* 35.1, Special Issue: Shell-Shock (Jan. 2000), pp. 101–108.

74 Stacy Aumonier, 'The Kidnapped "General"', *Adventure Stories from the 'Strand'*, ed. Geraldine Beare (London: Folio Society, 1995), p. 205. First published in the *Strand Magazine* issue for August 1923 and subsequently republished in various collections such as *Short Stories by Modern Writers*, ed. R.W. Jepson (London: Longmans, 1936).

75 Ibid.

76 Ibid.

77 Reid, *Broken Men*, pp. 76–7.

78 Of Robert Graves, Linda M. Shires suggests that his poems 'activate the horrors of recent war experiences and resort to creativity as a form of therapy'. Linda M. Shires, *British Poetry of the Second World War* (Basingstoke: Macmillan, 1985), p. 31. McLoughlin also notes the potentially healing effect of writing about war (McLoughlin, *Authoring War*, pp. 191–2).

79 Aumonier, 'The Kidnapped "General"', p. 205.

80 Ibid.

81 Reid, *Broken Men*, p. 168.

82 H.C. McNeile ['Sapper'], 'The Death Grip', *Sapper's War Stories: Collected in One Volume* (1930. London: Hodder & Stoughton, 1932), p. 895.

83 Ibid., pp. 895–6.

84 Joanna Bourke, 'Effeminacy, Ethnicity and the End of Trauma: the Sufferings of "Shell-Shocked" Men in Great Britain and Ireland, 1914–39', *Journal of Contemporary History* 35.1, Special Issue: Shell-Shock (2000), p. 62. The man's symptoms place him in Peter Leese's category of 'normal' shell-shock cases, with common symptoms such as 'violent outbursts and unpredictable or bizarre behaviour' (Leese, 'Problems Returning Home', p. 1061).

85 Winifred Holtby, 'Such a Wonderful Evening!', *Truth is Not Sober* (London: Collins, 1934), p. 270.

86 Ibid.

87 Ibid., p. 271.

88 Richard Aldington, 'The Case of Lieutenant Hall', *Roads to Glory* (1930. Freeport, NY: Books for Libraries Press, 1970), p. 286.

89 Ibid., pp. 287–8.

90 Bourke, 'Effeminacy, Ethnicity and the End of Trauma', p. 57.

91 Joanna Bourke, *An Intimate History of Killing* (London: Granta, 1999), p. 8.

92 Bourke, 'Effeminacy, Ethnicity and the End of Trauma', p. 65.

93 Charles Neville Brand, 'The Returned', *Best Short Stories of 1932*, ed. Edward J. O'Brien (London: Jonathan Cape, 1932), p. 65.

94 Ibid., pp. 68–9.

CHAPTER 5. NARRATIVE REHEARSALS OF MORAL
AND IDEOLOGICAL ALTERNATIVES

1 Bourke, 'Effeminacy, Ethnicity and the End of Trauma', p. 59.

2 Ibid.

3 Mosse, 'Shell-Shock as a Social Disease', p. 105.

4 Eden Phillpotts, 'A Touch of "Fearfulness"', *The Chronicles of St. Tid* (London: Skeffington, 1917), p. 273.

5 Ibid., p. 283.

6 Jessica Meyer, *Men of War: Masculinity and the First World War* (Basingstoke: Palgrave Macmillan, 2009), p. 2.

7 Edgar Jepson, 'Albert's Return', *Strand Magazine* 58 (October 1919), p. 384.

8 Ibid., p. 386.

9 Ibid., p. 387.

10 Meyer, *Men of War*, p. 3.

11 H.T. Dorling ['Taffrail'], 'Bad Hat', *26 Adventure Stories, Old and New, by Twenty and Six Authors*, eds. Ernest Rhys and Catharine Amy Dawson Scott (New York: Appleton, 1929), p. 214.

12 Barclay, *My Heart's Right There*, p. 10.

13 Ida Alexa Ross Wylie, 'All Dressed Up', *Some Other Beauty and Other Stories* (London: Cassell, 1930), p. 321. Subsequently published in March 1938 in *Harper's Bazaar*. Wylie (1885–1959) was a feminist writer of novels and short stories. See Elizabeth Crawford, *The Women's Suffrage Movement: A Reference Guide, 1866–1928* (London: Routledge, 2001), p. 36.

14 Bourke, 'Effeminacy, Ethnicity and the End of Trauma', p. 58.

15 Wylie, 'All Dressed Up', pp. 326–7.

16 Philip Gibbs, *Realities of War* (London: Heinemann, 1920), pp. 330–1, quoted in Snape, *God and the British Soldier*, p. 197. A 'Bantam soldier' was a recruit from a volunteer regiment of men under the required minimum height for soldiers on active service, formed in response to the need for additional manpower in the early stages of the war.

17 H.C. McNeile ['Sapper'], 'The Fatal Second', *Sapper's War Stories: Collected in One Volume* (1930. London: Hodder & Stoughton, 1932), p. 466. First collected in *Men, Women and Guns* (London: Hodder & Stoughton, 1916).

18 Maunder (ed.), *British Literature of World War I*, p. xxiii.

19 H. Marrot, *The Life and Letters of John Galsworthy* (London: Heinemann, 1935); quoted in Maunder (ed.), *British Literature of World War I*, p. 214.

20 John Galsworthy, 'Peace Meeting', *Tatterdemalion* (London: Heinemann, 1920), p. 142.

21 Will Ellsworth-Jones, *We Will Not Fight: The Untold Story of the First World War's Conscientious Objectors* (London: Aurum, 2008), p. 5.

22 Lois S. Bibbings, *Telling Tales about Men: Conscientious Objectors to Military Service during the First World War* (Manchester: Manchester University Press, 2009), pp. 15–16.

23 'House of Commons. Army (Annual) Bill', *The Times*, 30 March 1927, p. 8.

24 See Corrigan, *Mud, Blood and Poppycock*, p. 234.

25 Ibid., p. 216.

26 Ibid., p. 230.

27 A.P.M. is short for assistant provost marshal, the officer in charge of military police for a specific army unit.

28 Alfred Noyes, 'Court-Martial', *Hidden Player* (London: Hodder & Stoughton, 1924), p. 221.

29 Ibid., p. 225.
30 Ibid.
31 Ibid., p. 241.
32 Eric J. Leed, *No Man's Land: Combat and Identity in World War I* (Cambridge: Cambridge University Press, 1979), p. 9.
33 Noyes, 'Court-Martial', pp. 245–6.
34 Ibid., p. 230.
35 Ibid.
36 Reid, *Broken Men*, p. 82.
37 See Santanu Das, *Touch and Intimacy in First World War Literature* (Cambridge: Cambridge University Press, 2005), chapter 1.
38 See Jonathan Black, 'Thanks for the Memory: War Memorials, Spectatorship, and the Trajectories of Commemoration, 1919–2001', *Matters of Conflict: Material Culture, Memory, and the First World War*, ed. Nicholas J. Saunders (London: Routledge, 2004), pp. 134–48. Fiona Reid points to the fact that victims of shell shock likewise figured in the public consciousness as 'nerve-wracked boys', creating 'representational problems' with regard to older (and ageing) veterans (Reid, *Broken Men*, pp. 85–6).
39 See among others Cate Haste, *Keep the Home Fires Burning: Propaganda in the First World War* (London: Allen Lane, 1977); M.L. Sanders and Philip M. Taylor, *British Propaganda during the First World War, 1914–18* (London: Macmillan, 1982); Gary S. Messinger, *British Propaganda and the State in the First World War* (Manchester: Manchester University Press, 1992).
40 See Bergonzi, *Heroes' Twilight*, pp. 23–4.
41 Paris, *Over the Top*, p. 131.
42 The long-lived cultural trope of the incessantly eating German is explored in greater detail in chapter 5 of Petra Rau's study *English Modernism, National Identity and the Germans, 1890–1950* (Farnham: Ashgate, 2009).
43 Harold Hannyngton Child, Rev. of *Good Old Anna* by Marie Belloc Lowndes, *Times Literary Supplement*, 11 November 1915, p. 404. I am indebted to Potter's *Boys in Khaki* for alerting me to the review. The originally anonymous reviewer Harold Child is named in the *TLS Centenary Archive*.
44 Krista Cowman, '"There Are Kind Germans as Well as Brutal Ones": The Foreigner in Children's Literature of the First World War', *The Lion and the Unicorn* 31.2 (2007), p. 106.
45 Doyle's and other writers' work for the Propaganda Bureau and their support of the war effort are treated amongst others in Keith Grieves, 'Depicting the War on the Western Front: Sir Arthur Conan Doyle and the Publication of The British Campaign in France and Flanders', *Publishing in the First World War: Essays in Book History*, eds. Mary Hammond and Shafquat Towheed (Basingstoke: Palgrave Macmillan, 2007), pp. 215–32.
46 See also John G. Cawelti and Bruce A. Rosenberg, *The Spy Story* (Chicago: University of Chicago Press, 1987), p. 40.
47 Arthur Conan Doyle, 'His Last Bow', *The New Annotated Sherlock Holmes*, Vol. 2, ed. Leslie S. Klinger (New York: Norton, 2005), p. 1426. A similar description of the English as hard under a soft shell is provided by Alfred

Noyes's spy Krauss in 'Uncle Hyacinth', who finds himself unable to quite make out the character of the young naval officer who arrests him: 'The young officer smiled and saluted the ladies again. He was a very ladylike young man, Mr. Neilsen had thought, and an obvious example of the degeneracy of England. But Mr. Neilsen's plump arm was still bruised by the steely grip with which that lean young hand had helped him aboard, so his conclusions were mixed.' Alfred Noyes, 'Uncle Hyacinth', *Walking Shadows* (London: Cassell, 1918), p. 53.

48 Doyle, 'His Last Bow', p. 1443.

49 Ibid., p. 1428.

50 Buchan's own involvement in the war as a well-meaning writer of propaganda is outlined in Kate MacDonald, 'Translating Propaganda: John Buchan's Writing During the First World War', *Publishing in the First World War: Essays in Book History*, eds. Mary Hammond and Shafquat Towheed (Basingstoke: Palgrave Macmillan, 2007), pp. 181–202.

51 John Buchan, 'The Loathly Opposite', *Runagates Club* (1928. London: Hodder & Stoughton, 1930), p. 190.

52 Cawelti and Rosenberg, *The Spy Story*, pp. 44–5.

53 See Matthew Stibbe, *German Anglophobia and the Great War, 1914–1918* (Cambridge: Cambridge University Press, 2001).

54 In his recent cultural history of Britain at war, Adrian Gregory demonstrates through meticulous analysis of wartime newspapers that phenomena such as the urban myth and everyday gossip did far more to spread and exaggerate stories of German atrocities than any news reports or official statements. See Gregory, *The Last Great War*, chapter 2.

55 Frederick Britten Austin, 'A Problem in Reprisals', *Strand Magazine* 57 (March 1919), p. 165.

56 Paris, *Over the Top*, p. 18.

57 Blanche Wills Chandler, 'Our Catch', *Tommies Two* (London: Sampson Low, 1917), pp. 153–7, p. 155.

58 See Paul Delany, *D.H. Lawrence's Nightmare: The Writer and his Circle in the Years of the Great War* (Hassocks: Harvester, 1979), pp. 315–20. The episode is also addressed in Lawrence's post-war novel *Kangaroo* (1923).

59 John Galsworthy, 'The Bright Side', *Tatterdemalion* (London: Heinemann, 1920), p. 74.

60 Ibid., p. 77.

61 See Gerard De Groot, *Blighty: British Society in the Era of the Great War* (London: Longman, 1996), p. 157. In their oral history of the war, van Emden and Humphries document various experiences of Anglo-German families resembling closely those of the fictional Gerhardts; see Richard van Emden and Steve Humphries, *All Quiet on the Home Front: An Oral History of Life in Britain during the First World War* (London: Headline, 2003), chapter 3.

62 Alexander Waugh, 'An Autumn Gathering', *Pleasure* (London: Grant Richards, 1921), p. 139.

63 Ibid., p. 145.

64 Ibid., p. 156.

65 Flora Annie Steel, 'Sunrise', *King Albert's Gift Book: A Tribute to the Belgian King and People from Representative Men and Women throughout the World* (London: Daily Telegraph and Hodder & Stoughton, 1914), pp. 43–5. Quoted from Maunder (ed.), *British Literature of World War I*, p. 33.

66 Geoffrey Moss, 'Defeat', *English Short Stories of To-Day*, ed. The English Association (1924; London: Oxford University Press, 1939), p. 128. Interestingly, an earlier story by Galsworthy with the same title, which was first published in the United States in *Scribner's Magazine* (August 1917), similarly explores sympathy with Germans in the face of defeat, although its German protagonist is a German girl trapped in wartime London and forced to earn her living through prostitution.

67 Moss, 'Defeat', p. 162.

68 Bourke, *Intimate History of Killing*, p. 1.

69 See Paul Fussell's chapter 'A Satire on Circumstance' on irony and ironic contrast in Great War writing in *The Great War and Modern Memory* (Oxford: Oxford University Press, 2000), pp. 3–35.

70 Herbert Read, 'Killed in Action', *Short Stories of the First World War*, ed. George L. Bruce (London: Sidgwick & Jackson, 1971), p. 177. Previously published in *Naked Warriors* (1919), and in *Ambush* (London: Faber, 1930) as part of the *Criterion Miscellany* series.

71 Richard Aldington, 'Killed in Action', *Roads to Glory* (1930. Freeport, NY: Books for Libraries Press, 1970), pp. 131–43.

72 Read, 'Killed in Action', p. 178.

73 Ibid., pp. 178–80.

74 Ibid., pp. 183–4.

75 Ibid., p. 179.

76 Ibid., p. 183.

77 Ibid., p. 184.

78 Ibid., p. 181.

79 Ibid., p. 182.

80 Ibid., p. 181.

81 Ibid., p. 181.

82 Ibid., p. 183.

83 Ibid.

CHAPTER 6. COMMEMORATIVE NARRATIVES AND POST-WAR STORIES

1 Acton, *Grief in Wartime*, p. 48.

2 Jeffery Farnol, 'The Great Silence', *A Matter of Business, and Other Stories* (London: Sampson Low, 1940), p. 146.

3 Ibid., p. 141.

4 Winifred Holtby, 'The Casualty List', *Truth is Not Sober* (London: Collins, 1934), p. 243.

5 Ibid., p. 247.

6 Quoted in Shires, *British Poetry of the Second World War*, pp. 147–8.

7 On the decision to grant permanency to soldiers' graves in the wake of World War I, see Summers, *Remembered*, p. 17.

8 Michael Copp, *An Imagist at War: The Complete War Poems of Richard Aldington* (London: Associated University Press, 2002), p. 18. Copp also points out that Aldington was quite aware of the financial rewards of writing a war novel at that point in time, and was anxious to have it published as soon as possible after completion (p. 17).

9 See Norman T. Gates (ed.), *Richard Aldington: An Autobiography in Letters* (University Park, PA: Pennsylvania State University Press, 1992), p. 100.

10 George J. Zytaruk, and James T. Boulton (eds.), *The Letters of D.H. Lawrence*, Vol. II, *June 1913-October 1916* (Cambridge: Cambridge University Press, 1981), p. 644.

11 Cy Fox, 'Aldington and Wyndham Lewis – Allies Against the Fool-Farm', *Richard Aldington: Papers from the Reading Symposium*, ed. Lionel Kelly (Reading: University of Reading, 1987), p. 86.

12 Watson, *Fighting Different Wars*, pp. 3–5.

13 Cohen, *The War Come Home*, p. 47.

14 Richard Aldington, 'Farewell to Memories', *Roads to Glory* (1930. Freeport, NY: Books for Libraries Press, 1970), p. 304.

15 Ibid., p. 315.

16 Ibid., p. 316.

17 Ibid., p. 317.

18 Nathalie Blondel, '"It goes on happening": Frances Bellerby and the Great War', *Women's Fiction and the Great War*, eds. Suzanne Raitt and Trudi Tate (Oxford: Clarendon, 1997), p. 151.

19 Ibid., p. 153.

20 Frances Bellerby, 'The Green Cupboard', *A Breathless Child and Other Stories* (London: Collins, 1952), p. 12.

21 Ibid., p. 26.

22 Concerning the somewhat misleading setting of the story, Blondel explains: 'Whilst this opening [with the evacuee's hostel] might appear to be referring to Second World War evacuees, the story is set in the early 1920s and describes how three war orphans spend a few hours with a woman who gives them buns, pleased to have someone to talk to.' (Blondel, '"It goes on happening"', p. 161). Although 'Winter Afternoon' is set in the 1920s, it is included in this section because it was written after World War II and because its setting is vague enough to allow us to read it as a post-war, not an inter-war story.

23 Frances Bellerby, 'Winter Afternoon', *A Breathless Child and Other Stories* (London: Collins, 1952), p. 148.

24 Bellerby, 'Winter Afternoon', p. 150.

25 Compare Victoria Stewart, 'The Last War: The Legacy of the First World War in 1940s British Fiction', *British Popular Culture and the First World War*, ed. Jessica Meyer (Leiden: Brill, 2008), p. 260.

26 For varied discussions of the levels of allegory in the story, see Robert L. Calder, '"A More Sinister Troth": Elizabeth Bowen's "The Demon Lover" as Allegory', *Studies in Short Fiction* 31 (1994), pp. 91–7; Daniel V. Fraustino, 'Elizabeth Bowen's "The Demon Lover": Psychosis or Seduction', *Studies in Short Fiction* 17 (1980), pp. 483–7; Douglas A. Hughes, 'Cracks in the Psyche: Elizabeth Bowen's "The Demon Lover"', *Studies in Short Fiction* 10 (1973), pp. 411–13.

27 Bowen, *The Mulberry Tree*, p. 96.

28 See also Stewart, 'The Last War', pp. 271–3.

29 Winter, 'The Persistence of Tradition', p. 43.

30 Karlin ascribes this desire to Kipling, although Kipling did of course not live to see the Second World War (Karlin, 'Kipling and the Limits of Healing', p. 332).

31 Todman, *The Great War*, p. 35.

32 Julian Barnes, 'Evermore', *Cross Channel* (London: Jonathan Cape, 1996), p. 105. The story was previously published in the *New Yorker* on 13 November 1995.

33 Ibid., p. 105.

34 Also see Korte, Schneider and Sternberg, *Der Erste Weltkrieg und die Mediendiskurse der Erinnerung*, p. 236.

35 Miss Moss's Anglo-Jewish identity and her reflections on anti-semitic attitudes towards her brother on the part of fellow soldiers during the war, as well as later anti-semitic vandalism she encounters in the war cemeteries, add another dimension to Barnes's engagement with the war's mythology, particularly the perceived close comradeship of the trenches.

36 Barnes, 'Evermore', pp. 94–5.

37 Ibid., p. 95.

38 The full wording of this standard inscription for war cemeteries, 'Their name liveth for evermore', was in fact suggested to the Commonwealth War Graves Commission by another grieving relative, Rudyard Kipling (Karlin, 'Kipling and the Limits of Healing', p. 334).

39 Robert Pogue Harrison, *The Dominion of the Dead* (Chicago: University of Chicago Press, 2003), pp. 143–5.

40 Arthur Calder-Marshall, 'Before the War', *English Story*, eds. Woodrow and Susan Wyatt (London: Collins, 1941), p. 122.

41 Cohen, *The War Come Home*, p. 34.

42 Calder-Marshall, 'Before the War', pp. 124–5.

43 See Stewart, 'The Last War', pp. 263–7.

44 Calder-Marshall, 'Before the War', p. 126.

45 Cohen, *The War Come Home*, p. 131.

46 Eksteins, *The Rites of Spring*, p. 297.

47 J.M. Winter, *Remembering War: The Great War Between Memory and History in the 20th Century* (New Haven: Yale University Press, 2006), p. 26.

48 Ibid., pp. 26–8.

49 Ibid., p. 30.

50 Robert Graves, 'Christmas Truce', *Collected Short Stories* (London: Cassell, 1966), p. 101.
51 Ibid., pp. 111; 114.
52 Robert Westall, 'The Making of Me', *Echoes of War* (London: Kestrel-Viking, 1989), p. 82.
53 Ibid., p. 88.
54 Korte, Schneider and Sternberg, *Der Erste Weltkrieg und die Mediendiskurse der Erinnerung*, pp. 29–31.
55 Anne Perry, 'Heroes', *Murder & Obsession*, ed. Otto Penzler (London: Orion, 2000), p. 381.
56 Maunder (ed.), *British Literature of World War I*, p. xiii.
57 Todman, *The Great War*, p. 40.
58 Robert Grossmith, 'Company', *The Minerva Book of Short Stories* 3, eds. Giles Gordon and David Hughes (London: Mandarin, 1991), p. 70.
59 Ibid., p. 80.
60 Ibid.
61 Ibid., p. 70.
62 Ibid., p. 75.

Bibliography

PRIMARY SOURCES

SHORT STORIES

Please note that in many cases the bibliographical details presented in this section reflect the version used for research rather than that of first publication. Full bibliographical details for single-author story collections are only given once, with a short title used for subsequent entries.

'Miles'. 'Three Episodes of the War', *A Martial Medley: Fact and Fiction*, ed. Eric Partridge. London: Scholartis, 1931, pp. 21–45.

Aldington, Richard. 'At All Costs', *Roads to Glory*. 1930. Freeport, NY: Books for Libraries Press, 1970, pp. 55–83.

'Booby Trap', *Roads to Glory*, pp. 175–85.

'Bundle of Letters', *Roads to Glory*, pp. 147–71.

'Case of Lieutenant Hall', *Roads to Glory*, pp. 263–90.

'Deserter', *Roads to Glory*, pp. 87–100.

'Farewell to Memories', *Roads to Glory*, pp. 293–317.

'Killed in Action', *Roads to Glory*, pp. 131–43.

'Lads of the Village', *Roads to Glory*, pp. 219–35.

'Love for Love', *Roads to Glory*, pp. 239–60.

'Meditation on a German Grave', *Roads to Glory*, pp. 3–36.

'Of Unsound Mind', *Roads to Glory*, pp. 103–27.

'Sacrifice Post', *Roads to Glory*, pp. 189–215.

'Victory', *Roads to Glory*, pp. 39–51.

Allen, Raymund. 'Irregular Forces – A Story of Chess and War', *Strand Magazine* 50 (December 1915), pp. 698–705.

'The King's Enemy', *Strand Magazine* 51 (April 1916), pp. 412–17.

Allison, James Murray. 'Mr. Franklyn's Adventure', *Best British Short Stories of 1924*, ed. Edward J. O'Brien and John Cournos. Boston: Small Maynard, 1925, pp. 3–11.

Anstey, F. 'The Breaking-Point', *Strand Magazine* 58 (December 1919), pp. 534–42.

Armstrong, Martin Donisthorpe. 'The Defensive Flank', *The Bazaar, and Other Stories*. 1924. London: Jonathan Cape, 1928, pp. 81–100.

'On Patrol', *Best Short Stories of the War: An Anthology*, ed. H.M. Tomlinson. New York: Harper, 1931, pp. 317–26.

Ashton, Helen Rosaline. 'First-Floor Bedroom', *Belinda Grove*. London: Gollancz, 1932, pp. 168–96.

Atkey, Bertram. 'MacKurd: A Tale of the Aftermath', *Strand Magazine* 58 (November 1919), pp. 429–40.

Aumonier, Stacy. 'The Grayles', *English Review* 22 (March 1916), pp. 222–32.

'A Source of Irritation', *Strand Magazine* 55 (February 1918), pp. 99–107.

'Mrs Huggins' Hun', *Strand Magazine* 57 (February 1919), pp. 124–32.

'The Brothers', *Love-a-Duck, and Other Stories*. London: Hutchinson, 1921, pp. 275–88.

'Armistice Day', *Armistice Day and Evening Dress*, ed. F. Sefton Delmer and A. Kruse. Berlin: Weidmannsche Buchhandlung, 1930, pp. 1–32.

'Them Others', *Great Short Stories of the War*, ed. H.C. Minchin. London: Eyre & Spottiswoode, 1930, pp. 43–65.

'The Great Unimpressionable', *An Anthology of Modern Short Stories*, ed. J.W. Marriott. London: Thomas Nelson, 1938, pp. 170–94.

'The Match', *English Country Stories*, ed. Ronald Lewin. London: Paul Elek, 1949, pp. 190–200.

'The Kidnapped "General"', *Adventure Stories from the 'Strand'*, ed. Geraldine Beare. London: Folio Society, 1995, pp. 193–206.

Austin, Frederick Britten. 'A Battlepiece: New Style', *The War-God Walks Again*. London: Williams & Norgate, 1926, pp. 127–63.

'A Battlepiece: Old Style', *The War-God Walks Again*, pp. 91–124.

'The Air Scout', *Strand Magazine* 48 (November 1914), pp. 562–72.

'Panzerkraftwagen', *Strand Magazine* 53 (April 1917), pp. 314–25.

'"Nach Verdun!"', *Strand Magazine* 53 (June 1917), pp. 531–41.

'The Other Side', *Strand Magazine* 54 (July 1917), pp. 3–13.

'The Magic of Muhammed Din', *Strand Magazine* 54 (August 1917), pp. 99–107.

'They Come Back', *Strand Magazine* 54 (October 1917), pp. 366–75.

'For Greater Italy!', *Strand Magazine* 54 (September 1917), pp. 295–303.

'Brought Down in Flames', *Strand Magazine* 54 (December 1917), pp. 596–606.

'The Sea-Devil', *Strand Magazine* 55 (January 1918), pp. 3–13.

'Zu Befehl!' ('According to Order!') *Strand Magazine* 55 (March 1918), pp. 213–22.

'In the Hindenburg Line', *Strand Magazine* 55 (April 1918), pp. 303–13.

'Peace', *Strand Magazine* 56 (September 1918), pp. 213–22.

'A Problem in Reprisals', *Strand Magazine* 57 (March 1919), pp. 165–74.

'Held in Bondage', *Strand Magazine* 58 (July 1919), pp. 3–12.

'A Point of Ethics', *Strand Magazine* 58 (December 1919), pp. 555–64.

'From the Depth', *Strand Magazine* 59 (February 1920), pp. 179–87.

'Goliath', *The War-God Walks Again*, pp. 167–204.

'In the China Sea', *The War-God Walks Again*, pp. 51–88.

'The End of an Epoch', *Best Short Stories of the War: An Anthology*, ed. H.M. Tomlinson. New York: Harper, 1931, pp. 291–312.

'They Who Laughed', *The War-God Walks Again*, pp. 207–47.

'When the War-God Walks Again', *The War-God Walks Again*, pp. 11–47.

Avery, Stephen Morehouse. 'Mademoiselle from Armenteers', *C'est la Guerre! Best Stories of the World War*, ed. James Gerald Dunton. Boston: Stratford, 1927, pp. 174–89.

Balmer, Edwin. 'A Case of Lost Memory', *Strand Magazine* 57 (May 1919), pp. 426–34.

Barclay, Florence. 'In Hoc Vince', *King Albert's Gift Book: A Tribute to the Belgian King and People from Representative Men and Women throughout the World*. London: Daily Telegraph and Hodder & Stoughton, 1914, pp. 99–101. Reprinted in Maunder (ed.), *British Literature of World War I*, pp. 23–6.

My Heart's Right There. London: G.P. Putnam's Sons, 1914. Reprinted in Maunder (ed.), *British Literature of World War I*, pp. 5–21.

Barnes, Julian. 'Evermore', *Cross Channel*. London: Jonathan Cape, 1996, pp. 91–111.

'Tunnel', *Cross Channel*, pp. 191–211.

Barrie, J.M. 'A Well-Remembered Voice', *Echoes of the War*. London: Hodder & Stoughton, 1918, pp. 127–68.

'Barbara's Wedding', *Echoes of the War*, pp. 97–126.

'The New Word', *Echoes of the War*, pp. 59–96.

'The Old Lady Shows Her Medals', *Echoes of the War*, pp. 3–58.

Bell, J.J. 'For Belgium', *Strand Magazine* 50 (August 1915), pp. 161–9.

Bell, R.S. Warren. 'In the Dark', *Strand Magazine* 56 (August 1918), pp. 141–8.

'Master and Pupil', *Strand Magazine* 49 (March 1915), pp. 268–80.

Bellerby, Frances. 'The Green Cupboard', *A Breathless Child and Other Stories*. London: Collins, 1952, pp. 11–29.

'Winter Afternoon', *A Breathless Child*, pp. 139–52.

Bird, Richard. 'A Schoolboy Ranker. A Story of a Dipcote Boy who Saved a French Battalion from Destruction', *Captain* 32 (March 1915), pp. 403–11. Reprinted in Maunder (ed.), *British Literature of World War I*, pp. 63–75.

'Little Candles', *Strand Magazine* 51 (April 1916), pp. 384–92.

Blackwood, Algernon. 'Cain's Atonement', *Best Short Stories of the War: An Anthology*, ed. H.M. Tomlinson. New York: Harper, 1931, pp. 496–503.

Bland, E. 'Eileen', *Strand Magazine* 56 (December 1918), pp. 471–7.

Blunden, Edmund Charles. 'A Postscript', *Legion Book*, ed. James Humphrey Cotton Minchin. London: Cassell, 1929, pp. 136–44.

Bolitho, Hector. 'The Albatross', *Best Short Stories of 1932*, ed. Edward J. O'Brien. London: Jonathan Cape, 1932, pp. 44–57.

Borden, Mary. 'Belgium', *The Forbidden Zone*. London: Heinemann, 1929, pp. 1–4.

'Blind', *The Forbidden Zone*, pp. 136–59.

'Bombardment', *The Forbidden Zone*, pp. 5–10.

'Conspiracy', *The Forbidden Zone*, pp. 117–22.

'Enfant de Malheur', *The Forbidden Zone*, pp. 66–92.

'In the Operating Room', *The Forbidden Zone*, pp. 127–35.

'Moonlight', *The Forbidden Zone*, pp. 51–65.
'Paraphernalia', *The Forbidden Zone*, pp. 123–6.
'Rosa', *The Forbidden Zone*, pp. 93–106.
'Sentinels', *The Forbidden Zone*, pp. 17–20.
'The Beach', *The Forbidden Zone*, pp. 42–50.
'The Captive Balloon', *The Forbidden Zone*, pp. 11–12.
'The City in the Desert', *The Forbidden Zone*, pp. 109–16.
'The Priest and the Rabbi', *The Forbidden Zone*, pp. 160–66.
'The Regiment', *The Forbidden Zone*, pp. 21–41.
'The Square', *The Forbidden Zone*, pp. 13–16.
'The Two Gunners', *The Forbidden Zone*, pp. 167–72.
Bottome, Phyllis. 'The Tug-of-War', *Innocence and Experience*. London: John Lane, 1935, pp. 161–77.
Bowen, Elizabeth. 'The Demon Lover', *The Demon Lover and Other Stories*. London: Jonathan Cape, 1945, pp. 80–7.
Boyle, Jack. 'Miss Doris's "Raffles"', *Strand Magazine* 56 (August 1918), pp. 79–89.
Brand, Charles Neville. 'The Returned', *Best Short Stories of 1932*, ed. Edward J. O'Brien. London: Jonathan Cape, 1932, pp. 58–72.
Brighouse, Harold. 'Once a Hero', *Best British Short Stories of 1922*, eds. Edward J. O'Brien and John Cournos. Toronto: Longmans Green, 1923, pp. 56–72.
Brophy, John. 'The Perambulator of Wrath', *A Martial Medley: Fact and Fiction*, ed. Eric Partridge. London: Scholartis, 1931, pp. 47–58.
Buchan, John. 'Dr Lartius', *The Runagates Club*. 1928. London: Hodder & Stoughton, 1930, pp. 93–113.
'Tendebant Manus', *The Runagates Club*, pp. 265–85.
'The King of Ypres', *Scottish War Stories*, ed. Trevor Royle. Edinburgh: Polygon, 1999, pp. 112–23.
'The Loathly Opposite', *The Runagates Club*, pp. 171–90.
Bullett, Gerald William. 'Prentice', *The Baker's Cart, and Other Tales*. 1925. Freeport, NY: Books for Libraries Press, 1970, pp. 287–301.
Butts, Mary. 'Speed the Plough', *Women, Men and the Great War: An Anthology of Stories*, ed. Trudi Tate. Manchester: Manchester University Press, 1995, pp. 45–51.
Calder-Marshall, Arthur. 'Before the War', *English Story*, eds. Woodrow and Susan Wyatt. London: Collins, 1941, pp. 113–26.
Catterick, D.H. 'Reginald', *English Review* 27 (October 1918), pp. 268–72.
Cecil, Edward. 'Forty-Eight Hours', *Strand Magazine* 54 (November 1917), pp. 503–9.
Chandler, Blanche Wills. 'A Little Nest Egg', *Women's Writing on the First World War*, eds. Agnès Cardinal, Dorothy Goldman, and Judith Hattaway. Oxford: Oxford University Press, 1999, pp. 157–9.
'A Pattern of Propriety', *Women's Writing on the First World War*, pp. 154–6.
'A Trance in the Trenches', *Tommies Two*. London: Sampson Low, 1917, pp. 137–40.
'In Reply', *Tommies Two*, pp. 141–4.
'On Leave', *Tommies Two*, pp. 24–30.

'Our Catch', *Tommies Two*, pp. 153–7.

'Our Start for the Front', *Tommies Two*, pp. 21–3.

'The Hardship of Billets', *Tommies Two*, pp. 1–20.

'Zepp Proof', *Tommies Two*, pp. 34–7.

Clarke, Laurence. 'Flashlights. A Story of the East Coast', *Strand Magazine* 55 (May 1918), pp. 351–9.

Cleaver, Hylton. 'Dodson's Day', *Strand Magazine* 57 (March 1919), pp. 221–9.

'The Man Who Stole a Job', *Strand Magazine* 58 (October 1919), pp. 336–43.

'The Sporting Spirit', *Strand Magazine* 52 (December 1916), pp. 641–51.

'The Stake in Waiting', *Strand Magazine* 58 (July 1919), pp. 50–7.

Cleveland, John. 'The Key to Paradise', *Strand Magazine* 59 (May 1920), pp. 485–92.

Conrad, Joseph. 'The Tale', *Best Short Stories of the War: An Anthology*, ed. H.M. Tomlinson. New York: Harper, 1931, pp. 647–64.

De Selincourt, Hugh. 'The Passionate Time-Server', *Nine Tales*. 1917. Freeport, NY: Books for Libraries Press, 1969, pp. 107–26.

'The Sacrifice', *Nine Tales*, pp. 23–104.

Denison, Corrie. 'From Two Angles', *A Martial Medley: Fact and Fiction*, ed. Eric Partridge. London: Scholartis, 1931, pp. 59–102.

Dorling, H.T. ['Taffrail']. 'Bad Hat', *26 Adventure Stories, Old and New, by Twenty and Six Authors*, eds. Ernest Rhys and Catharine Amy Dawson Scott. New York: Appleton, 1929, pp. 201–16.

'The Night Patrol', *Short Stories of the First World War*, ed. George L. Bruce. London: Sidgwick & Jackson, 1971, pp. 129–49.

'The Story of Jonathan Rust', *Best Short Stories of the War: An Anthology*, ed. H.M. Tomlinson. New York: Harper, 1931, pp. 665–77.

Dorrington, Albert. 'The Man Who Strafed the Kaiser', *Strand Magazine* 53 (April 1917), pp. 402–9.

Doyle, Arthur Conan. 'His Last Bow', *The New Annotated Sherlock Holmes*, Vol. 2, ed. Leslie S. Klinger. New York: Norton, 2005, pp. 1424–43.

'The Prisoner's Defence', *Strand Magazine* 51 (February 1916), pp. 115–22.

Dudeney, Alice ['Mrs Henry Dudeney']. '"Missing"'. *Women's Writing on the First World War*, eds. Agnés Cardinal, Dorothy Goldman, and Judith Hattaway. Oxford: Oxford University Press, 1999, pp. 290–9.

Eckersley, Arthur. 'Casualty', *English Review* 24 (April 1917), pp. 310–16.

Edginton, May. 'Comfort for the Troops', *Strand Magazine* 54 (November 1917), pp. 480–8.

'The Job', *Strand Magazine* 54 (December 1917), pp. 554–62.

'There's a Silver Lining', *Strand Magazine* 54 (August 1917), pp. 146–54.

'War Workers', *Strand Magazine* 54 (October 1917), pp. 386–94.

Farnol, Jeffery. 'The Great Silence', *A Matter of Business, and Other Stories*. London: Sampson Low, 1940, pp. 139–46.

'Tomorrow', *A Matter of Business*, pp. 1–7.

Ford, Ford Madox. 'Fun! – It's Heaven', *Bystander* (24 November 1915), pp. 327–30. Reprinted in Maunder (ed.), *British Literature of World War I*, pp. 97–100.

'The Scaremonger', *Women, Men and the Great War: An Anthology of Stories*, ed. Trudi Tate. Manchester: Manchester University Press, 1995, pp. 268–74.

Frankau, Gilbert. 'A Ragtime Hero', *Men, Maids and Mustard-Pot: A Collection of Tales*. London: Hutchinson, 1923, pp. 167–76.

'Julius Schumacher, Englishman', *Men, Maids and Mustard-Pot*, pp. 45–62.

'My Friend Batstone', *Men, Maids and Mustard-Pot*, pp. 94–104.

Gallishaw, John. 'Jack Bolton, 551', *Only Two Ways to Write a Story*. New York: Putnam, 1928, pp. 91–110.

Galsworthy, John. '"A Green Hill Far Away"', *Tatterdemalion*. London: Heinemann, 1920, pp. 194–200.

'A Forsyte Encounters the People, 1917', *On Forsyte 'Change*. London: Heinemann, 1930, pp. 243–54.

'A Patriot', *Forsytes, Pendyces and Others. 1933*. London: Heinemann, 1936, pp. 135–41.

'Cafard', *Tatterdemalion*, pp. 104–14.

'Defeat', *Tatterdemalion*, pp. 27–50.

'Flotsam and Jetsam', *Tatterdemalion*, pp. 51–73.

'Heritage: An Impression', *Tatterdemalion*, pp. 186–93.

'Peace Meeting', *Tatterdemalion*, pp. 134–43.

'Poirot and Bidan: A Recollection', *Tatterdemalion*, pp. 175–82.

'Recorded', *Tatterdemalion*, pp. 115–22.

'Soames and the Flag', *On Forsyte 'Change*, pp. 257–92.

'The Bright Side', *Tatterdemalion*, pp. 74–103.

'The Dog It Was That Died', *Tatterdemalion*, pp. 144–64.

'The Grey Angel', *Tatterdemalion*, pp. 3–26.

'The Juryman', *Five Tales*. London: Heinemann, 1920, pp. 279–308. Reprinted in Maunder (ed.), *British Literature of World War I*, pp. 227–42.

'The Mother Stone', *Tatterdemalion*, pp. 169–74.

'The Muffled Ship', *Tatterdemalion*, pp. 183–5.

'The Nightmare Child', *Tatterdemalion*, pp. 275–87.

'The Recruit', *Tatterdemalion*, pp. 123–33.

'Told by the Schoolmaster', *Forsytes, Pendyces and Others*, pp. 145–62.

Garnett, David. 'The Old Dovecote', *English Review* 30 (February 1920), pp. 145–52.

Gibbon, Lewis Grassic. 'Shot at Dawn', *Scottish War Stories*, ed. Trevor Royle. Edinburgh: Polygon, 1999, pp. 145–8.

Gibbon, Perceval. 'Plain German', *Strand Magazine* 54 (December 1917), pp. 515–30.

Gibbons, John. 'At All Times and in All Places', *Twenty-Four Vagabond Tales*. London: Burns Oates & Washbourne, 1931, pp. 85–95.

'Confession Most Foul', *Twenty-Four Vagabond Tales*, pp. 75–84.

'The Curious Catholicity of Mr America', *Twenty-Four Vagabond Tales*, pp. 96–103.

'The Frailty of Father A', *Twenty-Four Vagabond Tales*, pp. 104–16.

Gibbs, Sir Philip Hamilton. 'Out of the Ruins', *Out of the Ruins, and Other Little Novels*. 1927. London: Hutchinson, 1930, pp. 9–39.

'The Fortunate Face', *Out of the Ruins*, pp. 155–205.

'The School of Courage', *Out of the Ruins*, pp. 209–75.

'The Supernatural Lady', *Out of the Ruins*, pp. 99–124.

'The Wandering Birds', *Out of the Ruins*, pp. 43–70.

Gordon, Lady. 'The National Lent', *Strand Magazine* 53 (April 1917), pp. 361–3.

Graham, R.B. Cunninghame. 'Brought Forward', *English Review* 19 (February 1915), pp. 285–9.

'In a Backwater', *English Review* 18 (October 1914), pp. 280–4.

Graham, Winifred. 'The Ballunatics', *Strand Magazine* 56 (August 1918), pp. 116–19.

Graves, Robert. 'Christmas Truce', *Collected Short Stories*. London: Cassell, 1966, pp. 100–18.

'You Win, Houdini!', *Collected Short Stories*, pp. 119–31.

Grossmith, Robert. 'Company', *The Minerva Book of Short Stories* 3, eds. Giles Gordon and David Hughes. London: Mandarin, 1991, pp. 70–80.

Grundy, C.W. 'Lost and Found', *A Martial Medley: Fact and Fiction*, ed. Eric Partridge. London: Scholartis, 1931, pp. 11–19.

Hall, Holworthy. 'Men Are Such Children', *Strand Magazine* 57 (April 1919), pp. 300–9.

Hall, Radclyffe. 'Fräulein Schwartz', *Women's Writing on the First World War*, eds. Agnés Cardinal, Dorothy Goldman, and Judith Hattaway. Oxford: Oxford University Press, 1999, pp. 13–31.

'Miss Ogilvy Finds Herself', *Women, Men and the Great War: An Anthology of Stories*, ed. Trudi Tate. Manchester: Manchester University Press, 1995, pp. 125–40.

Hanley, James. 'Greaser Anderson', *Men in Darkness: Five Stories*. London: John Lane, 1931, pp. 299–323.

Hannay, James Owen ['George A. Birmingham']. 'Getting Even', *Our Casualty, and Other Stories*. London: Skeffington, 1919, pp. 23–34.

'His Girl', *Our Casualty*, pp. 105–19.

'Our Casualty', *Our Casualty*, pp. 7–20.

'Sir Galahad', *Our Casualty*, pp. 123–37.

Harris, Frank. 'The Last Kindness', *Best Short Stories of the War: An Anthology*, ed. H.M. Tomlinson. New York: Harper, 1931, pp. 167–72.

Herbert, Alan Patrick. 'Indomitable Tweedy', *Best Short Stories of the War: An Anthology*, ed. H.M. Tomlinson. New York: Harper, 1931, pp. 78–83.

Heron-Maxwell, Beatrice. 'The Bat', *Strand Magazine* 52 (September 1916), pp. 345–52.

Hibbard, George. 'Woman's Wit', *Strand Magazine* 56 (December 1918), pp. 449–56.

Holme, Constance. 'Speeding Up, 1917', *Women's Writing on the First World War*, eds. Agnés Cardinal, Dorothy Goldman, and Judith Hattaway. Oxford: Oxford University Press, 1999, pp. 250–1.

Holtby, Winifred. 'So Handy for the Fun Fair', *Women, Men and the Great War: An Anthology of Stories*, ed. Trudi Tate. Manchester: Manchester University Press, 1995, pp. 52–67.

'Such a Wonderful Evening!' *Truth is Not Sober*. London: Collins, 1934, pp. 268–72.

'The Casualty List', *Truth is Not Sober*, pp. 242–8.

Horn, Holloway. 'The Lie', *Best British Short Stories of 1922*, eds. Edward J. O'Brien and John Cournos. Toronto: Longmans Green, 1923, pp. 165–7.

Howard, Keble. 'A Shock For Uncle Timothy', *Strand Magazine* 56 (October 1918), pp. 238–43.

'Miss Pett's Grand Chance', *Strand Magazine* 54 (November 1917), pp. 463–70.

'Needs Must when Love Drives', *Strand Magazine* 57 (April 1919), pp. 312–19.

'Nicholas and the "Old Bean"', *Strand Magazine* 57 (June 1919), pp. 478–84.

Hutten, Baroness von. 'Mothers', *English Review* 30 (January 1920), pp. 36–44.

Jameson, Annie Edith ['J.E. Buckrose']. '"Lights Out!"' *War-Time in Our Street: The Story of Some Companies Behind the Firing Line*. London: Hodder & Stoughton, 1917, pp. 9–16.

'Lovers', *War-Time in Our Street*, pp. 91–102.

'One of the Old Guard', *War-Time in Our Street*, pp. 149–58.

'Our Lad', *War-Time in Our Street*, pp. 29–38.

'Pie', *War-Time in Our Street*, pp. 41–51.

'The Alarm', *War-Time in Our Street*, pp. 119–30.

'The Captain', *War-Time in Our Street*, pp. 67–75.

'The Parcel', *War-Time in Our Street*, pp. 19–26.

'The Splendid Pretenders', *War-Time in Our Street*, pp. 79–88.

'The Spy', *War-Time in Our Street*, pp. 55–64.

'The Widow and the Specials', *War-Time in Our Street*, pp. 105–15.

'War Economy', *War-Time in Our Street*, pp. 133–45.

Jepson, Edgar. 'Albert's Return', *Strand Magazine* 58 (October 1919), pp. 384–92.

'Madderson's Mascot', *Strand Magazine* 52 (December 1916), pp. 583–9.

Jerrold, Ianthe. 'The Orchestra of Death', *Great English Short Stories*, eds. Lewis Melville and Reginald Hargreaves. London: Harrap, 1931, pp. 1031–42.

Johns, W.E. 'A Desperate Chance!' *Biggles in France*. 1935. London: Red Fox-Random House, 1993, pp. 19–27.

'Down to Earth', *Biggles in France*, pp. 9–18.

'One Bomb and Two Pockets', *Biggles in France*, pp. 28–39.

Kipling, Rudyard. 'A Friend of the Family', *Debits and Credits*. 1926. London: Macmillan, 1949, pp. 305–26.

'Madonna of the Trenches', *Debits and Credits*, pp. 239–61.

'Mary Postgate', *A Diversity of Creatures*. 1917. London: Macmillan, 1952, pp. 419–41.

'On the Gate', *Debits and Credits*, pp. 331–56.

'Sea Constables: A Tale of '15', *Debits and Credits*, pp. 25–49.

'Swept and Garnished', *Diversity of Creatures*, pp. 407–18.

'The Gardener', *Debits and Credits*, pp. 399–414.

'The Janeites', *Debits and Credits*, pp. 147–74.

'The Tender Achilles', *Limits and Renewals*, pp. 347–67.

Lawrence, D.H. 'England, my England', 1922. *England, my England, and Other Stories*. Leipzig: Tauchnitz, 1928, pp. 9–52.

'Monkey Nuts', *England, my England*, pp. 105–23.

'Samson and Delilah', *England, my England*, pp. 177–99.

'The Blind Man', *England, my England*, pp. 75–102.

'Tickets, Please', *England, my England*, pp. 55–72.

'Wintry Peacock', *England, my England*, pp. 127–48.

Lewis, Wyndham. 'Cantleman's Spring Mate', *Unlucky for Pringle: Unpublished and Other Stories*. London: Vision, 1973, pp. 77–84.

'The Countryhouse Party, Scotland', *Unlucky for Pringle*, pp. 45–9.

'The French Poodle', *Unlucky for Pringle*, pp. 53–9.

'The King of the Trenches', *Unlucky for Pringle*, pp. 60–72.

'The War Baby', *Unlucky for Pringle*, pp. 85–108.

Locke, William John. 'A Spartan of the Hills', *Stories Near and Far*. 1926. London: Bodley Head-John Lane, 1928, pp. 59–92.

'Echo of the Past', *Stories Near and Far*, pp. 135–62.

'The Apostle', *Stories Near and Far*, pp. 165–93.

Lowndes, Marie A. Belloc. 'The Parcel', *The Grim Thirteen: Stories by Thirteen Authors*, ed. Frederick Stuart Greene. London: Hurst & Blackett, 1918, pp. 179–94.

'What Happened in Berlin', *Strand Magazine* 52 (August 1916), pp. 201–12.

Lucas, Frank Laurence. 'Glory', *The Woman Clothed With the Sun, and Other Stories*. London: Cassell, 1937, pp. 131–46.

Lucas, St John Welles. 'My Son, My Son', *Georgian Stories, 1924*. New York: Putnam; London: Chapman & Hall, 1924, pp. 180–231.

Lyons, Albert Michael Neil. 'An Over-Seas Contingent', *Kitchener Chaps*. London: John Lane, 1915, pp. 205–22.

'First and Second Rations', *Kitchener Chaps*, pp. 77–85.

'Jack the Lion', *Kitchener Chaps*, pp. 141–53.

'Mr Bogle's Toast', *Kitchener Chaps*, pp. 181–89.

'Old Nitch: A Story from the Pickle-Works, Written Down and Punctuated', *Kitchener Chaps*, pp. 35–56.

'Private Blood', *Kitchener Chaps*, pp. 59–73.

'Sar'nt Majaw', *Kitchener Chaps*, pp. 21–32.

'The Belgian Officer', *Kitchener Chaps*, pp. 193–201.

'The Mutiny of Sludge Lane', *Kitchener Chaps*, pp. 3–18.

'The Nerve of John Phipps', *Kitchener Chaps*, pp. 89–103.

'The Pyjama Suit', *Kitchener Chaps*, pp. 169–78.

'The Queen Anne's Westminsters', *Kitchener Chaps*, pp. 157–65.

'What They Can Do', *Kitchener Chaps*, pp. 107–16.

'Why Sidney Joined', *Kitchener Chaps*, pp. 119–137.

MacGill, Patrick. 'The Raiders', *Strand Magazine* 53 (January 1917), pp. 86–94.

Machen, Arthur. 'The Bowmen', *The Collected Arthur Machen*. London: Duckworth, 1988, pp. 300–302.

'The Soldier's Rest', *The Bowmen and Other Legends of the War*. London: Simpkin, Marshall, Hamilton, Kent & Co., 1915, pp. 39–50. Reprinted in Maunder (ed.), *British Literature of World War I*, pp. 57–60.

Macnair, Wilson. 'On Record', *Strand Magazine* 56 (September 1918), pp. 223–7.

McNeile, H.C. ['Sapper']. 'A Point of Detail', *Strand Magazine* 54 (July 1917), pp. 39–48.

'An Arrow at a Venture', *Strand Magazine* 59 (February 1920), pp. 105–13.

'James Henry', *Sapper's War Stories: Collected in One Volume*. 1930. London: Hodder & Stoughton, 1932, pp. 909–29.

'Jim Brent's V.C.', *Sapper's War Stories*, pp. 505–34.

'Private Meyrick – Company Idiot', *Sapper's War Stories*, pp. 418–42.

'Retribution', *Sapper's War Stories*, pp. 480–504.

'Spud Trevor of the Red Hussars', *Sapper's War Stories*, pp. 85–104.

'The Death Grip', *Sapper's War Stories*, pp. 885–908.

'The Fatal Second', *Sapper's War Stories*, pp. 461–80.

'The Land of Topsy Turvy', *Sapper's War Stories*, pp. 537–97.

'The Man-Trap', *Strand Magazine* 53 (May 1917), pp. 418–28.

'The Man Who Would Not Play Cards', *Strand Magazine* 59 (June 1920), pp. 541–9.

'The Motor-Gun', *Sapper's War Stories*, pp. 104–26.

'The Sixth Drunk', *Sapper's War Stories*, pp. 345–51.

Macnicol, Eona. 'Grey Boy', *Scottish War Stories*, ed. Trevor Royle. Edinburgh: Polygon, 1999, pp. 149–64.

Mander, A.E. '"For it"', *English Review* 29 (October 1919), pp. 331–40.

Mansfield, Katherine. 'An Indiscreet Journey', *Women's Writing on the First World War*, eds. Agnés Cardinal, Dorothy Goldman, and Judith Hattaway. Oxford: Oxford University Press, 1999, pp. 255–67.

'The Fly', *Women, Men and the Great War: An Anthology of Stories*, ed. Trudi Tate. Manchester: Manchester University Press, 1995, pp. 68–72.

Marsh, Richard. 'Scandalous!', *Strand Magazine* 52 (August 1916), pp. 172–81.

Martin, J. Sackville. 'A Plain Man', *Strand Magazine* 54 (November 1917), pp. 450–55.

Maugham, W.S. 'Giulia Lazzari', *Ashenden Or, The British Agent*. 1928. London: Heinemann, 1956, pp. 121–48.

'Gustav', *Women, Men and the Great War: An Anthology of Stories*, ed. Trudi Tate. Manchester: Manchester University Press, 1995, pp. 275–80.

'The Greek', *Ashenden Or, The British Agent*, pp. 82–98.

'The Hairless Mexican', *Ashenden Or, The British Agent*, pp. 48–69.

'The Traitor', *Ashenden Or, The British Agent*, pp. 157–97.

Maxwell, W.B. 'Joan of Arc', *Strand Magazine* 57 (January 1919), pp. 58–65.

'The Widow', *Strand Magazine* 56 (November 1918), pp. 331–7.

Mayne, Ethel Colburn. 'The Difference', *Transatlantic Review* 1.5 (May 1924), pp. 318–320.

McKenna, Stephen. 'The Latest Raid', *Strand Magazine* 54 (December 1917), pp. 536–9.

McWilliam, Candia. 'Sweetie Rationing', *The Penguin Book of Contemporary Women's Short Stories*, ed. Susan Hill. Harmondsworth: Penguin, 1995, pp. 243–7.

Mill, Arthur. 'Wreckage of War', *English Review* 28 (March 1919), pp. 234–5.

Montague, C.E. 'A Trade Report Only', *Fiery Particles*. 1923. London: Chatto & Windus, 1936, pp. 211–33.

'A Cock and Bull Story', *Action, and Other Stories*. London: Chatto & Windus, 1928, pp. 32–50.

'A Pretty Little Property', *Action*, pp. 100–120.

'Action', *Action*, pp. 1–31.

'All for Peace and Quiet', *Fiery Particles*, pp. 150–75.

'Didn't Take Care of Himself', *Action*, pp. 234–64.

'Honours Easy', *Great Short Stories of the War*, ed. H.C. Minchin. London: Eyre & Spottiswoode, 1930, pp. 829–67.

'Judith', *Action*, pp. 64–88.

'Man Afraid', *Action*, pp. 171–84.

'My Friend the Swan', *Fiery Particles*, pp. 70–88.

'Sleep, Gentle Sleep', *Action*, pp. 51–63.

'Ted's Leave', *Action*, pp. 185–209.

'The First Blood Sweep', *Fiery Particles*, pp. 107–34.

'Wodjabet', *Action*, pp. 141–61.

Morden, Simon. 'Brilliant Things', *Brilliant Things: A Short Story Collection*. Bristol: Subway, 2004, pp. 7–13.

Morgan, John Hartman ['Centurion']. 'A Day on the Somme', *Gentlemen At Arms*. London: Heinemann, 1918, pp. 94–107.

'Hot Air', *Gentlemen At Arms*, pp. 85–93.

'The Allies', *Gentlemen At Arms*, pp. 233–45.

'The Lieutenant', *Gentlemen At Arms*, pp. 1–12.

Moss, Geoffrey. 'Defeat', *English Short Stories of To-Day*, ed. The English Association. London: Oxford University Press, 1939, pp. 128–62.

Mottram, R.H. 'The Chink', *Ten Years Ago: Armistice and Other Memories Forming a Pendant to 'The Spanish Farm Trilogy'*. London: Chatto & Windus, 1928, pp. 140–53.

'The Common Secretary', *Ten Years Ago*, pp. 34–49.

'The Darkest Day', *Ten Years Ago*, pp. 113–25.

'The Devil's Own', *Ten Years Ago*, pp. 101–12.

'The Horse Marines', *Ten Years Ago*, pp. 90–100.

'I-Grec, Emm, Cé, A', *Ten Years Ago*, pp. 160–69

'The Old Man's Chair', *Ten Years Ago*, pp. 75–89.

'Virginia', *Ten Years Ago*, pp. 50–61.

'Why Ever?', *Ten Years Ago*, pp. 170–80.

'Young Hamilton Tighe', *Ten Years Ago*, pp. 126–39.

Munro, H.H. ['Saki']. 'Birds on the Western Front', *The Square Egg, and Other Sketches*. 1924. London: Bodley Head-John Lane, 1929, pp. 113–17.

'For the Duration of the War', *The Complete Works of Saki*. London: Bodley Head, 1989, pp. 532–6.

'The Square Egg', *The Square Egg, and Other Sketches*, pp. 104–112.

Munro, Neil. 'The Oldest Air in the World', *Scottish War Stories*, ed. Trevor Royle. Edinburgh: Polygon, 1999, pp. 102–11.

Newberry, Linda. 'The Christmas Tree', *Gripping War Stories*, ed. Tony Bradman. London: Corgi, 1999, pp. 97–117.

Noyes, Alfred. 'Court-Martial', *Hidden Player*. London: Hodder & Stoughton, 1924, pp. 216–48.

'May Margaret', *Walking Shadows*. London: Cassell, 1918, pp. 201–42.

'Peaches', *Walking Shadows*, pp. 173–98.

'The Creative Impulse', *Walking Shadows*, pp. 105–37.

'The Hand of the Master', *Walking Shadows*, pp. 285–96.

'The Lighthouse', *Walking Shadows*, pp. 245–70.

'The Man from Buffalo', *Walking Shadows*, pp. 57–74.

'Uncle Hyacinth', *Walking Shadows*, pp. 3–54.

O'Flaherty, Liam. 'The Alien Skull', *An Anthology of Modern Short Stories*, ed. J.W. Marriott. London: Thomas Nelson, 1938, pp. 146–55.

Ollivant, Alfred. 'The Indian Hospital', *The Brown Mare*. London: Allen & Unwin, 1916, pp. 85–101.

Pain, Barry. 'Incidents Photography', *Strand Magazine* 50 (September 1915), pp. 273–82.

'Owing to the War', *Strand Magazine* 53 (January 1917), pp. 61–3.

Panter-Downes, Mollie. 'Battle of the Greeks', *Good Evening, Mrs. Craven: The Wartime Stories of Mollie Panter-Downes*, intro. Gregory LeStage. 1941. London: Persephone, 2008, pp. 59–65.

'Meeting at the Pringles", *Good Evening, Mrs. Craven*, pp. 7–13.

Perry, Anne. 'Heroes', *Murder & Obsession*, ed. Otto Penzler. London: Orion, 2000, pp. 379–94.

Pertwee, Roland. 'The Man with the Plough', *Strand Magazine* 53 (February 1917), pp. 106–11.

'Camouflage', *Strand Magazine* 53 (May 1917), pp. 502–506.

'A Matter for Boccaccio', *Strand Magazine* 56 (December 1918), pp. 413–21.

'Mr. Flintheart', *Strand Magazine* 60 (October 1920), pp. 292–303.

Phillpotts, Eden. 'A Touch of "Fearfulness"', *The Chronicles of St Tid*. London: Skeffington, 1918, pp. 272–83.

'Cornwallis and Me and Fate', *The Human Boy and the War*. 1916. Freeport, NY: Books for Libraries Press, 1970, pp. 225–48.

'For the Red Cross', *The Human Boy and the War*, pp. 249–72.

'Percy Minimus and his Tommy', *The Human Boy and the War*, pp. 141–59.

'Silver Thimble Farm', *The Chronicles of St Tid*, pp. 28–46.

'The "Turbot's" Aunt', *The Human Boy and the War*, pp. 205–24.

'The Battle of the Sand-Pit', *The Human Boy and the War*, pp. 3–25.

'The Countryman of Kant', *The Human Boy and the War*, pp. 45–67.

'The Fight', *The Human Boy and the War*, pp. 115–40.

'The Hutchings Testimonial', *The Human Boy and the* War, pp. 91–114.

'The Mystery of Fortescue', *The Human Boy and the War*, pp. 26–44.

'The Prize Poem', *The Human Boy and the War*, pp. 160–82.

'Travers minor, Scout', *The Human Boy and the* War, pp. 68–90.

Pollard, Hugh. 'Hazard', *English Review* 26 (May 1918), pp. 415–18.

'Morphine', *English Review* 26 (February 1918), pp. 113–6.

Pope, Jessie. 'Cornstalks', *Pearson's Magazine* 42 (1916), pp. 530–6; subsequently published in *Love on Leave*. London: C.A. Pearson, 1919, pp. 59–69. Reprinted in Maunder (ed.), *British Literature of World War I*, pp. 175–82.

'The Allotment Bride', *Pearson's Magazine*, 44 (September 1917), pp. 231–5; subsequently published in *Love on Leave*, pp. 14–23. Reprinted in Maunder (ed.), *British Literature of World War I*, pp. 183–90.

Powell, G.H. 'The End of Judas', *Strand Magazine* 51 (January 1916), pp. 50–53.

Priestley, John Boynton. 'The Town Major of Miraucourt', *The Second Mercury Story Book*. London: Longmans, 1931, pp. 235–49.

Read, Herbert. 'Cloud-Form', *Ambush*, Criterion Miscellany No. 16. London: Faber & Faber, 1930, pp. 27–29.

'Cupid's Everlasting Honeymoon', *Ambush*, pp. 40–43.

'First Blood', *Ambush*, pp. 9–13.

'Killed in Action', *Short Stories of the First World War*, ed. George L. Bruce. London: Sidgwick & Jackson, 1971, pp. 177–84.

'Man, Melodion, Snowflakes', *Ambush*, pp. 14–16.

'The Raid', *Ambush*, pp. 30–39.

Redman, Ben Ray. 'Down in Flames', *Down in Flames*. New York: Payson & Clarke, 1930, pp. 31–73.

'From Above', *Down in Flames*, pp. 285–96.

'Morale', *Down in Flames*, pp. 3–28.

'The Enduring Image', *Down in* Flames, pp. 267–82.

Reynolds, Mrs Baillie. 'Cazalet's Secretary', *Strand Magazine* 59 (March 1920), pp. 225–34.

'Counting the Steps', *Strand Magazine* 60 (August 1920), pp. 163–70.

'The Lych-Gate', *Strand Magazine* 59 (January 1920), pp. 3–11.

'The Moonlight Raider', *Strand Magazine* 55 (February 1918), pp. 115–23.

Ricci, Lewis Anselm da Costa ['Bartimeus']. '"Arma Virumque…"', *The Long Trick*. London: Cassell, 1917, pp. 153–71.

'Carrying On', *The Long Trick*, pp. 130–52.

'Mystery', *Strand Magazine* 56 (September 1918), pp. 168–72.

'The English Way', *Strand Magazine* 57 (January 1919), pp. 49–53.

'The Epic of St. George's Day, 1918', *Navy Eternal, which is the Navy-That-Floats, the Navy-That-Flies and the Navy-Under the Sea*. London: Hodder & Stoughton, 1918, pp. 289–307.

'The Feet of the Young Men', *Strand Magazine* 55 (June 1918), pp. 489–92.

'The Lonely Sailor', *Strand Magazine* 51 (March 1916), pp. 277–82.

'The Navy-That-Flies', *Navy Eternal*, pp. 89–117.

'The Navy-Under-The-Sea', *Navy Eternal*, pp. 190–212.

'The Port Lookout', *Best Short Stories of the War: An Anthology*, ed. H.M. Tomlinson. New York: Harper, 1931, pp. 678–81.

'Crab-Pots', *Great English Short Stories*, eds. Lewis Melville and Reginald Hargreaves. London: Harrap, 1931, pp. 988–99.

'Wet Bobs', *The Long Trick*, pp. 109–29.

Richards, Frank [Charles Hamilton], 'Coker's Conscript', *Magnet* (29 April 1916), pp. 1–8. Reprinted in Maunder (ed.), *British Literature of World War I*, pp. 101–56.

Ridge, W. Pett. 'In the Service', *Strand Magazine* 51 (June 1916), pp. 621–5.

'Before and After', *Strand Magazine* 53 (January 1917), pp. 50–54.

'Corporal's Guard', *Strand Magazine* 56 (October 1918), pp. 276–9.

Roberts, Morley. 'The Man Who Lost His Likeness', *Strand Magazine* 52 (December 1916), pp. 684–94.

'Rumpity Pusher', *Strand Magazine* 57 (January 1919), pp. 3–10.

Rodney, David. 'Murder in the Front Line', *Modern Short Stories*. London: Luker & Hill, 1938, pp. 22–8.

Ruck, Berta. 'The Purple of the Shoulder Strap', *Khaki and Kisses*. London: Hutchinson, 1915, pp. 39–51. Reprinted in Maunder (ed.), *British Literature of World War I*, pp. 47–53.

'The Shirker', *Khaki and Kisses*. London: Hutchinson, 1915, pp. 196–203. Reprinted in Maunder (ed.), *British Literature of World War I*, pp. 41–5.

Ryan, Thomas. 'The Soldier', *Men in Chains*. London: Peter Davies, 1939, pp. 188–219.

Samuel, Edwin Herbert. 'Company Office', *A Cottage in Galilee*. London: Vallentine Mitchell, 1957, pp. 7–12.

Sedgwick, Anne Douglas. 'Hepaticas', *Atlantic Narratives: Modern Short Stories*, ed. Charles Swain Thomas. Boston: Atlantic Monthly, 1918, pp. 30–55.

Sharp, Evelyn. 'Frightfulness', *Herald* (4 September 1915), p. 6; subsequently published in *A Communion of Sinners*. London: George, Allen & Unwin, 1917, pp. 131–7. Reprinted in Maunder (ed.), *British Literature of World War I*, pp. 81–3.

'The Apple Tree', *Herald* (18 September 1915), p. 4; subsequently published in *A Communion of Sinners*, pp. 12–18. Reprinted in Maunder (ed.), *British Literature of World War* I, pp. 85–7.

'The Patriot's Day', *Herald* (4 November 1916), p. 6; subsequently published in *A Communion of Sinners*, pp. 139–44. Reprinted in Maunder (ed.), *British Literature of World War* I, pp. 89–91.

Sinclair, May. 'Red Tape', *Women, Men and the Great War: An Anthology of Stories*, ed. Trudi Tate. Manchester: Manchester University Press, 1995, pp. 199–209.

Sitwell, Sir Osbert. 'The Machine Breaks Down', *Best British Short Stories of 1923*, eds. Edward J. O'Brien and John Cournos. Boston: Small Maynard, 1924, pp. 279–89.

'Defeat', *Collected Stories*. 1953. London: Duckworth, 1974, pp. 1–6.

Smith, Iain Crichton. 'Greater Love', *Scottish War Stories*, ed. Trevor Royle. Edinburgh: Polygon, 1999, pp. 312–20.

Spark, Muriel. 'The First Year of My Life', *The Penguin Book of British Comic Short Stories*, ed. Patricia Craig. London: Viking-Penguin, 1990, pp. 341–7.

St Mars, F. 'Watchers of the Mud', *Great English Short Stories*, eds. Lewis Melville and Reginald Hargreaves. London: Harrap, 1931, pp. 970–88.

Steel, Flora Annie. 'Sunrise', *King Albert's Gift Book: A Tribute to the Belgian King and People from Representative Men and Women throughout the World*. London: Daily Telegraph and Hodder & Stoughton, 1914, pp. 43–5. Reprinted in Maunder (ed.), *British Literature of World War I*, pp. 31–4.

Steevens, Harold. 'The Sentry Post at Cowman's Curl', *Strand Magazine* 49 (June 1915), pp. 603–14.

'Schmitt's Pigeons', *Strand Magazine* 51 (March 1916), pp. 306–16.

'The Service Revolver', *Strand Magazine* 58 (July 1919), pp. 18–27.

Swayne, Martin. 'The Sleep-Beam', *Strand Magazine* 55 (March 1918), pp. 187–93.

Thurston, E. Temple. 'The Nature of the Beast', *Strand Magazine* 56 (December 1918), pp. 383–96.

Tomlinson, H.M. 'A Raid Night', *Best Short Stories of the War: An Anthology*, ed. H.M. Tomlinson. New York: Harper, 1931, pp. 17–23.

'Armistice', *Best Short Stories of the War: An Anthology*, ed. H.M. Tomlinson. New York: Harper, 1931, pp. 779–80.

Townend, William. 'No Quarter', *Best Short Stories of the War: An Anthology*, ed. H.M. Tomlinson. New York: Harper, 1931, pp. 376–99.

Updale, Eleanor. 'Not a Scratch', *War: Stories of Conflict*, ed. Michael Morpurgo. Basingstoke: Macmillan's Children, 2005, pp. 147–61.

Wakefield, Herbert Russell. 'Day-Dream in Macedon', *Imagine a Man in a Box*. London: Philip Allan, 1931, pp. 125–36.

Wallace, Edgar. 'The Despatch-Rider', *Strand Magazine* 48 (December 1914), pp. 716–21.

'Code No. 2', *Strand Magazine* 51 (April 1916), pp. 369–77.

'Mr. Miller & the Kaiser', *Strand Magazine* 58 (August 1919), pp. 103–10.

'The Magnificent Ensign Smith', *Strand Magazine* 57 (May 1919), pp. 367–71.

Walpole, Hugh. 'Bombastes Furioso', *The Thirteen Travellers*. London: Hutchinson, 1921, pp. 258–86.

'Fanny Close', *The Thirteen Travellers*, pp. 33–49.

'Hon. Clive Torby', *The Thirteen Travellers*, pp. 50–67.

'Lois Drake', *The Thirteen Travellers*, pp. 154–178.

'Major Wilbraham', *Best British Short Stories of 1922*, eds. Edward J. O'Brien and John Cournos. Toronto: Longmans Green, 1923, pp. 293–309.

'Miss Morganhust', *The Thirteen Travellers*, pp. 68–85.

'Mr. Nix', *The Thirteen Travellers*, pp. 179–203.

'Nobody', *The Thirteen Travellers*, pp. 226–57.

'Peter Westcott', *The Thirteen Travellers*, pp. 86–107.

Warner, Sylvia Townsend. 'A Love Match', *Women, Men and the Great War: An Anthology of Stories*, ed. Trudi Tate. Manchester: Manchester University Press, 1995, pp. 10–28.

Watson, H.B. Marriott. 'The Lighthouse', *Strand Magazine* 52 (November 1916), pp. 521–8.

'The Safe', *Strand Magazine* 52 (September 1916), pp. 358–66.

Waugh, Alexander Raban. 'A Stranger', *Pleasure*. London: Grant Richards, 1921, pp. 181–232.

'An Autumn Gathering', *Pleasure*, pp. 139–57.

Wells, Arthur Walter. '"Chanson Triste"', *Best Short Stories of 1925*, ed. Edward J. O'Brien. London: Jonathan Cape, 1925, pp. 239–48.

West, Edward Sackville. 'The Lock', *Best British Short Stories of 1927*, ed. Edward J. O'Brien. New York: Dodd Mead, 1927, pp. 184–209.

Westall, Robert. 'The Making of Me', *Echoes of War*. London: Kestrel-Viking, 1989, pp. 80–90.

White, Antonia. 'Surprise Visit', *Women's Writing on the First World War*, eds. Agnés Cardinal, Dorothy Goldman, and Judith Hattaway. Oxford: Oxford University Press, 1999, pp. 334–41.

Whyte, A.F. 'Sunk', *Scottish War Stories*, ed. Trevor Royle. Edinburgh: Polygon, 1999, pp. 134–44.

Wodehouse, P.G. 'A Prisoner of War', *Strand Magazine* 49 (March 1915), pp. 305–14.

Wylie, I.A.R. '"All Dressed Up"', *Some Other Beauty*. London: Cassell, 1930, pp. 295–328.

Young, Blamires. 'Clarence', *English Review* 27 (December 1928), pp. 409–12.

Young, Francis Brett. 'Armistice', *Cage Bird, and Other Stories*. London: Heinemann, 1933, pp. 127–44.

'Marching on Tanga', *Short Stories of the First World War*, ed. George L. Bruce. London: Sidgwick & Jackson, 1971, pp. 151–63.

NOVELS, POETRY AND REVIEWS

Aldington, Richard. *Death of a Hero*. London: Heinemann, 1929.

Barbusse, Henri. *Under Fire: The Story of a Squad*, trans. Fitzwater Wray. London: Dent, 1917.

Barker, Pat. *Regeneration*. London: Viking, 1991.

The Eye in the Door. London: Viking, 1993.

The Ghost Road. London: Viking, 1995.

Beith, John Hay ['Ian Hay']. *The First Hundred Thousand*. Edinburgh: Blackwood, 1915.

Carrying On – After the First Hundred Thousand. Edinburgh: Blackwood, 1917.

'Petit-Jean', *Strand Magazine* 53 (June 1917), pp. 596–606.

Binyon, Laurence. 'For the Fallen', *The Penguin Book of First World War Poetry*, ed. George Walter. London: Penguin, 2006, pp. 235–6.

Blunden, Edmund. *Undertones of War. 1928*. Harmondsworth: Penguin, 1984.

Brittain, Vera. *Testament of Youth: An Autobiographical Study of the Years 1900–1925*, ed. Mark Bostridge. 1933. London: Virago, 2004.

Bunyan, John. *The Pilgrim's Progress*. Oxford: Oxford University Press, 2003.

Child, Harold Hannyngton. Rev. of *Good Old Anna* by Marie Belloc Lowndes, *Times Literary Supplement*, 11 November 1915, p. 404.

Cole, Margaret Postgate. 'The Veteran', *The Penguin Book of First World War Poetry*, ed. George Walter. London: Penguin, 2006, p. 213.

Doolittle, Hilda ['H.D.']. *Kora and Ka, with Mira-Mare*. 1934. New York: New Directions, 1996.

Falls, Cyril. Rev. of *Debits & Credits*, by Rudyard Kipling, *Times Literary Supplement*, 16 September 1926, p. 611.

Graves, Robert. *Goodbye To All That: An Autobiography*. London: Jonathan Cape, 1929.

Hanley, James. *The German Prisoner*. London: [private publication], [1935].

Hill, Susan. *Strange Meeting*. London: Hamilton, 1971.

Lawrence, T.E. *Seven Pillars of Wisdom: A Triumph*. London: Jonathan Cape, 1926.

Leighton, Marie Connor. *Boy of My Heart: A Biography*. London: Hodder & Stoughton, 1916.

Macaulay, Rose. *Non-Combatants and Others*. 1916. London: Methuen, 1986.

Manning, Frederic ['Private 19022']. *Her Privates We*. London: Peter Davies, 1930.

Masefield, John. 'August, 1914', *The Penguin Book of First World War Poetry*, ed. George Walter. London: Penguin, 2006, pp. 8–11.

Owen, Wilfred. 'Disabled', *The Penguin Book of First World War Poetry*, ed. George Walter. London: Penguin, 2006, p. 252.

'Mental Cases', *The Penguin Book of First World War Poetry*, ed. George Walter. London: Penguin, 2006, pp. 218–19.

Pope, Jessie. 'Short Leave', *More War Poems*. London: Grant Richards, 1915, p. 26.

'The Beau Ideal', *More War Poems*. London: Grant Richards, 1915, p. 43.

Raymond, Ernest. *Tell England: A Study in a Generation*. 1922. London: Cassell, 1973.

Remarque, Erich Maria. *All Quiet on the Western Front*, trans. A.W. Wheen. London: Putnam, 1929.

Sassoon, Siegfried. *Memoirs of an Infantry Officer*. London: Faber, 1930.

Scannell, Vernon. 'The Great War', *Collected Poems 1950–1993*. London: Robson Books, 1993, pp. 68–9.

West, Rebecca. *The Return of the Soldier*. 1918. London: Virago, 2008.

Williamson, Henry. *The Patriot's Progress: Being the Vicissitudes of Private John Bullock*. 1930. Stroud: Sutton in Association with the Imperial War Museum, 1999.

ANTHOLOGIES OF WAR STORIES

Adcock, Arthur St John (ed.). *In the Firing Line: Stories of the War by Land and Sea*. London: Hodder & Stoughton, 1914.

Aldine War Stories. London: Aldine, 1930–31.

Allan, Junior (ed.). *Humorous Scottish War Stories: Selected from the 'Daily Mail'*. Dundee: Valentine, 1930.

Best War Stories. Twickenham: Hamlyn, 1985.

Bradman, Tony (ed.). *Gripping War Stories*. London: Corgi, 1999.

Bruce, George L. (ed.). *Short Stories of the First World War*. London: Sidgwick & Jackson, 1971.

Cardinal, Agnés, Dorothy Goldman, and Judith Hattaway (eds.). *Women's Writing on the First World War*. Oxford: Oxford University Press, 1999.

Christopher, Jane (ed.). *War Stories: Major Writers of the 19th and 20th Centuries*. Harlow: Longman, 1999.

Dunton, James Gerald (ed.). *C'est la Guerre! Best Stories of the World War*. Boston: Stratford, 1927.

Faulks, Sebastian, and Jörg Hensgen (eds.). *The Vintage Book of War Stories*. London: Vintage, 1999.

Fifty Amazing Stories of the Great War. London: Odhams, 1936.

Foster, John L. (ed.) *Twelve War Stories*. Harlow: Longman, 1980.

Glover, Jon, and Jon Silkin (eds.). *The Penguin Book of First World War Prose*. Harmondsworth: Penguin, 1989.

Great First World War Stories. London: Chancellor, 1994.

Hemingway, Ernest (ed.). *Men at War: The Best War Stories of All Time*. New York: Crown, 1942.

Heroic War Stories. London: Treasure Press, 1988.

Higonnet, Margaret R. (ed.). *Lines of Fire: Women Writers of World War I*. London: Plume, 1999.

Korte, Barbara, and Ann-Marie Einhaus (eds.). *The Penguin Book of First World War Stories*. London: Penguin, 2007.

Lewis, Jon E. (ed.). *The Mammoth Book of Modern War Stories*. London: Robinson, 1993.

Maunder, Andrew. *British Literature of World War I*, Vol. I: *The Short Story and the Novella*. London: Chatto & Pickering, 2011.

McAllister, Hayden (ed.). *War Stories*. London: Octopus, 1997.

Minchin, H.C. (ed.). *Great Short Stories of the War*. London: Eyre & Spottiswoode, 1930.

Morpurgo, Michael (ed.). *War: Stories About Conflict*. London: Macmillan's Children, 2005.

Parrott, James Edward (ed.). *The Path of Glory: Heroic Stories of the Great War*. London: Nelson, 1921.

Partridge, Eric (ed.). *A Martial Medley: Fact and Fiction*. London: Scholartis, 1931.

Riordan, James (ed.). *The Young Oxford Book of War Stories*. Oxford: Oxford University Press, 2001.

Royle, Trevor (ed.). *Scottish War Stories*. Edinburgh: Polygon, 1999.

Smith, Angela K. (ed.). *Women's Writing of the First World War: An Anthology*. Manchester: Manchester University Press, 2000.

Tate, Trudi (ed.). *Women, Men and the Great War: An Anthology of Stories*. Manchester: Manchester University Press, 1995.

Thrilling Deeds of Valour: Stories of Heroism in the Great War. London: Blackie, 1916.

Tomlinson, H.M. (ed.). *Best Short Stories of the War.* New York: Harper, 1931.

Underwood, Lamar (ed.). *The Greatest War Stories Ever Told.* Guilford, CO: Lyons, 2001.

Urquhart, Fred (ed.). *Men at War: The Best War Stories of All Time.* London: Arco, 1957.

Willson, Wingrove (ed.). *Naval Stories of the Great War.* London: Aldine, 1931.

Wilson, Richard (ed.). *The Post of Honour: Stories of Daring Deeds Done by Men of the British Empire in the Great War.* London: Dent, 1917.

Wonderful Stories: Winning the V.C. in the Great War. London: Hutchinson, 1917.

Wood, Walter (ed.). *Soldiers' Stories of the War.* London: Chapman and Hall, 1915.

In the Line of Battle: Soldiers' Stories of the War. London: Chapman & Hall, 1916.

GENERAL ANTHOLOGIES AND COLLECTIONS

Adrian, Jack (ed.). *Detective Stories from The Strand.* Oxford: Oxford University Press, 1992.

Allen, E.E., and A.T. Mason (eds.). *Twelve Modern Short Stories.* London: Edward Arnold, 1958.

Baker, Denys Val (ed.). *Modern Short Stories.* London: Staples, 1944.

Worlds Without End: A Book of Short Stories. London: Sylvan, 1945.

Beare, Geraldine (ed.). *Crime Stories from the 'Strand'.* London: Folio Society, 1991.

Short Stories from the 'Strand'. London: Folio Society, 1992.

Adventure Stories from the 'Strand'. London: Folio Society, 1995.

Best, Andrew, and Mark Cohen (eds.). *The World of the Short Story.* London: Longman, 1975.

Bowen, Elizabeth (ed.). *The Faber Book of Modern Short Stories.* London: Faber, 1937.

Bradbury, Malcolm (ed.). *The Penguin Book of Modern British Short Stories.* London: Viking-Penguin, 1987.

Bradbury, Malcolm and Judy Cooke (eds.). *New Writing.* London: Minerva in association with the British Council, 1992–2001.

Buchan, John (ed.). *Modern Short Stories.* London: Nelson, 1926.

Bullocke, J.G. (ed.). *The Harrap Book for Modern Short Stories.* London: Harrap, 1968.

Byatt, A.S. (ed.). *The Oxford Book of English Short Stories.* Oxford: Oxford University Press, 1998.

Byram, R.S. (ed.). *Junior Short Story Anthology.* Harlow: Longman, 1990.

Craig, Patricia (ed.). *The Penguin Book of British Comic Stories.* London: Viking-Penguin, 1990.

Davin, Dan (ed.). *English Short Stories of Today*. Second Series. London: Oxford University Press, 1958.

Dolley, Christopher (ed.). *The Penguin Book of English Short Stories*. Harmondsworth: Penguin, 1967.

The Second Penguin Book of English Short Stories. Harmondsworth: Penguin, 1972.

Dorsch, T.S. (ed.). *English Short Stories of Today*. Third Series. London: Oxford University Press, 1965.

Drabble, Margaret, and Charles Osborne (eds.). *New Stories 1: An Anthology*. London: Arts Council of Great Britain, 1976.

English Association. *English Short Stories of To-Day*. London: Oxford University Press, 1939.

Evans, H.B. (ed.). *Modern Story*. Edgware: Anthology Publications, 1946.

Fadiman, Clifton (ed.). *The World of the Short Story: A Twentieth-Century Collection*. London: Pan, 1987.

Finn, Frederick Edward Simpson (ed.). *In Short: An Anthology of Short Stories*. London: Murray, 1981.

Glaskin, Gerald Marcus (ed.). *A Small Selection of Short Stories*. London: Barrie & Rockcliff, 1962.

Gordon, Giles (ed.). *Modern Short Stories 2: 1940–1980*. London: Dent, 1982.

Modern Short Stories. London: Everyman, n.d.

Greco, Sheena (ed.). *The New Windmill Book of Short Stories*. Oxford: Heinemann, 2000.

Hadfield, John and Charles Heywood (eds.). *Modern Short Stories*. London: Dent, 1939.

Hadfield, John (ed.). *Modern Short Stories: 20 Masters of the English Short Story*. London: Dent, 1964.

Modern Short Stories to 1940. London: Dent, 1984.

Hamlin, Mike, Christine Hall, and Jane Browne (eds.). *The New Windmill Book of Classic Short Stories*. Oxford: New Windmills-Heinemann, 1997.

Harrison, Michael (ed.). *Under Thirty: An Anthology*. London: Rich & Gowan, 1939.

Hendry, James Findlay (ed.). *The Penguin Book of Scottish Short Stories*. Harmondsworth: Penguin, 1979.

Hill, Susan (ed.). *Contemporary Women's Short Stories: An Anthology*. London: Penguin, 1995.

The Second Penguin Book of Modern Women's Short Stories. Harmondsworth: Penguin, 1995.

Holbrook, David (ed.). *People & Diamonds: An Anthology of Modern Short Stories for Use in Secondary Schools*. Cambridge: Cambridge University Press, 1962.

Howard, Ivan (ed.). *Things*. London: Mayflower-Dell, 1965.

Hudson, Derek (ed.). *Modern English Short Stories*. Oxford: Oxford University Press, 1972.

Hunter, Jim (ed.). *Modern Short Stories*. London: Faber, 1977.

Modern Short Stories 2. London: Faber, 1994.

International Short Story Anthology. London: Jonathan Cape, 1967.

Isherwood, Christopher (ed.). *Great English Short Stories.* New York: Dell, 1957.

Jackson, David (ed.). *Springboard: Modern Short Stories for the Middle School.* 1970. Walton-on-Thames: Nelson, 1987.

Jessup, Alexander, and Henry Seidel Canby (eds.). *The Book of the Short Story.* New York: Appleton, 1924.

Jones, Phyllis M. (ed.). *Modern English Short Stories,* Vol. 1. London: Oxford University Press, 1963.

English Short Stories 1888–1937. Oxford: Oxford University Press, 1973.

Kneebone, Richard, and Melvin Taylor (eds.). *New Writing.* London: Cassell, 1962.

Le Gallienne, Richard (ed.). *The World's Best Short Stories.* New Delhi: Srishti, 2000.

Lehmann, John (ed.). *New Writing* 1 (Spring 1936). London: Laurence & Wishart. 1937.

New Writing: New Series. Part 3. London: John Lane, 1939.

English Stories from New Writing. London: John Lehmann, 1951.

Marland, Eileen, and Michael Marland (eds.). *Friends and Families: A Collection of Modern Short Stories.* London: Longman, 1973.

Marriott, James William (ed.). *An Anthology of Modern Short Stories.* London: Nelson, 1938.

Marshall, Sarah (ed.). *Story Break: A Collection of Short Stories.* Peterborough: New Fiction, 2004.

Martin, Alex, and Robert Hill (eds.). *Modern Short Stories.* London: Cassell, 1991.

Martin, Augustine (ed.). *An Anthology of Short Stories for Intermediate Certificate.* Dublin: Gill, 1967.

Martin, Richard (ed.). *Modern English Short Stories,* Vol. 1. London: Macmillan, 1966.

Melville, Lewis, and Reginald Hargreaves (eds.). *Great English Short Stories.* London: Harrap, 1931.

Milford, Humphrey (ed.). *Selected English Short Stories.* Oxford: Oxford University Press, 1927.

Modern Short Stories. London: University of London Press, 1931.

Modern Short Stories: Beveney Selection Number Two. London: Luker & Hill, 1946.

More Modern Short Stories. London: Lovat Dickson, 1936.

Murray, Ian (ed.). *The New Penguin Book of Scottish Short Stories.* London: Penguin, 1983.

O'Brien, Edward J. (ed.). *Modern English Short Stories.* London: Jonathan Cape, 1930.

The Best British Short Stories. Boston: Houghton Mifflin, 1922–37.

Pocock, Guy Noel (ed.). *Modern Short Stories.* London: Dent, 1929.

Pudney, John (ed.). *Pick of Today's Short Stories.* London: Odhams, 1949–52; London: Putnam, 1953–57.

Rayner, Jacqueline (ed.). *Companions: A Short Story Collection*. Maidenhead: Big Finish, 2003.

Rhys, Ernest (ed.). *English Short Stories from the Fifteenth to the Twentieth Century*. 1921. London: Dent, 1926.

Richards, Alun (ed.). *The Penguin Book of Sea Stories*. Harmondsworth: Penguin, 1977.

The Second Penguin Book of Sea Stories. Harmondsworth: Penguin, 1980.

The Second Penguin Book of Welsh Short Stories. Harmondsworth: Penguin, 1993.

Roberts, Kaye (ed.). *What's the story?: A Collection of Fiction Stories*. Llangollen: Fiction Today, 1998.

Robertson, Wendy, and Heather Bennett (eds.). *Headlines: The Write Around Short Story Anthology*. Middlesbrough: Write Around, 1994.

Royston, Mike (ed.). *Fast and Curious: A New Windmill Book of Short Stories*. Oxford: New Windmills-Heinemann, 1999.

Ways With Words: A New Windmill Book of Short Stories. Oxford: New Windmills-Heinemann, 2001.

Sharrock, Roger (ed.). *English Short Stories of Today*. Fourth Series. London: Oxford University Press, 1976.

Smith, Albert James and William H. Mason (eds.). *Short Story Study: A Critical Anthology*. London: Edward Arnold, 1961.

Stern, Gladys Bronwyn (ed.). *Long Short Story: A Collection*. London: Cassell, 1939.

Taylor, Peter J.W. (ed.). *More Modern Short Stories: For Students of English*. Oxford: Oxford University Press, 1981.

The 'Strand' Best Stories. London: George Newnes, 1915.

Thomas, Charles Swain (ed.). *Atlantic Narratives: Modern Short Stories*. Boston: Atlantic Monthly, 1918.

Tomlinson, H.M. (ed.). *Great Sea Stories of All Nations*. 1930. London: Spring Books, 1967.

Watson, James, and John Watson (eds.). *Modern Short Stories*. Glasgow: John Watson, 1943.

Welsh Short Stories: An Anthology. London: Faber, 1949.

Whitehead, Frank (ed.). *Moments of Truth: Modern Short Stories*. St. Albans: Hart-Davis Educational, 1974.

Wilson, Richard (ed.). *English Short Stories: An Anthology*. London: Dent, 1962.

Wyatt, Woodrow, and Susan Wyatt (eds.). *English Story*. London: Collins, 1941–50.

SECONDARY SOURCES

Acton, Carol. *Grief in Wartime: Private Pain, Public Discourse*. Basingstoke: Palgrave Macmillan, 2007.

'Best Boys and Aching Hearts: The Rhetoric of Romance as Social Control in Wartime Magazines for Young Women', *British Popular Culture and the First World War*, ed. Jessica Meyer. Leiden: Brill, 2008, pp. 173–93.

Adams, Hazard. 'Canons: Literary Criteria/Power Criteria', *Critical Inquiry* 14 (1988), pp. 748–64.

Ardis, Ann L. *Modernism and Cultural Conflict 1880–1922*. Cambridge: Cambridge University Press, 2002.

Assmann, Aleida, and Jan Assmann (eds.). *Kanon und Zensur: Archäologie der literarischen Kommunikation II*. München: Wilhelm Fink, 1987.

Assmann, Aleida. 'Canon and Archive', *Cultural Memory Studies: An International and Interdisciplinary Handbook*, eds. Astrid Erll and Ansgar Nünning. Berlin: de Gruyter, 2008, pp. 97–107.

'Funktionsgedächtnis und Speichergedächtnis – Zwei Modi der Erinnerung.' *Generation und Gedächtnis: Erinnerungen und kollektive Identitäten*, eds. Kristin Platt and Mihran Dabag. Opladen: Leske & Budrich, 1995, pp. 169–85.

'Vier Formen des Gedächtnisses.' *Erwägen Wissen Ethik* 13.2 (2002), pp. 183–90.

Assmann, Jan. 'Communicative and Cultural Memory.' *Cultural Memory Studies: An International and Interdisciplinary Handbook*, eds. Astrid Erll and Ansgar Nünning. Berlin: de Gruyter, 2008, pp. 109–18.

Aumonier, Stacy. Foreword. *Short Story Writing for Profit*, by Michael Joseph. 2nd edition. London: Hutchinson, 1923, pp. vii-xii.

Barlow, Adrian. *The Great War in British Literature*. Cambridge: Cambridge University Press, 2000.

Beare, Geraldine. *Index to the Strand Magazine, 1891–1950*. Westport, CO: Greenwood, 1982.

Becker, Annette. 'The Avant-Garde, Madness and the Great War.' *Journal of Contemporary History* 35.1, Special Issue: Shell-Shock (January 2000), pp. 71–84.

Berger, Arthur Asa. *An Anatomy of Humor*. New Brunswick, NJ: Transaction, 1993.

Bergonzi, Bernard. *Heroes' Twilight: A Study of the Literature of the Great War*. London: Constable, 1965.

Bibbings, Lois S. *Telling Tales about Men: Conscientious Objectors to Military Service during the First World War*. Manchester: Manchester University Press, 2009.

Black, Jonathan. 'Thanks for the Memory: War Memorials, Spectatorship, and the Trajectories of Commemoration, 1919–2001', *Matters of Conflict: Material Culture, Memory, and the First World War*, ed. Nicholas J. Saunders. London: Routledge, 2004, pp. 134–48.

Blondel, Nathalie. '"It goes on happening": Frances Bellerby and the Great War.' *Women's Fiction and the Great War*, eds. Suzanne Raitt and Trudi Tate. Oxford: Clarendon, 1997, pp. 151–73.

Bloom, Clive. *Bestsellers: Popular Fiction since 1900*. Basingstoke: Palgrave, 2002.

Bloom, Harold. *The Western Canon: The Books and School of the Ages*. New York: Riverhead, 1995.

Bond, Brian. *The Unquiet Western Front: Britain's Role in Literature and History*. Cambridge: Cambridge University Press, 2002.

Bonheim, Helmut. *The Narrative Modes: Techniques of the Short Story*. Cambridge, MA: Brewer, 1992.

Boulton, James T. *The Letters of D.H. Lawrence*, Vol. I: *September 1901-May 1913*. Cambridge: Cambridge University Press, 1979.

Bourdieu, Pierre. *The Field of Cultural Production: Essays on Art and Literature*. Cambridge: Polity, 1993.

Bourke, Joanna. *An Intimate History of Killing*. London: Granta, 1999.

'Effeminacy, Ethnicity and the End of Trauma: the Sufferings of "Shell-Shocked" Men in Great Britain and Ireland, 1914–39', *Journal of Contemporary History* 35.1, Special Issue: Shell-Shock (January 2000), pp. 57–69.

Bowen, Elizabeth. *The Mulberry Tree: Writings of Elizabeth Bowen*, ed. Hermione Lee. London: Virago, 1986.

Bracco, Rosa Maria. *Merchants of Hope: British Middlebrow Writers and the First World War; 1919–1939*. Providence: Berg, 1993.

Braybon, Gail. 'Women and the War.' *The First World War in British History*, eds. Stephen Constantine, Maurice W. Kirby and Mary B. Rose. London: Arnold, 1995, pp. 141–67.

Breen, Judith Puchner. 'D.H. Lawrence, World War I, and the Battle between the Sexes: A Reading of "The Blind Man" and "Tickets, Please".' *Women's Studies: An Interdisciplinary Journal* 13.1–2 (1986), pp. 63–74.

Brooks, Cleanth, and Robert Penn Warren, *Understanding Fiction*. 1943. Englewood Cliffs, NJ: Prentice-Hall, 1959.

Buchholz, Sabine. *Narrative Innovationen in der Modernistischen Britischen Short Story*. Trier: WVT, 2003.

Buitenhuis, Peter. *The Great War of Words: Literature as Propaganda, 1914–18 and After*. London: Batsford, 1989.

Cadogan, Mary, and Patricia Craig. *Women and Children First: The Fiction of Two World Wars*. London: Gollancz, 1978.

Calder, Robert L. '"A More Sinister Troth": Elizabeth Bowen's "The Demon Lover" as Allegory', *Studies in Short Fiction* 31 (1994), pp. 91–7.

Cannadine, David. 'War and Death, Grief and Mourning in Modern Britain', *Mirrors of Mortality: Studies in the Social History of Death*, ed. Joachim Whaley. London: Europa, 1981, pp. 187–242.

Cawelti, John G. *Adventure, Mystery, and Romance: Formula Stories as Art and Popular Culture*. Chicago: University of Chicago Press, 1976.

Cawelti, John G. and Bruce A. Rosenberg. *The Spy Story*. Chicago: University of Chicago Press, 1987.

Clark, Timothy. 'Not Seeing the Short Story: A Blind Phenomenology of Reading', *The Oxford Literary Review* 26 (2004), pp. 5–30.

Clarke, I.F. *Voices Prophesying War: Future Wars 1763–1984*. 1966. Oxford: Oxford University Press, 1992.

Cobley, Evelyn. *Representing War: Form and Ideology in First World War Narratives.* Toronto: University of Toronto Press, 1993.

Cohen, Deborah. *The War Come Home.* Berkeley: University of California Press, 2001.

Cohen, Debra Rae. *Remapping the Home Front: Locating Citizenship in British Women's Great War Fiction.* Boston: Northeastern University Press, 2002.

Cole, Sarah. *Modernism, Male Friendship, and the First World War.* Cambridge: Cambridge University Press, 2003.

Constantine, Stephen, Maurice W. Kirby, and Mary B. Rose (eds.). *The First World War in British History.* London: Arnold, 1995.

Copp, Michael. *An Imagist at War: The Complete War Poems of Richard Aldington.* London: Associated University Press, 2002.

Corrigan, Gordon. *Mud, Blood and Poppycock: Britain and the First World War.* London: Cassell, 2003.

Cowman, Krista. '"There Are Kind Germans as Well as Brutal Ones": The Foreigner in Children's Literature of the First World War', *The Lion and the Unicorn* 31.2 (April 2007), pp. 103–15.

Crawford, Elizabeth. *The Women's Suffrage Movement: A Reference Guide, 1866–1928.* London: Routledge, 2001.

Daly, Nicholas. *Modernism, Romance and the Fin de Siècle: Popular Fiction and British Culture.* Cambridge: Cambridge University Press, 2006.

Darrohn, Christine. '"Blown to Bits!": Katherine Mansfield's "The Garden Party" and the Great War', *Modern Fiction Studies* 44.3 (1998), pp. 513–39.

Das, Santanu (ed.). *Touch and Intimacy in First World War Literature.* Cambridge: Cambridge University Press, 2005.

'Sepoys, Sahibs and Babus: India, the Great War and Two Colonial Journals', *Publishing in the First World War: Essays in Book History*, eds. Mary Hammond and Shafquat Towheed. Basingstoke: Palgrave Macmillan, 2007, pp. 61–77.

Race, Empire and First World War Writing. Cambridge: Cambridge University Press, 2011.

De Groot, Gerard. *Blighty: British Society in the Era of the Great War.* London: Longman, 1996.

Delany, Paul. *D.H. Lawrence's Nightmare: The Writer and his Circle in the Years of the Great War.* Hassocks: Harvester, 1979.

Dettmar, Kevin J.H., and Stephen Watt (eds.). *Marketing Modernisms: Self-Promotion, Canonization, Rereading.* Ann Arbor, MI: University of Michigan Press, 1999.

Duffet, Rachael. 'A War Unimagined: Food and the Rank and File Soldier of the First World War', *British Popular Culture and the First World War*, ed. Jessica Meyer. Leiden: Brill, 2008, pp. 47–70.

Eby, Cecil. *The Road to Armageddon: The Martial Spirit in English Popular Literature 1870–1914.* Durham, SC: Duke University Press, 1988.

Eksteins, Modris. *Rites of Spring: The Great War and the Birth of the Modern Age.* New York: Houghton Mifflin-Mariner, 2000.

Ellsworth-Jones, Will. *We Will Not Fight: The Untold Story of the First World War's Conscientious Objectors.* London: Aurum, 2008.

Falls, Cyril. *War Books: A Critical Guide*. London: Peter Davies, 1930.

Felski, Rita. *The Gender of Modernity*. Cambridge, MA: Harvard University Press, 1995.

Ferguson, Niall. *The Pity of War*. London: Allen Lane, 1998.

Ferguson, Suzanne. 'The Rise of the Short Story in the Hierarchy of Genres', *Short Story Theory at a Crossroads*, ed. Susan Lohafer and Jo Ellyn Clarey. Baton Rouge: Louisiana State University Press, 1989, pp. 176–92.

Flothow, Dorothea. 'Popular Children's Literature and the Memory of the First World War, 1919–1939', *The Lion and the Unicorn* 31.2 (2007), pp. 147–61.

Fowler, Alastair. *Kinds of Literature: An Introduction to the Theory of Genres and Modes*. Oxford: Clarendon, 1982.

Fox, Cy. 'Aldington and Wyndham Lewis – Allies Against the Fool-Farm', *Richard Aldington: Papers from the Reading Symposium*, ed. Lionel Kelly. Reading: University of Reading, 1987, pp. 85–97.

Fraustino, Daniel V. 'Elizabeth Bowen's "The Demon Lover": Psychosis or Seduction', *Studies in Short Fiction* 17 (1980), pp. 483–7.

Freedman, Ariela. 'Mary Borden's *Forbidden Zone*: Women's Writing from No-Man's-Land', *Modernism/Modernity* 9.1 (2002), pp. 109–24.

Friedman, Norman. 'Recent Short Story Theories: Problems in Definition', *Short Story Theory at a Crossroads*, eds. Susan Lohafer and Jo Ellyn Clarey. Baton Rouge: Louisiana State University Press, 1989, pp. 13–31.

Fussell, Paul. *The Great War and Modern Memory*. Oxford: Oxford University Press, 2000.

Gates, Norman T. (ed.). *Richard Aldington: An Autobiography in Letters*. University Park, PA: Pennsylvania State University Press, 1992.

Gelder, Ken. *Popular Fiction: The Logics and Practices of a Literary Field*. London: Routledge, 2004.

Gorak, Jan. *The Making of the Modern Canon: Genesis and Crisis of a Literary Idea*. London: Athlone, 1991.

Grayzel, Susan R. *Women's Identities at War: Gender, Motherhood, and Politics in Britain and France during the First World War*. Chapel Hill: University of North Carolina Press, 1999.

Gregory, Adrian. *The Last Great War: British Society and the First World War*. Cambridge: Cambridge University Press, 2008.

Guillory, John. *Cultural Capital: The Problem of Literary Canon Formation*. Chicago: University of Chicago Press, 1993.

Gullason, Thomas A. 'The Short Story: An Underrated Art', *Short Story Theories*, ed. Charles E. May. Athens, OH: Ohio University Press, 1976, pp. 13–31.

Hall, W. David. *Paul Ricoeur and the Poetic Imperative: The Creative Tension between Love and Justice*. Albany, NY: State University of New York Press, 2007.

Hammond, Mary, and Shafquat Towheed (eds.). *Publishing in the First World War: Essays in Book History*. Basingstoke: Palgrave Macmillan, 2007.

Hanson, Claire. *Re-Reading the Short Story*. Basingstoke: Macmillan, 1989.

Short Stories and Short Fiction, 1880–1980. Basingstoke: Macmillan, 1985.

Harrison, Robert Pogue. *The Dominion of the Dead*. Chicago: University of Chicago Press, 2003.

Haste, Cate. *Keep the Home Fires Burning: Propaganda in the First World War*. London: Allen Lane, 1977.

Head, Dominic. *The Modernist Short Story: A Study in Theory and Practice*. Cambridge: Cambridge University Press, 1992.

Hibberd, Dominic, and John Onions, eds. *Poetry of the Great War: An Anthology*. Basingstoke: Macmillan, 1986.

Hibberd, Dominic. *The First World War*. Basingstoke: Macmillan, 1990.

Higbee, Douglas. 'Practical Memory: Organized Veterans and the Politics of Commemoration', *British Popular Culture and the First World War*, ed. Jessica Meyer. Leiden: Brill, 2008, pp. 197–216.

Higonnet, Margaret R. (ed.). *Behind the Lines: Gender and the Two World Wars*. New Haven: Yale University Press, 1987.

Hopkins, Chris. 'Registering War: Modernism, Realism, and the Can(n)on', *Focus on Robert Graves and His Contemporaries* 2.5 (1996), pp. 38–43.

Hughes, Douglas A. 'Cracks in the Psyche: Elizabeth Bowen's "The Demon Lover"', *Studies in Short Fiction* 10 (1973), pp. 411–13.

Hynes, Samuel. *A War Imagined: The First World War and English Culture*. London: Pimlico, 1992.

The Soldiers' Tale: Bearing Witness to Modern War. New York: Allen Lane, 1997.

Jahr, Christoph. 'Der lange Weg nach München. Britische Außenpolitik unter dem Eindruck von Versailles', *Versailles 1919: Ziele – Wirkung – Wahrnehmung*, eds. Gerd Krumeich and Silke Fehlemann. Essen: Klartext, 2001, pp. 113–25.

Jauss, Hans Robert. *Toward an Aesthetic of Reception*, transl. Timothy Bahti, intro. Paul de Man. Minneapolis: University of Minnesota Press, 1982.

Jeffcoate, Robert. 'Teaching Poetry of the First World War in the Secondary School', *Critical Survey* 2.2 (1990), pp. 151–59.

Jones, Edgar, and Simon Wessely. *Shell Shock to PTSD: Military Psychiatry from 1900 to the Gulf War*. Maudsley Monographs 47. Hove: Psychology Press, 2005.

Joseph, Michael. *Short Story Writing for Profit*. 2nd edition. London: Hutchinson, 1923.

Jubb, Michael. 'Rudyard Kipling and the Message of Sympathy to the Relatives of Soldiers Killed in the First World War', *Notes and Queries* 32.3 (September 1985), p. 377.

Kaplan, Carola M., and Anne B. Simpson. 'Edwardians and Modernists: Literary Evaluation and the Problem of History', *Seeing Double: Revisioning Edwardian and Modernist Literature*, eds. Carola M. Kaplan and Anne B. Simpson. Basingstoke: Macmillan, 1996, pp. vii–xxi.

Karlin, Daniel. 'Kipling and the Limits of Healing', *Essays in Criticism: A Quarterly Journal of Literary Criticism* 48.4 (1998), pp. 331–56.

Kearl, Michael C. *Endings: A Sociology of Death and Dying*. Oxford: Oxford University Press, 1989.

Grieves, Keith. 'Depicting the War on the Western Front: Sir Arthur Conan Doyle and the Publication of The British Campaign in France and Flanders', *Publishing in the First World War: Essays in Book History*, eds. Mary Hammond and Shafquat Towheed. Basingstoke: Palgrave Macmillan, 2007, pp. 215–32.

Kermode, Frank. 'Canons', *Dutch Quarterly Review* 18 (1988), pp. 258–70.

Kingsbury, Celia M. '"Infinities of Absolution": Reason, Rumor, and Duty in Joseph Conrad's "The Tale"', *Modern Fiction Studies* 44.3 (1998), pp. 715–29.

Knightley, Phillip. *The First Casualty: The War Correspondent as Hero and Myth-Maker from the Crimea to Iraq*. Baltimore: Johns Hopkins University Press, 2004.

Korte, Barbara, Ralf Schneider, and Claudia Sternberg. *Der Erste Weltkrieg und die Mediendiskurse der Erinnerung in Großbritannien: Autobiographie – Roman – Film (1919–1999)*. Würzburg: Königshausen & Neumann, 2005.

Korte, Barbara. *The Short Story in Britain: A Historical Sketch and Anthology*. Tübingen: Francke, 2003.

'Being Engaged: The War Correspondent in British Fiction', *Anglia* 124 (2006), pp. 432–48.

Krockel, Carl. *War Trauma and English Modernism: T.S. Eliot and D.H. Lawrence*. Basingstoke: Palgrave Macmillan, 2011.

Leed, Eric J. *No Man's Land: Combat and Identity in World War I*. Cambridge: Cambridge University Press, 1979.

Leese, Peter. 'Problems Returning Home: The British Psychological Casualties of the Great War', *The Historical Journal* 40.4 (1997), pp. 1055–67.

Leete, Alfred. *Schmidt the Spy and his Messages to Berlin*. London: Duckworth, 1916.

Lewis, Wyndham. *Unlucky for Pringle: Unpublished and Other Stories*, eds. C.J. Fox and Robert T. Chapman. London: Vision, 1973.

Blasting and Bombardiering. 1937. London: John Calder; New York: Riverrun, 1982.

Liggins, Emma, Andrew Maunder, and Ruth Robbins. *The British Short Story*. Basingstoke: Palgrave Macmillan, 2010.

Lohafer, Susan, and Jo Ellyn Clarey (eds.). *Short Story Theory at a Crossroads*. Baton Rouge: Louisiana State University Press, 1989.

Lowe, Rodney. 'Government', *The First World War in British History*, eds. Stephen Constantine, Maurice W. Kirby, and Mary B. Rose. London: Arnold, 1995, pp. 29–50.

MacArthur, Brian. *For King and Country: Voices from the First World War*. London: Little Brown, 2008.

MacCallum-Stewart, Esther. '"If they ask us why we died": Children's Literature and the First World War, 1970–2005', *The Lion and the Unicorn* 31.2 (2007), pp. 176–88.

MacDonald, Kate. 'Translating Propaganda: John Buchan's Writing During the First World War', *Publishing in the First World War: Essays in Book History*, eds. Mary Hammond and Shafquat Towheed. Basingstoke: Palgrave Macmillan, 2007, pp. 181–202.

March-Russell, Paul. *The Short Story: An Introduction*. Edinburgh: Edinburgh University Press, 2009.

Martin, Christopher. 'British Prose Writing of the First World War', *Critical Survey* 2.2 (1990), pp. 137–43.

Maunder, Andrew. Introduction. *British Literature of World War I*, Vol. I: *The Short Story and the Novella*. London: Chatto & Pickering, 2011, pp. xxxiii–lxiii.

May, Charles E. *Short Story Theories*. Athens, OH: Ohio University Press, 1976.

The New Short Story Theories. Athens, OH: Ohio University Press, 1994.

The Short Story: The Reality of Artifice. New York, London: Routledge, 2002.

McLoughlin, Kate. *Authoring War: The Literary Representation of War from the Iliad to Iraq*. Cambridge: Cambridge University Press, 2011.

McGowan, Marcia Phillips. '"A Nearer Approach to the Truth": Mary Borden's *Journey Down a Blind Alley*', *War, Literature, and the Arts: An International Journal of the Humanities* 16.1–2 (2004), pp. 198–210.

Messinger, Gary S. *British Propaganda and the State in the First World War*. Manchester: Manchester University Press, 1992.

Meyer, Jessica (ed.). 'The Tuition of Manhood: "Sapper's" War Stories and the Literature of War', *Publishing in the First World War: Essays in Book History*, eds. Mary Hammond and Shafquat Towheed. Basingstoke: Palgrave Macmillan, 2007, pp. 113–28.

British Popular Culture and the First World War. Leiden: Brill, 2008.

Men of War: Masculinity and the First World War. Basingstoke: Palgrave Macmillan, 2009.

Michail, Eugene. '"A Sting of Remembrance!": Collective Memory and its Forgotten Armies', *British Popular Culture and the First World War*, ed. Jessica Meyer. Leiden: Brill, 2008, pp. 237–57.

Miller, Alisa. 'Poetry, Politics and Propaganda: Rupert Brooke and the Role of "Patriotic Poetry" in Great Britain, 1914–1918', DPhil thesis, University of Oxford (2008).

Miller, David, and Richard Price (eds.). *British Poetry Magazines 1914–2000: A History and Bibliography of 'Little Magazines'*. London: British Library-Oak Knoll, 2006.

Mosse, George L. 'Shell-Shock as a Social Disease', *Journal of Contemporary History* 35.1, Special Issue: Shell-Shock (January 2000), pp. 101–108.

Motion, Andrew (ed.). *First World War Poems*. London: Faber, 2003.

Afterword. *101 Poems against War*, eds. Matthew Hollis and Paul Keegan. London: Faber, 2003, p. 135.

Myszor, Frank. *The Modern Short Story*. Cambridge: Cambridge University Press, 2001.

Onions, John. *English Fiction and Drama of the Great War, 1918–39*. Basingstoke: Macmillan, 1990.

Orel, Harold. *Popular Fiction in England, 1914–1918*. New York: Harvester Wheatsheaf, 1992.

Ouditt, Sharon. *Fighting Forces, Writing Women: Identity and Ideology in the First World War*. London: Routledge, 1994.

Parfitt, George. *Fiction of the First World War: A Study*. London: Faber, 1988.

Paris, Michael. *Over the Top: The Great War and Juvenile Literature in Britain*. Westport, CO: Praeger, 2004.

The First World War and Popular Cinema: 1914 to the Present. Edinburgh: Edinburgh University Press, 1999.

Warrior Nation: Images of War in British Popular Culture, 1850–2000. London: Reaktion, 2000.

Peppis, Paul. '"Surrounded by a Multitude of Other Blasts": Vorticism and the Great War', *Modernism/Modernity* 4.2 (1997), pp. 39–66.

Phillips, Gordon. 'The Social Impact', *The First World War in British History*, eds. Stephen Constantine, Maurice W. Kirby and Mary B. Rose. London: Arnold, 1995, pp. 106–40.

Potter, Jane. '"A Great Purifier": The Great War in Women's Romances and Memoirs 1914–1918', *Women's Fiction and the Great War*, eds. Suzanne Raitt and Trudi Tate. Oxford: Clarendon, 1997, pp. 85–106.

Boys in Khaki, Girls in Print: Women's Literary Responses to the Great War 1914–1918. Oxford: Oxford University Press, 2005.

'For Country, Conscience and Commerce: Publishers and Publishing, 1914–18', *Publishing in the First World War: Essays in Book History*, eds. Mary Hammond and Shafquat Towheed. Basingstoke: Palgrave Macmillan, 2007, pp. 11–26.

'The Great War Poets', *The Blackwell Companion to the Bible in Literature*, ed. Rebecca Lemon et al. Oxford: Wiley-Blackwell, 2009, pp. 681–95.

Pound, Reginald. *The Strand Magazine, 1891–1950*. London: Heinemann, 1966.

Pratt, Mary Louise. 'The Short Story: The Long and the Short of It', *The New Short Story Theories*, ed. Charles E. May. Athens, OH: Ohio University Press, 1994, pp. 91–113.

Radford, Jean. *The Progress of Romance: The Politics of Popular Fiction*. London: Routledge & Kegan Paul, 1986.

Raitt, Suzanne, and Trudi Tate (eds.). *Women's Fiction and the Great War*. Oxford: Clarendon Press, 1997.

Rau, Petra. *English Modernism, National Identity and the Germans, 1890–1950*. Farnham: Ashgate, 2009.

Reid, Fiona. *Broken Men: Shell Shock, Treatment and Recovery in Britain 1914–1930*. London: Continuum, 2010.

Read, Mike. *Forever England: The Life of Rupert Brooke*. Edinburgh: Mainstream, 1997.

Reilly, Catherine. *Scars Upon My Heart: Women's Poetry and Verse of the First World War*. London: Virago, 1981.

Ricoeur, Paul. *Oneself as Another*. Chicago: University of Chicago Press, 1992.

Robert, Krisztina. '"All That Is Best Of The Modern Woman"? Representations of Female Military Auxiliaries in British Popular Culture, 1914–1919', *British Popular Culture and the First World War*, ed. Jessica Meyer. Leiden: Brill, 2008, pp. 97–122.

Rodden, John. 'Canonization and the Curriculum: George Orwell in the Anglo-American Classroom', *REAL: The Yearbook of Research in English and American Literature* 7 (1990), pp. 221–43.

Roper, Michael. 'Re-Remembering the Soldier Hero: The Psychic and Social Construction of Memory in Personal Narratives of the Great War', *History Workshop Journal* 50 (2000), pp. 181–204.

Sanders, M.L. and Philip M. Taylor, *British Propaganda during the First World War, 1914–18*. London: Macmillan, 1982.

Saunders, Nicholas J. 'Material Culture and Conflict: The Great War, 1914–2003', *Matters of Conflict: Material Culture, Memory, and the First World War*, ed. Nicholas J. Saunders. London: Routledge, 2004, pp. 5–25.

Scannell, Vernon. *Not Without Glory: Poets of the Second World War*. London: Woburn, 1976.

Schweitzer, Richard. *The Cross and the Trenches: Religious Faith and Doubt among British and American Great War Soldiers*. Westport, CT: Praeger, 2003.

Scutts, Joanna. 'Battlefield Cemeteries, Pilgrimage and Literature after the First World War: The Burial of the Dead', *ELT* 52.4 (2009), pp. 387–416.

Shaw, Valerie. *The Short Story: A Critical Introduction*. London: Longman, 1995.

Sherry, Vincent (ed.). *The Cambridge Companion to the Literature of the First World War*. Cambridge: Cambridge University Press, 2000.

The Great War and the Language of Modernism. Oxford: Oxford University Press, 2003.

Shires, Linda M. *British Poetry of the Second World War*. London: Macmillan, 1985.

Simmers, George. 'Military Fictions: Stories about Soldiers, 1914–1930', PhD thesis, Oxford Brookes University (2009).

Smith, Angela K. *The Second Battlefield: Women, Modernism and the First World War*. Manchester: Manchester University Press, 2000.

Suffrage Discourse in Britain during the First World War. Aldershot: Ashgate, 2005.

Smith, Malcolm. 'The War and British Culture', *The First World War in British History*, eds. Stephen Constantine, Maurice W. Kirby, and Mary B. Rose. London: Arnold, 1995, pp. 168–83.

Snape, Michael. *God and the British Soldier: Religion and the British Army in the First and Second World Wars*. London: Routledge, 2005.

Stephen, Martin (ed.). *Never Such Innocence: A New Anthology of Great War Verse*. London: Buchan & Enright, 1988.

Stephenson, John S. *Death, Grief, and Mourning: Individual and Social Realities*. New York: Free Press, 1985.

Stewart, Victoria. "'War Memoirs of the Dead": Writing and Remembrance in the First World War', *Literature and History* 14.2 (October 2005), pp. 37–52.

'The Last War: The Legacy of the First World War in 1940s British Fiction', *British Popular Culture and the First World War*, ed. Jessica Meyer. Leiden: Brill, 2008, pp. 259–281.

Stibbe, Matthew. *German Anglophobia and the Great War, 1914–1918*. Cambridge: Cambridge University Press, 2001.

Summerfield, Penny. *Reconstructing Women's Wartime Lives: Discourse and Subjectivity in Oral Histories of the Second World War*. Manchester: Manchester University Press, 1998.

Summers, Julie. *Remembered: The History of the Commonwealth War Graves Commission*. London: Merrell-Commonwealth War Graves Commission, 2007.

Tate, Trudi. *Modernism, History and the First World War*. Manchester: Manchester University Press, 1998.

Todman, Dan. *The Great War: Myth and Memory*. London: Hambledon, 2005.

Trout, Steven. 'Christ in Flanders?: Another Look at Rudyard Kipling's "The Gardener"', *Studies in Short Fiction* 35.2 (1998), pp. 169–78.

Tylee, Claire M. *The Great War and Women's Consciousness: Images of Militarism and Womanhood in Women's Writings, 1914–64*. Iowa City: University of Iowa Press, 1990.

Van Emden, Richard, and Steve Humphries. *All Quiet on the Home Front: An Oral History of Life in Britain during the First World War*. London: Headline, 2003.

Vannatta, Dennis P. *The English Short Story: 1945–1980, A Critical History*. Boston, MA: Twayne, 1985.

Vogeler, Martha S. *Austin Harrison and the English Review*. Columbia: University of Missouri Press, 2008.

'Harrison, Austin Frederic (1873–1928)', *Oxford Dictionary of National Biography*, Oxford University Press, http://www.oxforddnb.com/view/article/40734. Accessed 5 February 2008.

Ward, Alfred C. *Aspects of the Modern Short Story: English and American*. London: University of London Press, 1924.

Ware, Fabian Arthur Goulstone. *The Immortal Heritage: An Account of the Work and Policy of the Imperial War Graves Commission During Twenty Years, 1917–1937*. Cambridge: Cambridge University Press, 1937.

Watson, Alexander. *Enduring the Great War: Combat, Morale and Collapse in the German and British Armies, 1914–1918*. Cambridge: Cambridge University Press, 2008.

Watson, Janet S.K. *Fighting Different Wars: Experience, Memory, and the First World War in Britain*. Cambridge: Cambridge University Press, 2004.

Williams, David. *Media, Memory, and the First World War*. Montreal: McGill-Queen's University Press, 2009.

Williams, Raymond. *The Politics of Modernism: Against the New Conformists*. London: Verso, 1989.

Winter, J.M. *Sites of Memory, Sites of Mourning: The Great War in European Cultural History*. Cambridge: Cambridge University Press, 1995.

'The Great War and the Persistence of Tradition: Languages of Grief, Bereavement, and Mourning', *War, Violence, and the Modern Condition*, ed. Bernd Hüppauf. Berlin: De Gruyter, 1997, pp. 33–45.

Remembering War: The Great War Between Memory and History in the 20th Century. New Haven: Yale University Press, 2006.

Zytaruk, George J., and James T. Boulton (eds.). *The Letters of D.H. Lawrence*, Vol. II, *June 1913-October 1916*. Cambridge: Cambridge University Press, 1981.

Index

academy, 7, 11–12, 20, 23, 27, 30–1, 35–6, 67, 70, 135, 155
accessibility, 3–4, 19–21, 23, 26, 41, 67–9, 149, *See also* readability
adaptability, 16, 25, 71, 78, 90, *See also* universality
adventure fiction, 12, 17, 19, 43–8, 52–3, 64, 72, 109, 154
aesthetics, 8, 10, 13, 19, 23–4, 27, 29, 30, 72
Aldington, Richard, 2, 18, 28, 37, 57–8, 61–2, 65–7, 69, 88–9, 103–5, 131, 133, 137–9
Allatini, Rose, 113
Allison, J.M., 54
American Civil War, 61, 66
anthologies, 3–4, 6, 10–12, 15–17, 20, 25, 38, 41–2, 48, 53–70, 139, 150, 153
anti-war, 3, 15–16, 30, 41, 60–1, 102, 114, *See also* pacifism
archives, 6, 21–3, 26–7, 37–8, 69, 117, 152
armistice, 47, 77, 81, 90, 104, 111, 113, 135–6, 138
Armistice Day, 77, 81, 135–6
Asquith, H.H., 50
Assmann, Aleida, 11, 20–1, 26
audiences, 8, 12, 17–19, 22, 24–8, 30, 33–4, 38, 41–2, 45–6, 49, 53, 60, 63–4, 69, 70–2, 83, 86, 119–20, 129, 142, 148–9, 151–4
Aumonier, Stacy, 33, 51, 58, 85–6, 101–2
Austin, Frederick Britten, 40, 46–7, 49, 124–5, 130
authenticity, 27–9, 35, 37, 55, 57, 61–2, 65, 123, 139, 149, *See also* truthfulness
autobiography, 7, 18, 28–9, 30, 37, 55, 66–7, 140, 151, 153, *See also* memoirs
avant-garde, 8, 11, 25, 26, 33–4, 44, 133

Balkans, 56, 63
Barbusse, Henri, 58, 62, 67
Barclay, Florence, 69, 94, 110
Barker, Pat, 13, 60, 62, 153
Barnes, Julian, 144–6, 153–4
Barrie, J.M., 121

'Bartimeus', 58, 62, *See also* Ricci, L.A. da Costa
Beith, John Hay. *See* Hay, Ian
Belgium, 47, 49, 56, 87, 93, 101, 104, 113, 123–4, 135
Bellerby, Frances, 140–3, 148, 152
Bennett, Arnold, 121
bereavement, 14, 73, 76–8, 80–2, 84, 87, 91, 135, 140, 145–6
best-sellers, 2, 43, 71, 94
Binyon, Laurence, 81, 136, 145
Bird, Richard, 69, 91
Blackwood's Magazine, 18, 59
Blast, 44
blindness, 51, 96, 98–9
Blunden, Edmund, 18, 30, 41, 58, 67, 140
Boer War, 66
Borden, Mary, 9, 96–7, 130, 133
Bourdieu, Pierre, 30, 41, 71
Bowen, Elizabeth, 26, 142–3, 148
Brand, Charles Neville, 105–6
Brittain, Vera, 2, 31, 67, 96
Brooke, Rupert, 2, 15, 29, 86
Bryce Report, 124
Buchan, John, 69, 123
Buckrose, J.E. *See* Jameson, Annie Edith
Butts, Mary, 68

Calder-Marshall, Arthur, 142, 146, 148
Campaign for Nuclear Disarmament, 135, 150
canonicity, 3–4, 6–7, 10–12, 14–15, 17, 19–21, 24, 26–7, 29–31, 33–7, 42, 55–6, 59–61, 66, 68, 70, 72, 130, 134, 139, 149
Catterick, D.H., 51
cemeteries, 87–8, 135, 145
'Centurion'. *See* Morgan, James Hartman
Chandler, Blanche Wills, 68, 76–7, 125
Chekhov, Anton, 34, 52
children, 13, 16, 43, 55–7, 63–4, 91, 95, 116–17, 125–6, 140–2, 149, 151–2, 155
children's literature, 13, 16, 43, 55–7, 63–4, *See also* juvenile literature
Christianity, 87–8, 114